IMAGES
of America

ALBEMARLE

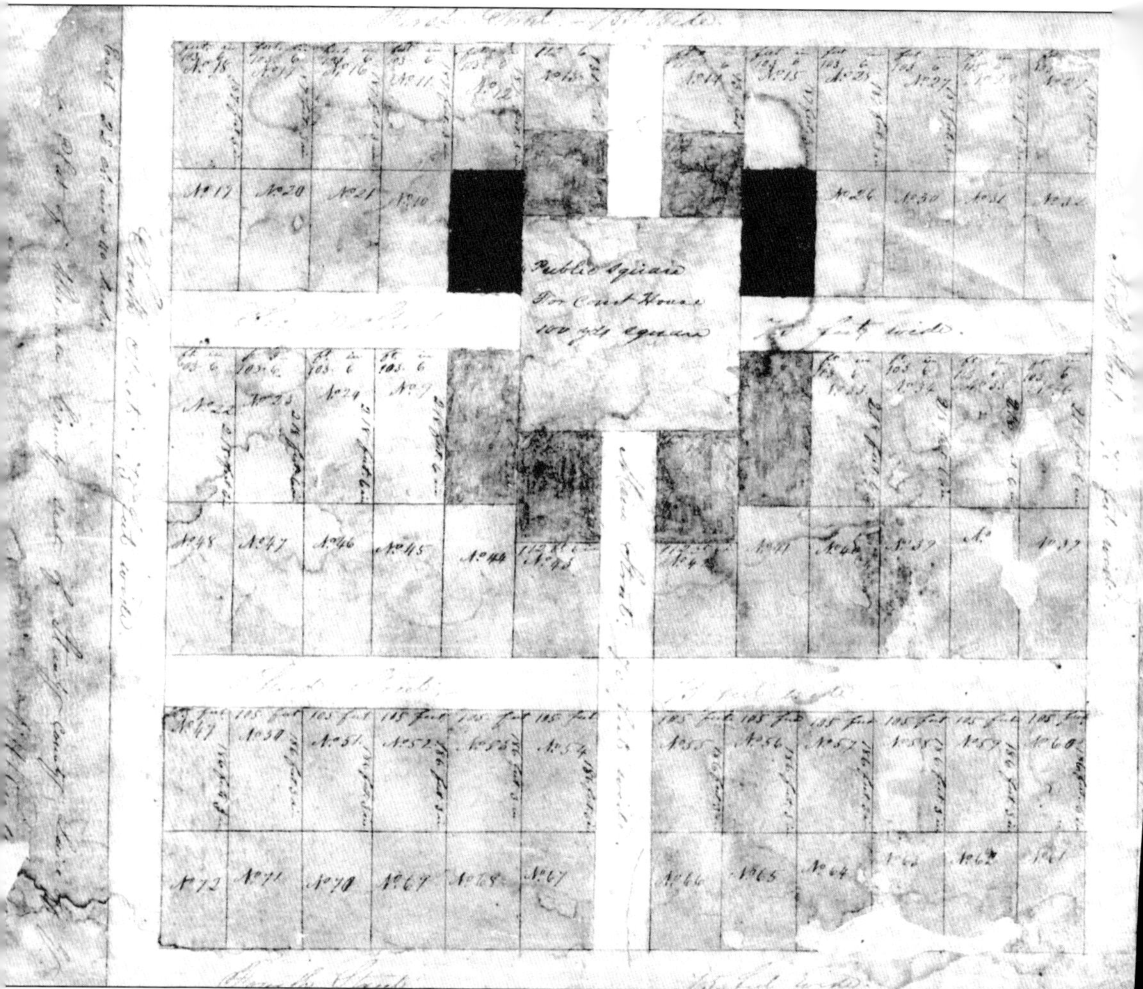

In 1841, streets surround the courthouse square in a grid on a map of downtown Albemarle. (Courtesy of the Stanly County Public Library.)

IMAGES
of America

ALBEMARLE

Elizabeth Chantale Varner
Stanly County Museum

ARCADIA
PUBLISHING

ISBN 978-0-7385-1696-7

Published by Arcadia Publishing
Charleston, South Carolina

Printed in the United States of America

Library of Congress Catalog Card Number: 2004107562

For all general information contact Arcadia Publishing at:
Telephone 843-853-2070
Fax 843-853-0044
E-mail sales@arcadiapublishing.com
For customer service and orders:
Toll-Free 1-888-313-2665

Visit us on the Internet at www.arcadiapublishing.com

This book is dedicated to my parents and sister for their continual support.

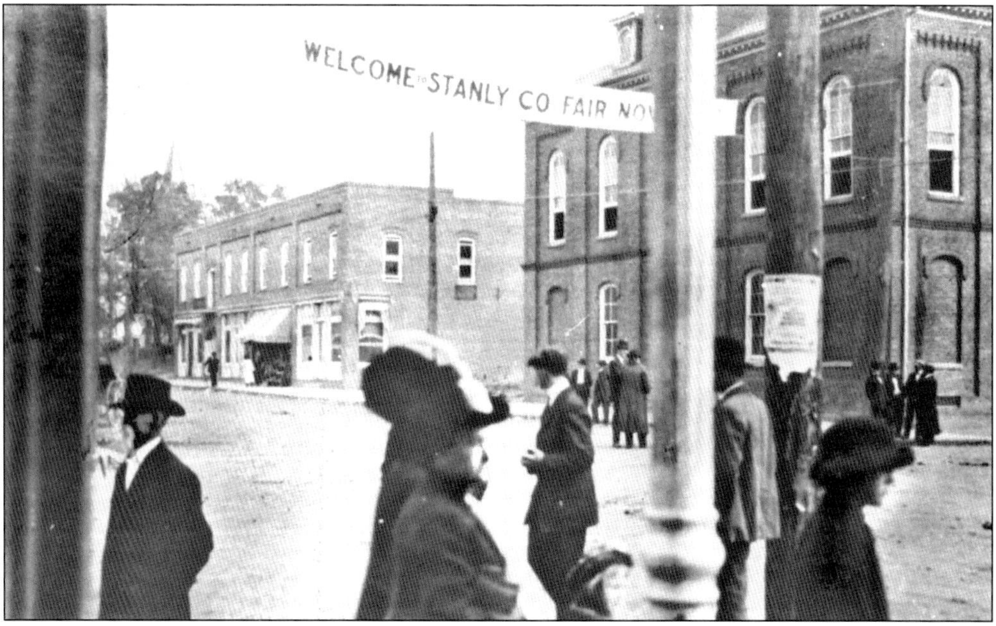

Welcome to the Stanly County Fair! In this image from November 1914, the banner spans the entire town square. (Courtesy of the Stanly County Museum.)

Contents

Acknowledgments

I would like to thank the following for their contributions and assistance in completing this book: Lessie Huneycutt, Abbie Rudolph, B.J. Garrison, Ticka Morrow, Dotty Plyler, National Association of Civilian Conservation Corps Alumni, *The Stanly News & Press*, the Boardroom, Gene Starnes, Jane Rogers, John T. Williams Jr., David's Frame Shop, Albemarle Fire Department, Hannah Hearne, the Stanly County Public Library, Tim Pressley, Terry Hamra, Roger Thomas, Dent Turner, the Patterson family, Joe Kluttz, Dr. and Mrs. Whitman Smith, Zelma Eudy, the Dr. Hill family, the Morgan family, Larry Bowers, and Daniel Harkey.

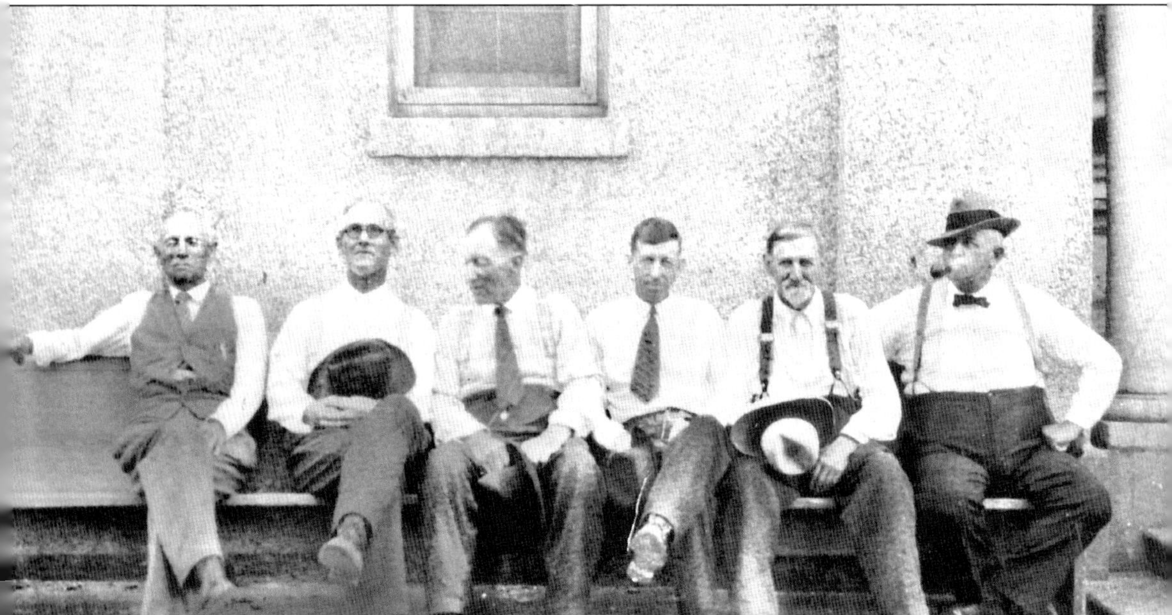

A group of gentlemen regularly met outside the courthouse and discussed matters of the day in the 1930s and 1940s. (Courtesy of the Stanly County Museum.)

Introduction

Like buried treasure, photographs are infinitely precious. Each holds a glimpse of the past waiting to be uncovered. Also, like buried treasure, photographs are often difficult to locate. One must navigate through dusty photograph albums, forgotten letters, and musty family Bibles to discover photographic treasures. Once found, however, each is a cache of riches. Together they form a map to connect all pieces of found information for future generations.

The riches contained in this book are treasures from Albemarle's past. These photographs are windows that provide a view of historic Albemarle. Photographs tell a story. They show what the past was like and how it evolved to the present. Many of the people and scenes depicted in this book are gone but are still remembered through photographs. They are visual images of recorded history and silent testaments to life in Albemarle for the past 160 years.

Albemarle is the county seat of Stanly County, which was created from Montgomery County on January 11, 1841. The city of Albemarle was named in honor of Albemarle County, the first county formed in North Carolina. That county was established in 1663 and was named after Gen. George Monck, the Duke of Albemarle as well as one of the eight "Lord Proprietors of Carolina."

The first commissioners of Stanly County were Parham Kirk, Daniel Palmer, Mathias Moose, John Little, Jacob Efird, Edward Davis, Richard Stoker, Sen. James Allen, and William Swaringen. These men were responsible for selecting a location for the county seat. Nancy Hearne, the widow of Nehemiah Hearne, donated 51 acres of land for the county seat. Of the 51 acres, 1 acre was reserved for the courthouse and the jail. The remaining 50 acres were sectioned off into 79 equal lots by W.H. Randle, the county surveyor, and auctioned off to raise money for constructing the courthouse, jail, and other public buildings.

From the time of its founding in 1857 through the present day, Albemarle has grown and changed. This photographic treasury documents the people and events that have shaped this Southern Piedmont town. While these images document Albemarle's past, they are not completely representative of the city's history. Not all classes and ethnic groups could afford a photographer's fee. Thus, many citizens are not photographically represented in proportion to their historical significance.

Photographs are a treasure map to the past. It is our hope that *Images of America: Albemarle* will inspire local citizens to begin their own treasure hunt for family photos, each of which will further illuminate the rich history of Albemarle, North Carolina.

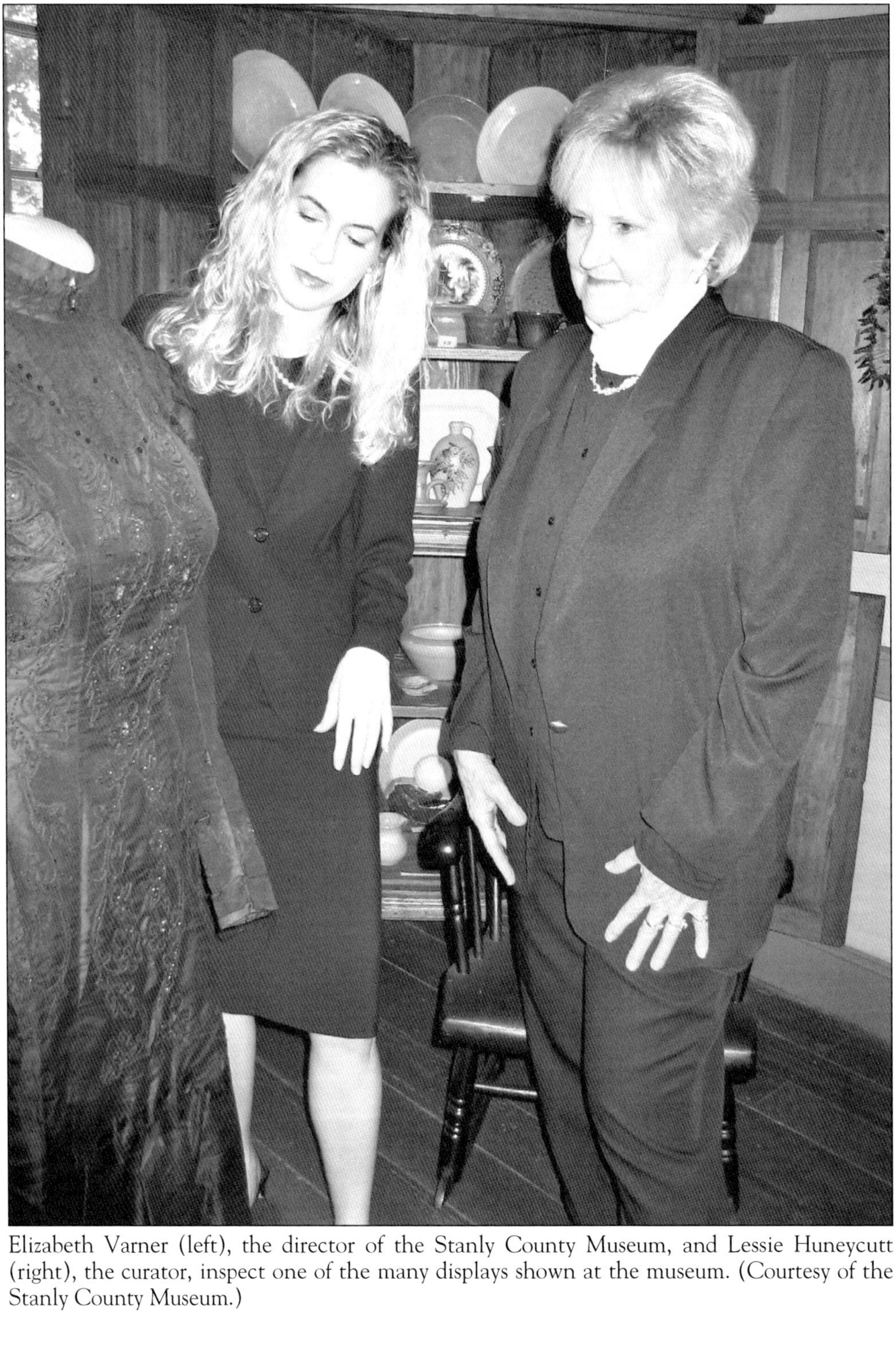

Elizabeth Varner (left), the director of the Stanly County Museum, and Lessie Huneycutt (right), the curator, inspect one of the many displays shown at the museum. (Courtesy of the Stanly County Museum.)

One

ALBEMARLE

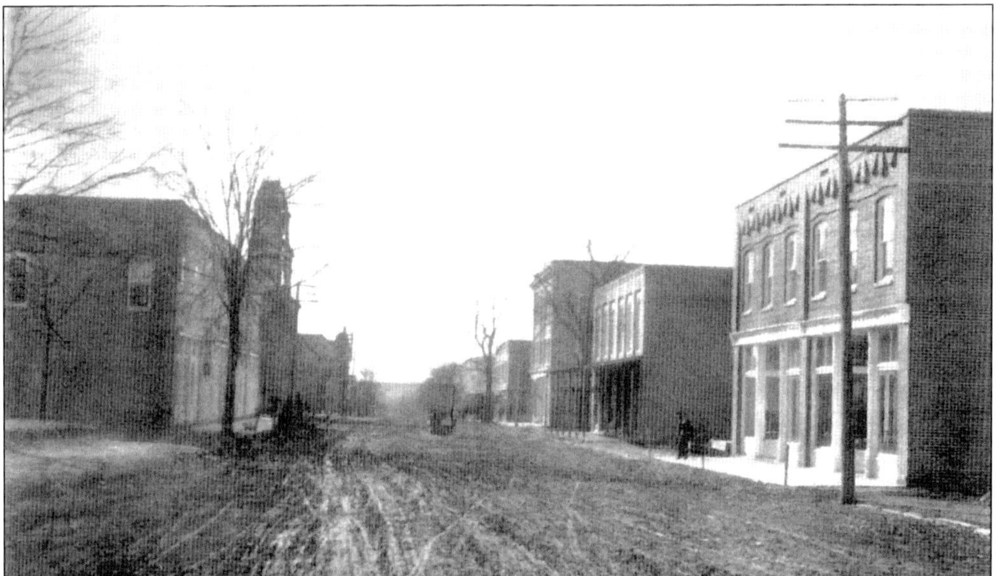

Looking south on Second Street in 1917, the well, located in the middle of the road, can clearly be seen. The courthouse on the left, the hitching post, and the wooden sidewalks can also be viewed in this photograph. (Courtesy of the Stanly County Museum.)

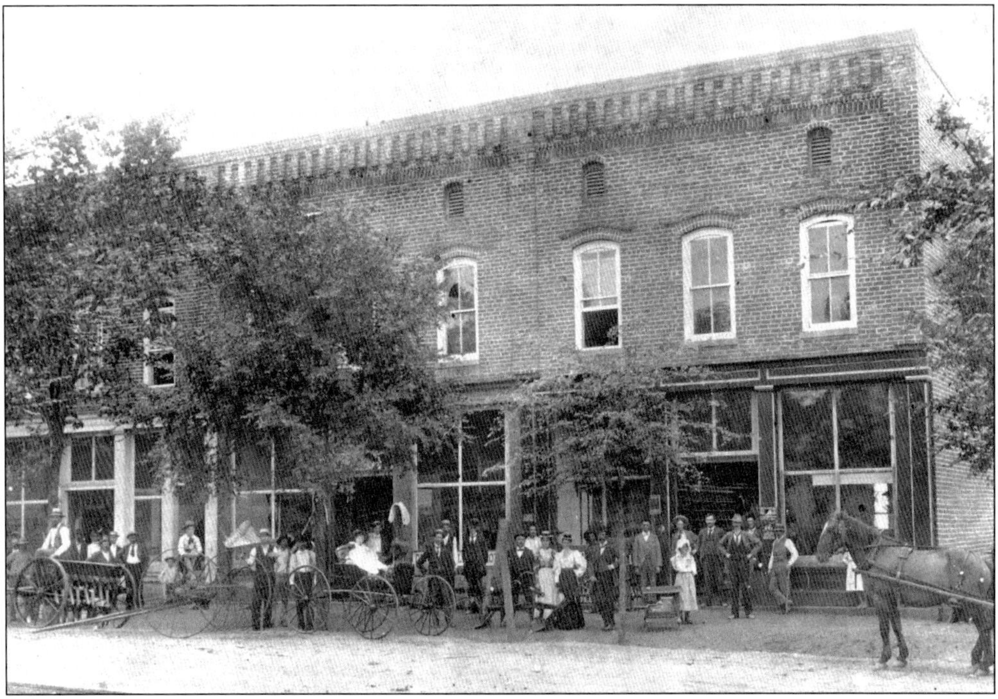

In 1895, traffic slows to a halt in front of the original Morrow Brothers and Heath Store, founded in the late 1800s. Farming equipment and goods were sold there, such as lamps, nails, seeds, hardware, and building materials. (Courtesy of the Stanly County Museum.)

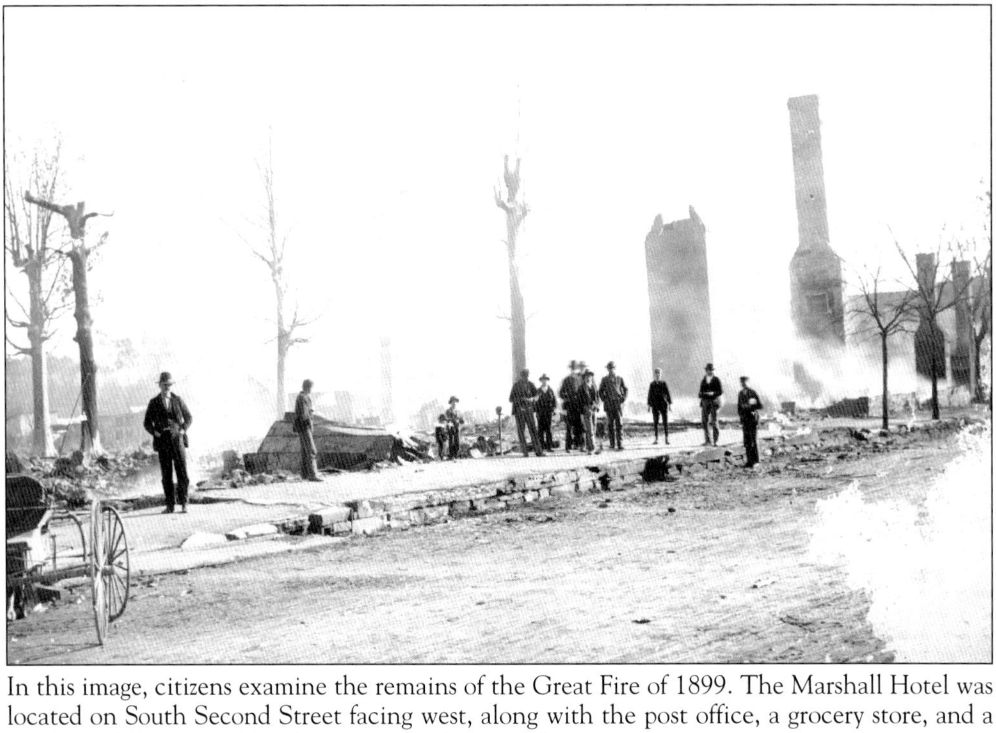

In this image, citizens examine the remains of the Great Fire of 1899. The Marshall Hotel was located on South Second Street facing west, along with the post office, a grocery store, and a boutique. (Courtesy of the Stanly County Museum.)

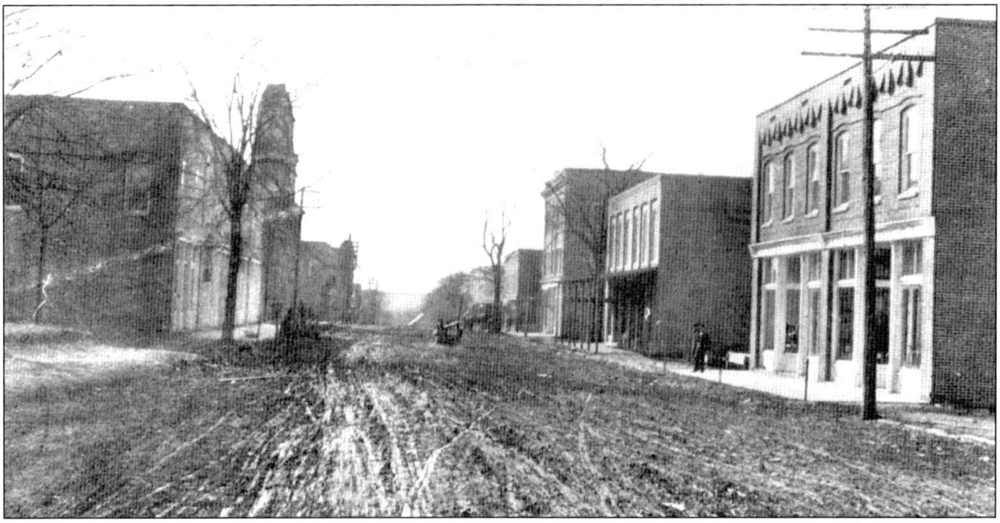

The Marks and Hearne buildings are shown in this 1907 image on the left of Second Street facing south. The tall building on the right is the Stanly County Loan & Trust Company. Again notice the well in front of the courthouse. (Courtesy of the Stanly County Museum.)

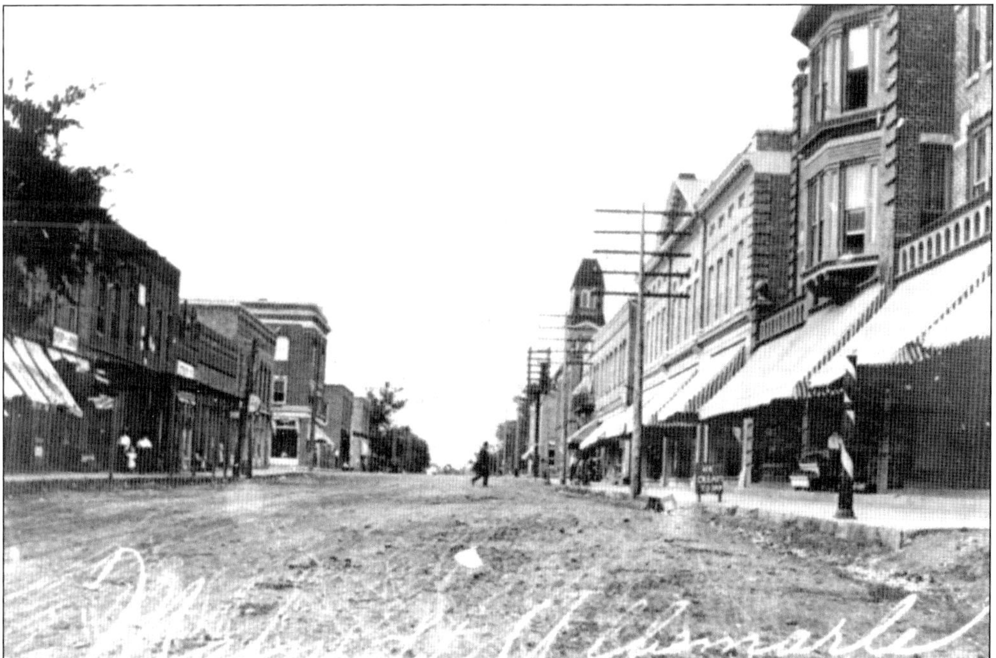

In 1909, this scene looking north on Second Street could have been viewed. Central Hotel and the second courthouse stand on the right side of the dirt road. (Courtesy of the Stanly County Museum.)

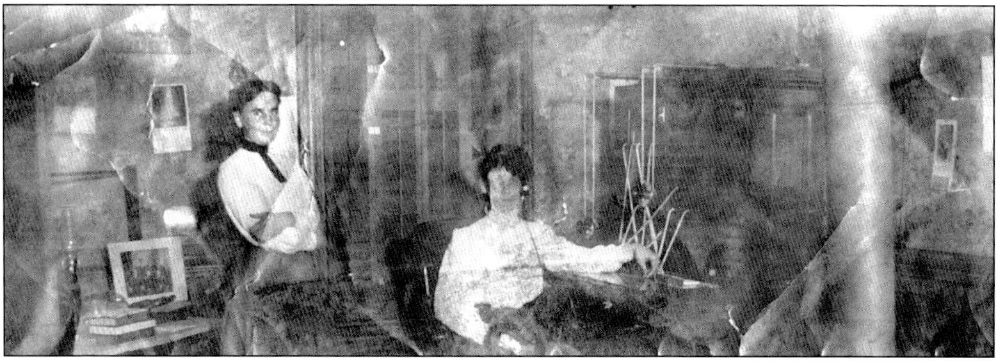

Sallie Marks and Fannie Harris operate the first telephone switchboard in the county *c.* 1910. Sallie Marks later became the first female professor at the University of North Carolina at Chapel Hill, teaching English literature. (Courtesy of the Stanly County Museum.)

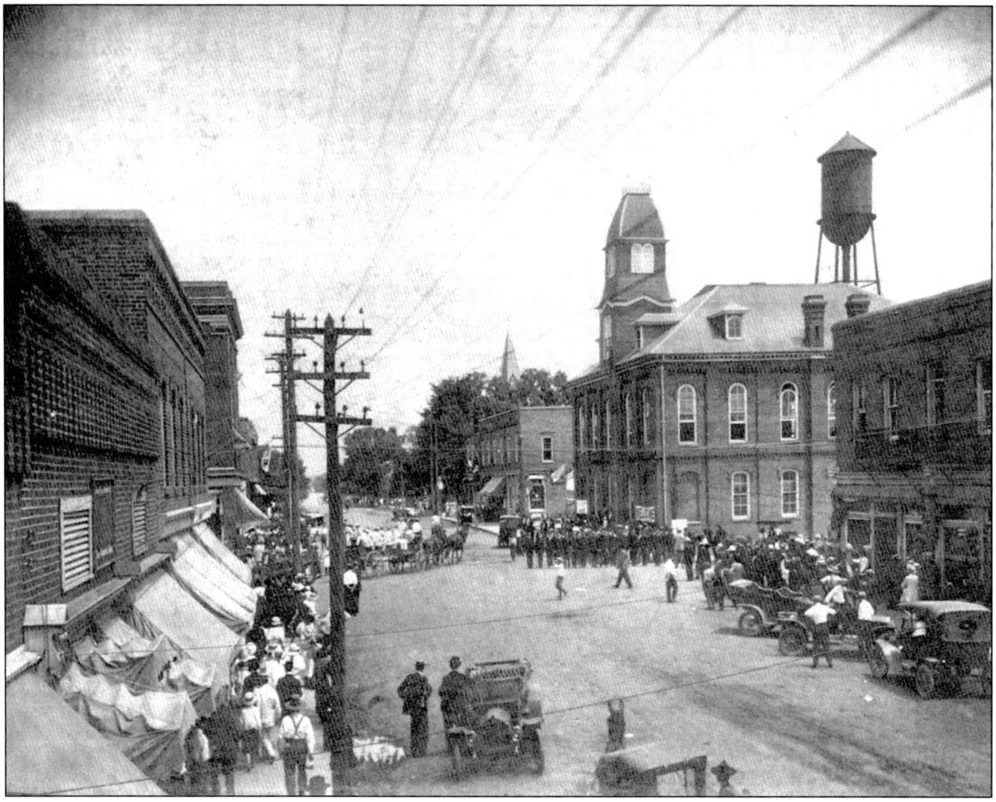

In 1912, citizens joined together for Fourth of July festivities in the town square. The courthouse is in the background beneath the water tower. (Courtesy of the Stanly County Museum.)

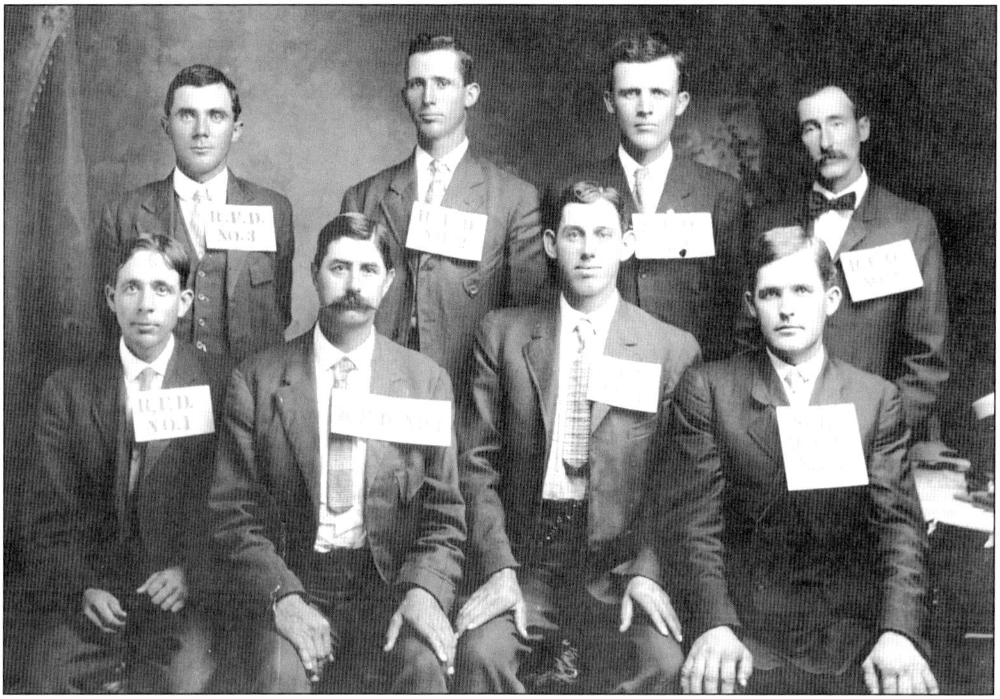

Albemarle rural mail carriers pose with their routes pinned to their lapels in 1913. From left to right are the following: (front row) Ernest Ritchie, unidentified, George Pickler, and unidentified; (back row) unidentified, Garrett Pickler, unidentified, and Luke Ritchie. (Courtesy of the Stanly County Museum.)

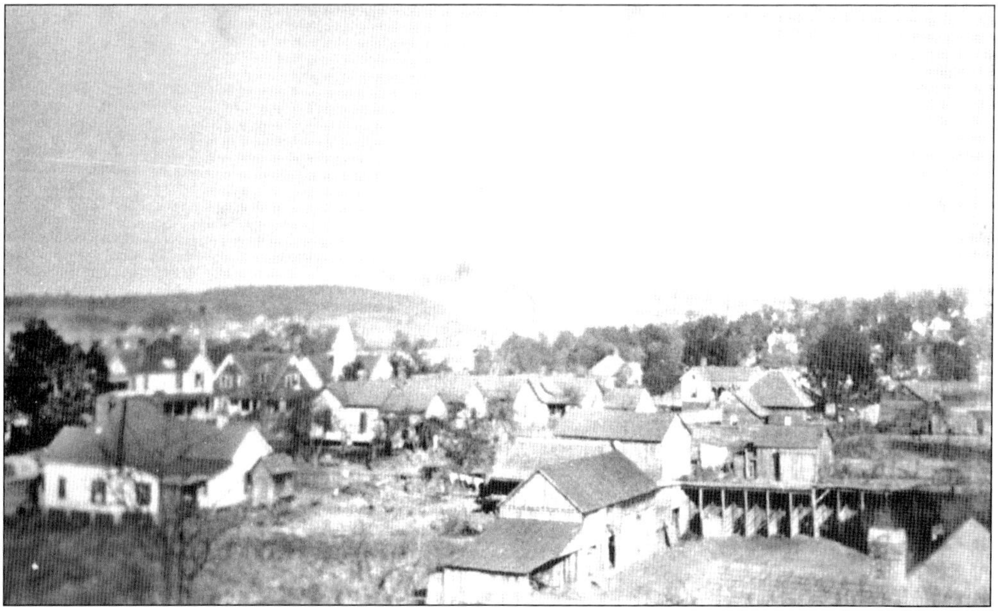

In 1914, this view could be seen from the top of the Stanly County Loan & Trust Building at the square. You may have noticed the stables in the photograph; it is believed that they belonged to P.J. Huneycutt Furniture and Undertakers. The stables would have housed the horses needed to pull the hearse. (Courtesy of the Stanly County Museum.)

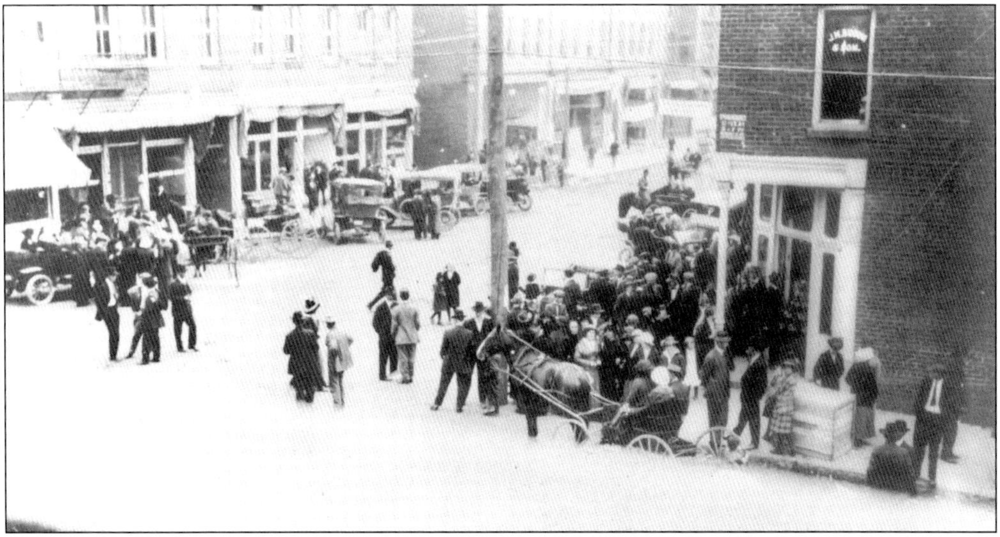

This 1915 view of Second Street is from the top of Stanly County Loan & Trust Building at the town square. The Lyric Theatre is pictured in the background. Shoppers enter Allen's entrance. Allen's, founded in 1906 by H.B. Allen and T.C. Rivers, sold clothing. (Courtesy of the Stanly County Museum.)

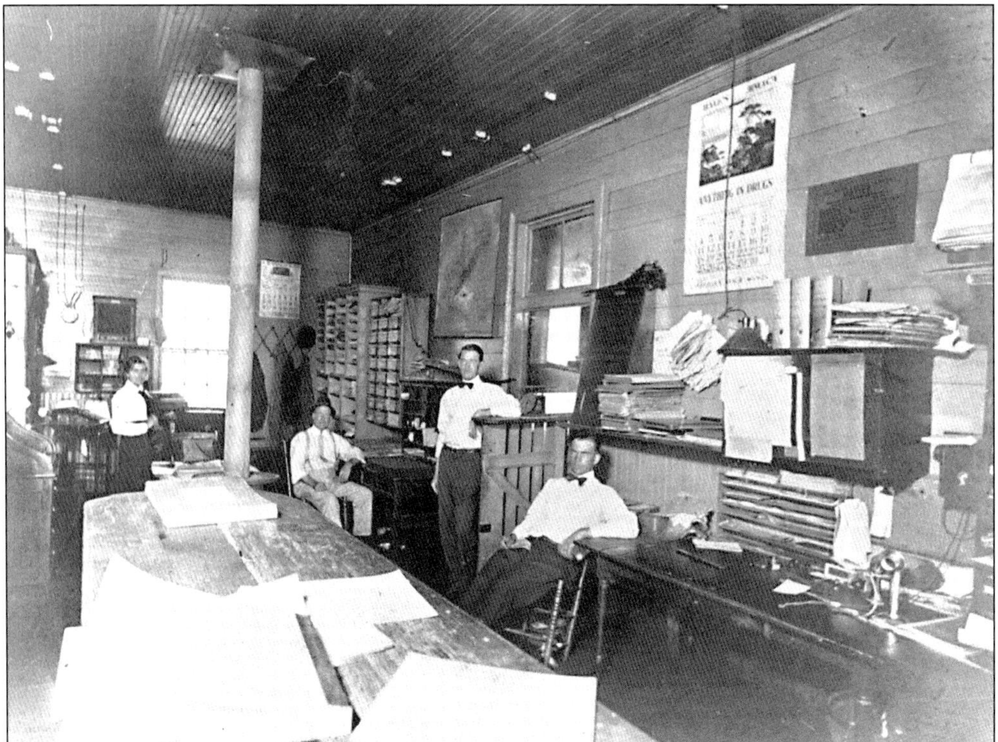

Workers pause in 1915 for this photograph of the interior of Albemarle's Yadkin Railroad Depot. Note the calendar on the right wall from Hall's Pharmacy as well as the iron stove. Pictured here are, from left to right, Mary Ella Austin, L.S. Whitworth, O.D. Shoe, and an unidentified man. (Courtesy of the Stanly County Museum.)

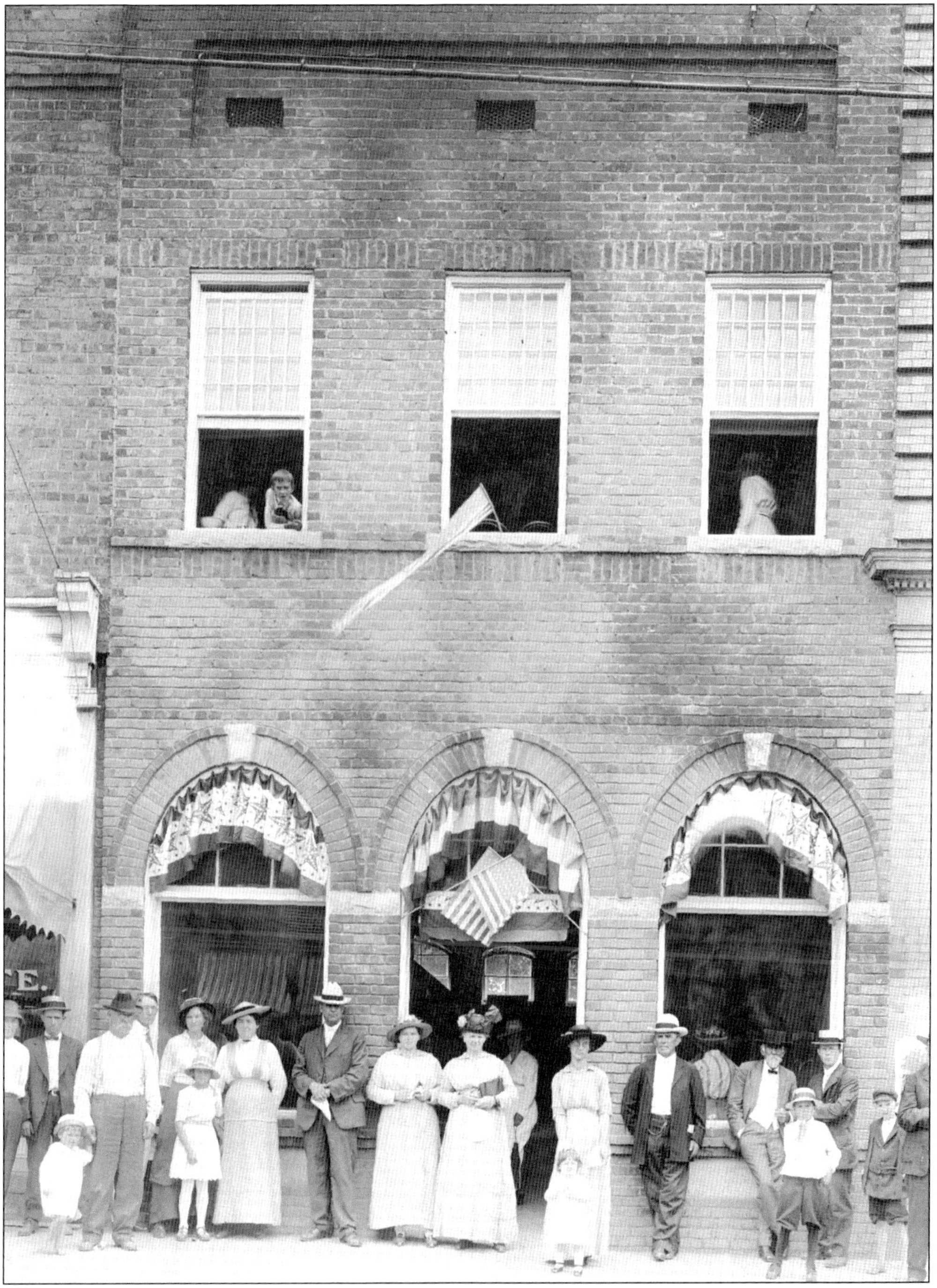

The Stanly County Community Building was built on South Second Street and dedicated on June 30, 1915. This community building was the first one in North Carolina built exclusively for the use of women and children. Albemarle Library, later Stanly County Library, was located in the Stanly County Community Building from 1916 until 1939. (Courtesy of the Stanly County Museum.)

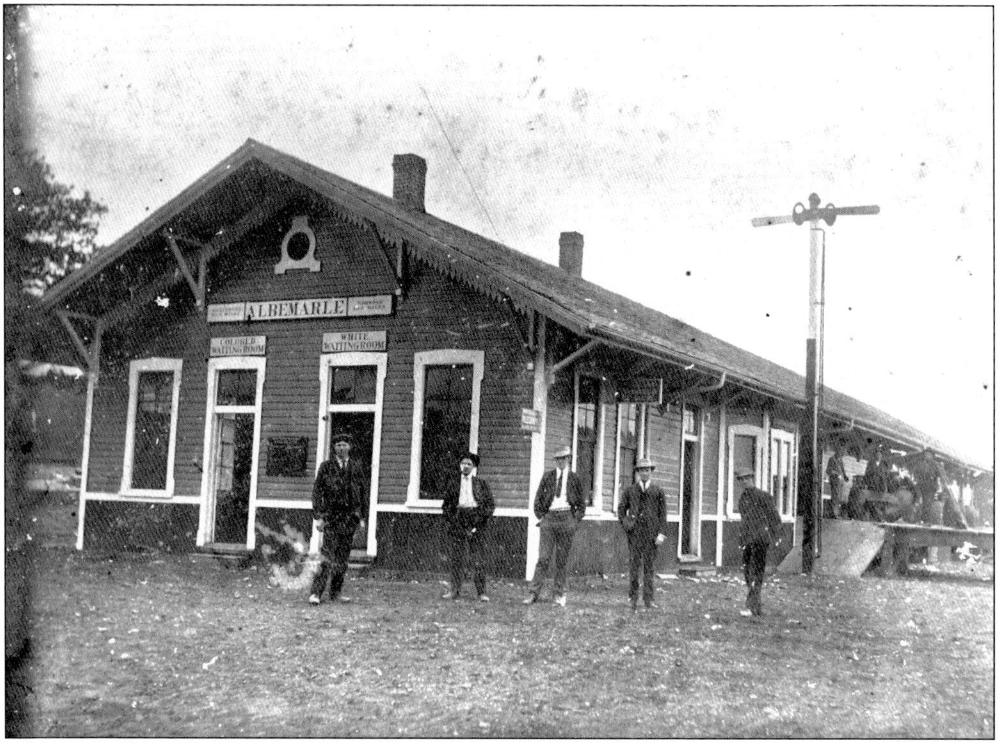

Passengers wait for the Southern Railroad train to arrive in this image from 1915. The Yadkin Railroad, constructed in 1891, was the first railroad built in Stanly County. Notice the signs over the doorways indicating segregated waiting rooms. (Courtesy of the Stanly County Museum.)

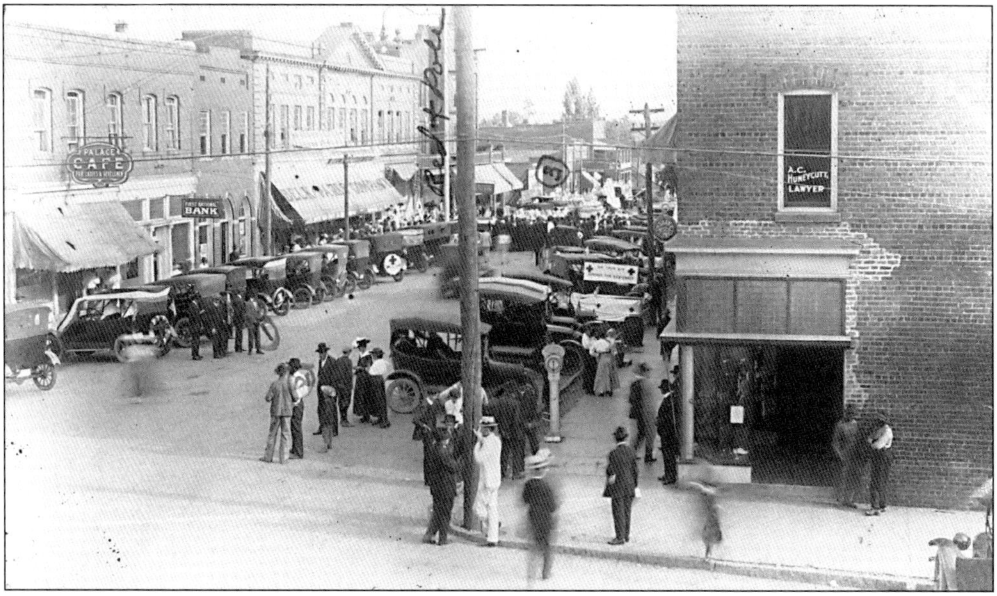

On May 18, a Red Cross flag is raised in front of the Dennings and James building on Second Street, c. 1917. The façade of the Belks-Parks building, where the current courthouse is located, can also be seen in this photograph. (Courtesy of the Stanly County Museum.)

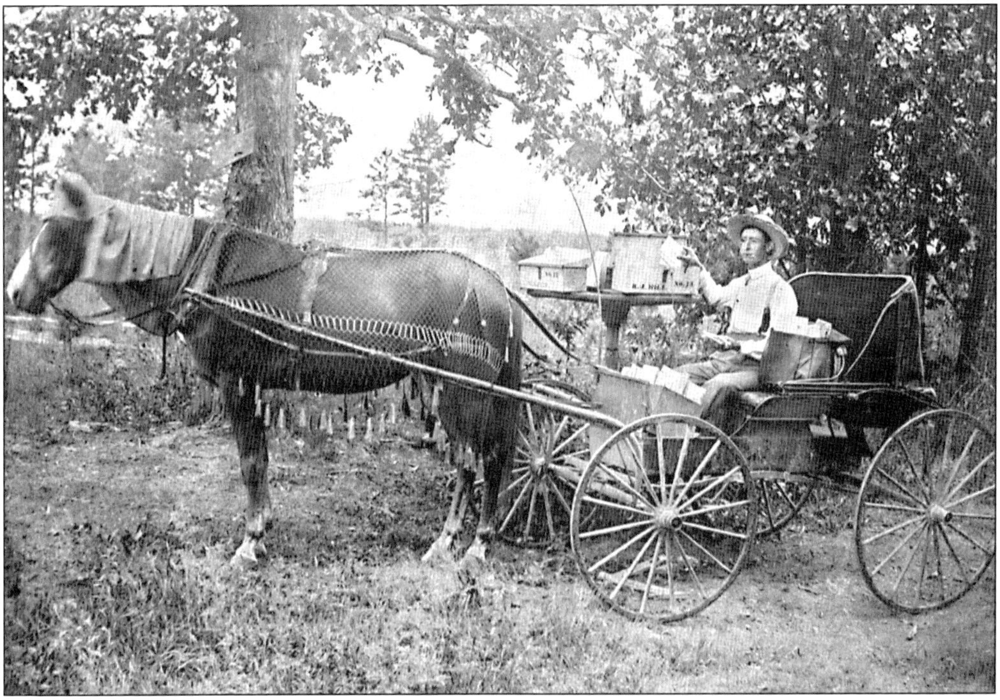

Mail carrier Martin L. James delivered mail via horse and buggy, beginning when he was 18 or 19 years old. (Courtesy of the Stanly County Museum.)

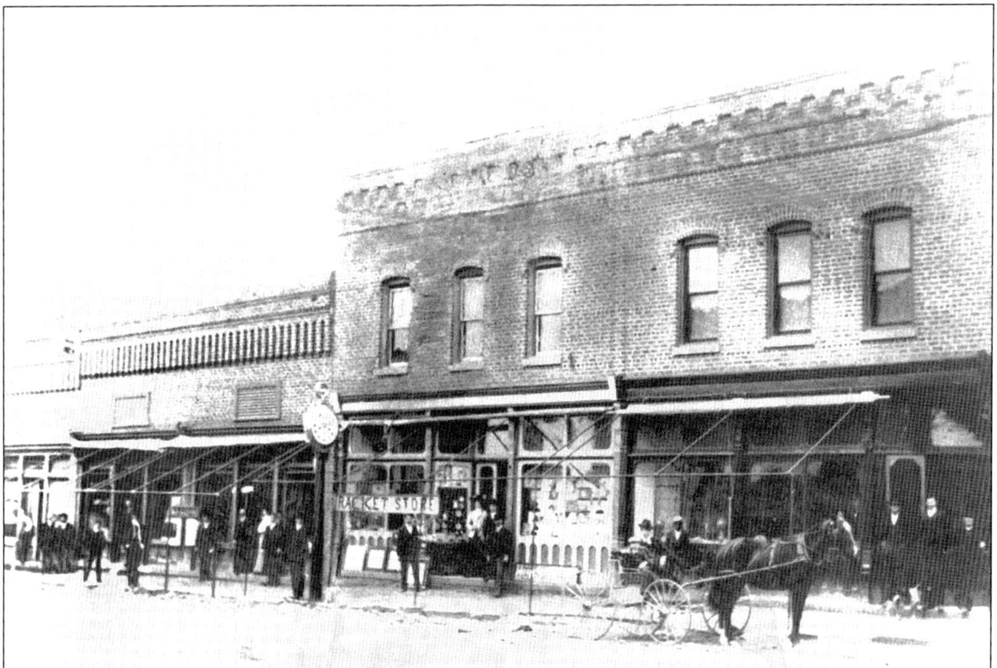

Allen's Clothing Store and the Racket Store were located on the west side of the first block of South Second Street. Notice the iron frames used for the hitching posts in this turn-of-the-century photograph. (Courtesy of the Stanly County Museum.)

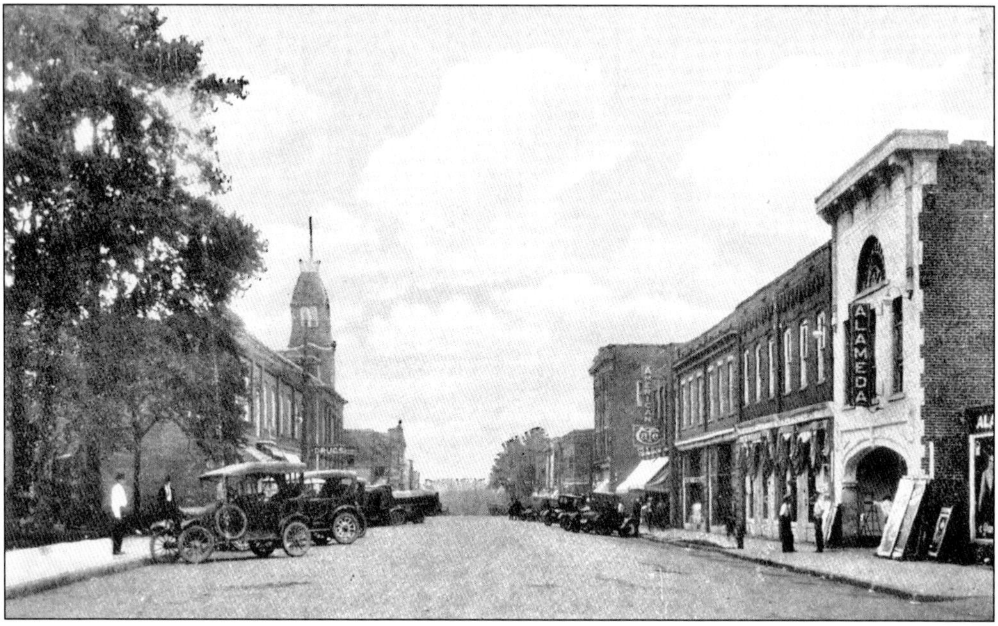

This 1923 view of Second Street depicts the oldest part of the business section of Albemarle. The population of Albemarle in 1893 was 200. In 1923, some 30 years later, the population had swelled to 10,000. (Courtesy of David's Frame Shop.)

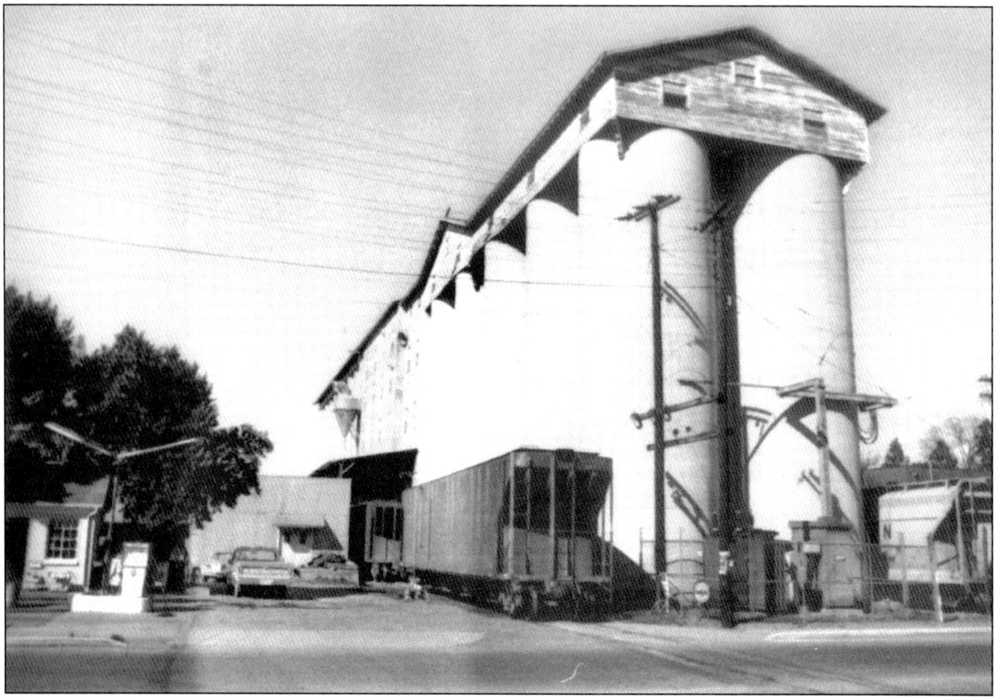

Known as the "Gateway to Albemarle," the concrete silos and grain elevators of the All Star Flour Mills extend 70 feet above downtown Albemarle. The All Star Flour Mills moved to Albemarle in 1918. (Courtesy of the Stanly County Museum.)

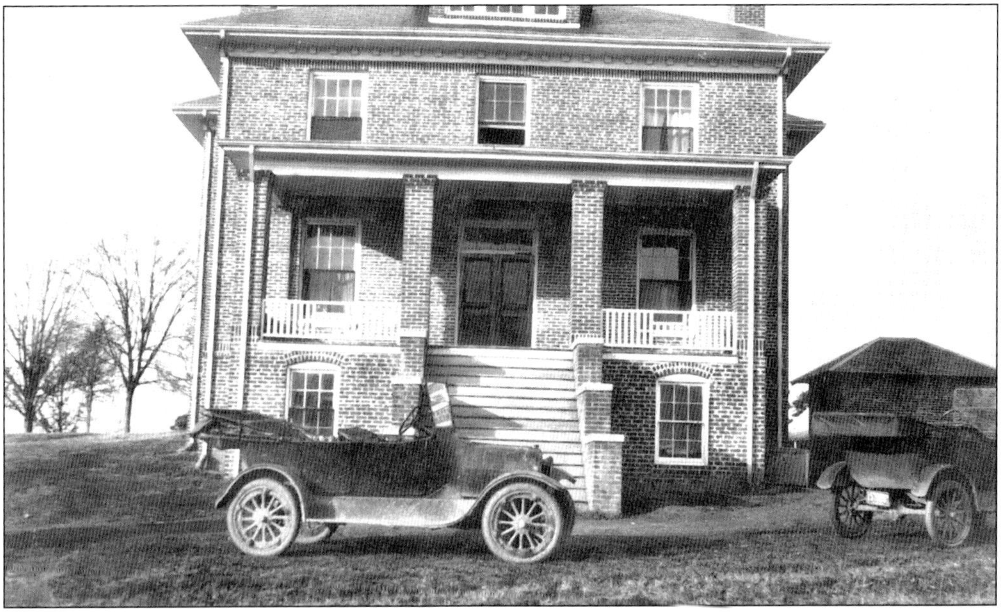

The County Home on Old Salisbury Road was a place for the elderly and infirm. In 1927, J.C. Burleson was elected keeper of the County Home. Slate from the roof of this building is now on the building located at 211 East Main Street. (Courtesy of the Stanly County Museum.)

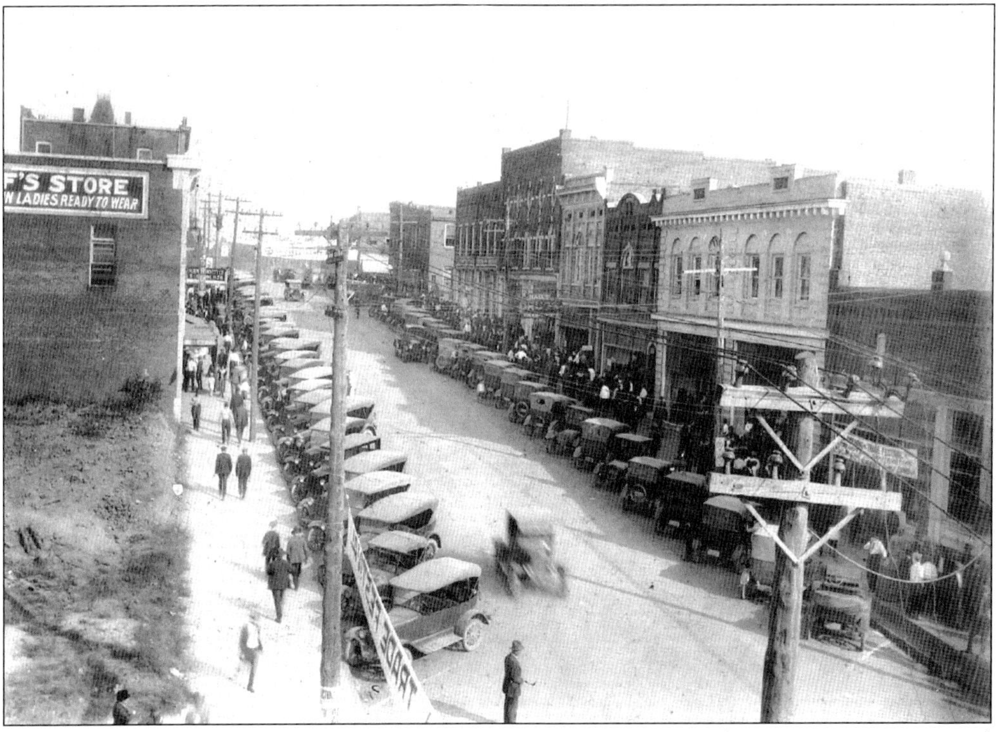

Crowds gather in the 1920s for a trade show sponsored by Efird Mill on Main Street. Located on the right side of the street, starting in the foreground, are Cabarrus Bank, Efird's Department Store, G.M. Dry, Dr. J.C. Hall's drugstore, Starnes Jewelry, and Huneycutt Furniture and Undertakers. (Courtesy of the Stanly County Museum.)

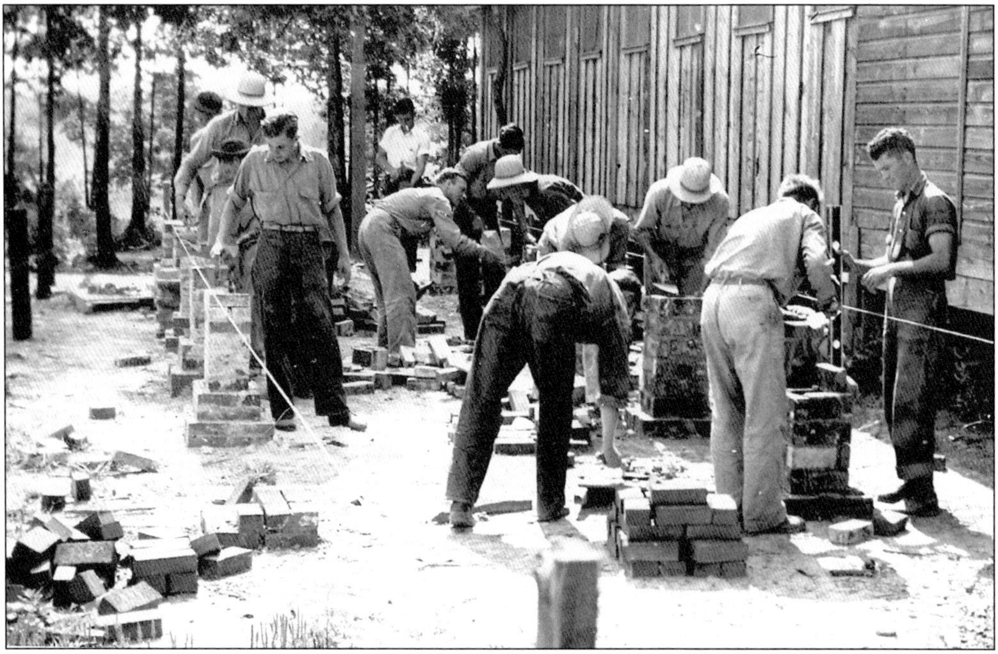

Workers build the structures at Camp Doughton for the United States Civilian Conservation Corps (CCC) in 1936. This camp was located at the corner of East Main Street and Coggins Avenue. One of the many aid programs created by President Roosevelt's New Deal, the CCC was instrumental in building roads and trails at Morrow Mountain State Park. (Courtesy of the National Association of Civilian Conservation Corps Alumni.)

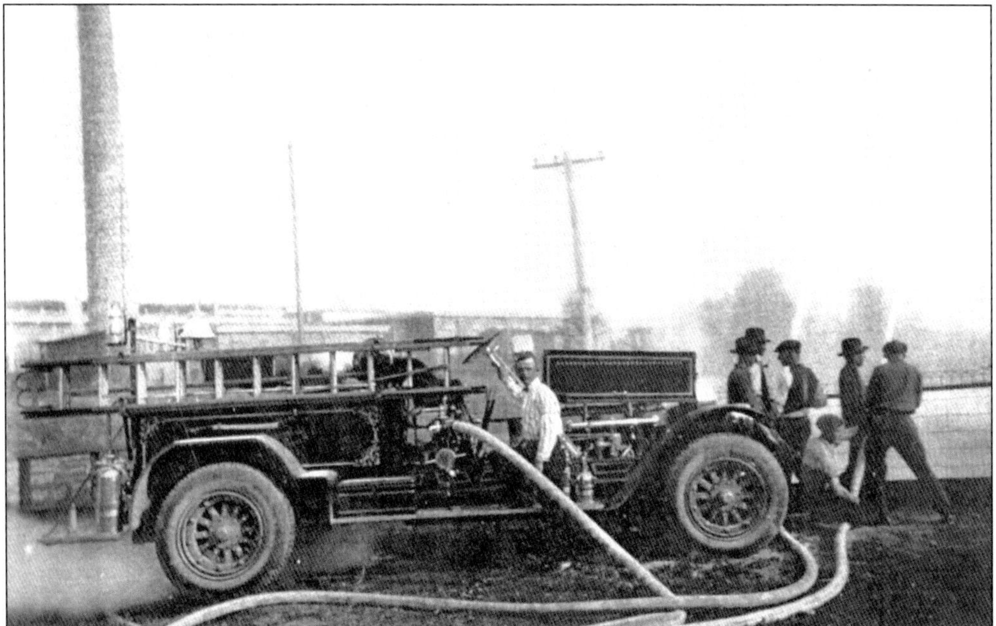

Members of the Albemarle Fire Department train with a fire hose at the Albemarle football field in 1938. Wiscassett Mill can be seen in the background. (Courtesy of the Albemarle Fire Department.)

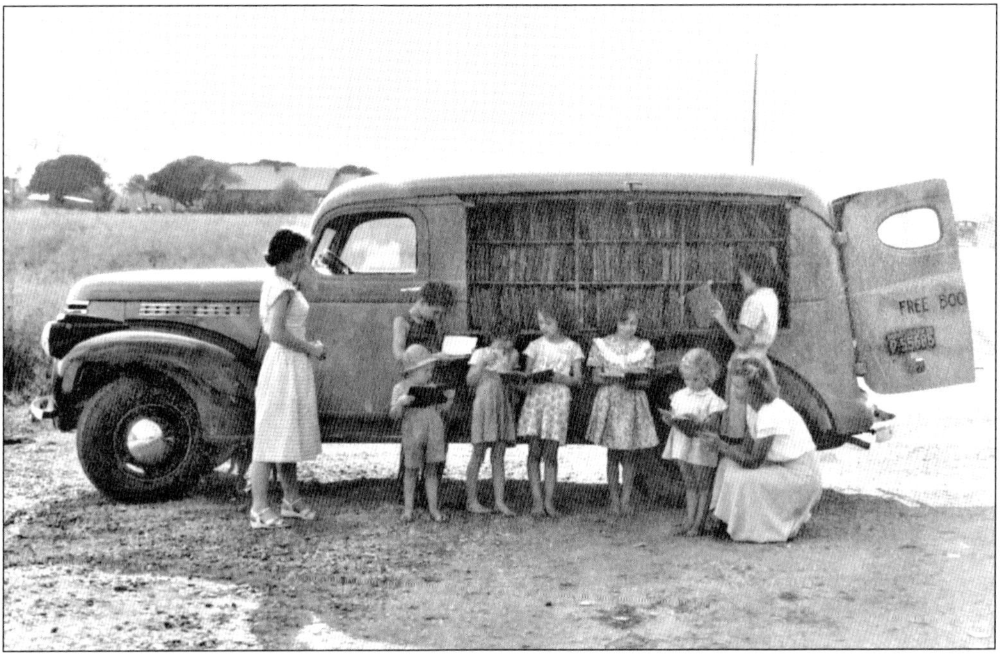

The first bookmobiles were used on June 23, 1947, by Mrs. Paul Williams. There were 32 book distribution locations throughout the county. Over $1,000 had been raised to purchase the bookmobile by 1941, but delays ensued as a result of World War II. (Courtesy of the Stanly County Public Library.)

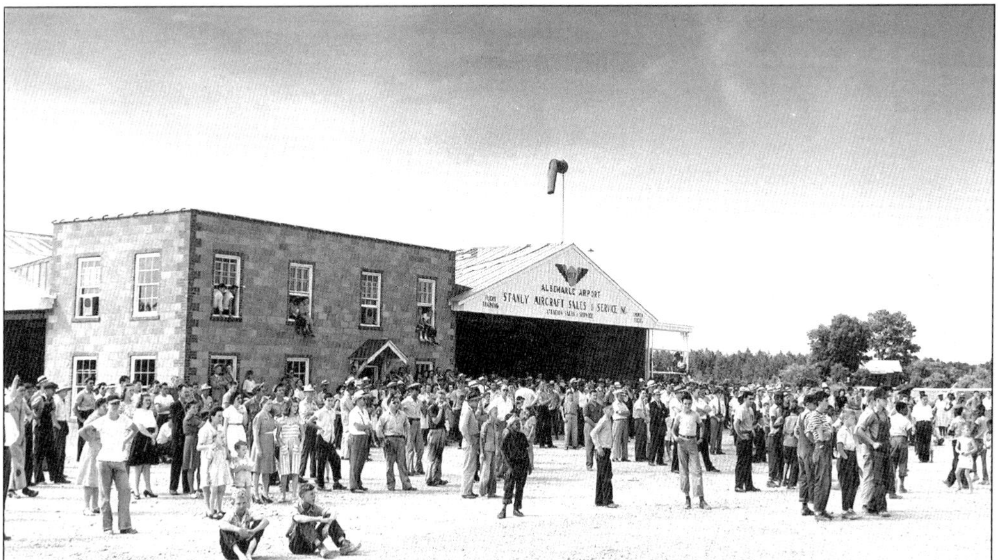

A crowd gathers for the opening of Albemarle's new airport in the summer of 1947. For the opening of the airport, there was an air show that featured acrobatic displays as well as military aircraft. The owners of the airport were Hazel L. "Chunk" Smith, J.C. Holbrook, Chad Efird, and Silas Dennis. (Courtesy of the Stanly County Museum.)

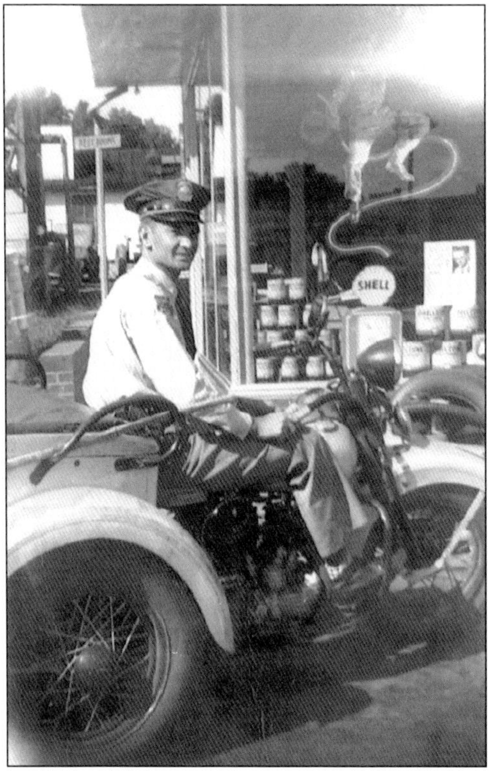

Albemarle police officer Will A. Calloway sits on a Harley Davidson three-wheeler outside of Herlocker's Service Station on West Main Street in 1950. (Courtesy of the Stanly County Museum.)

An Albemarle police officer cited a donkey tied outside the Democratic headquarters, located on the first floor of the Albemarle Hotel on North Second Street, during the May 1972 Presidential primary election. (Courtesy of *The Stanly County News & Press.*)

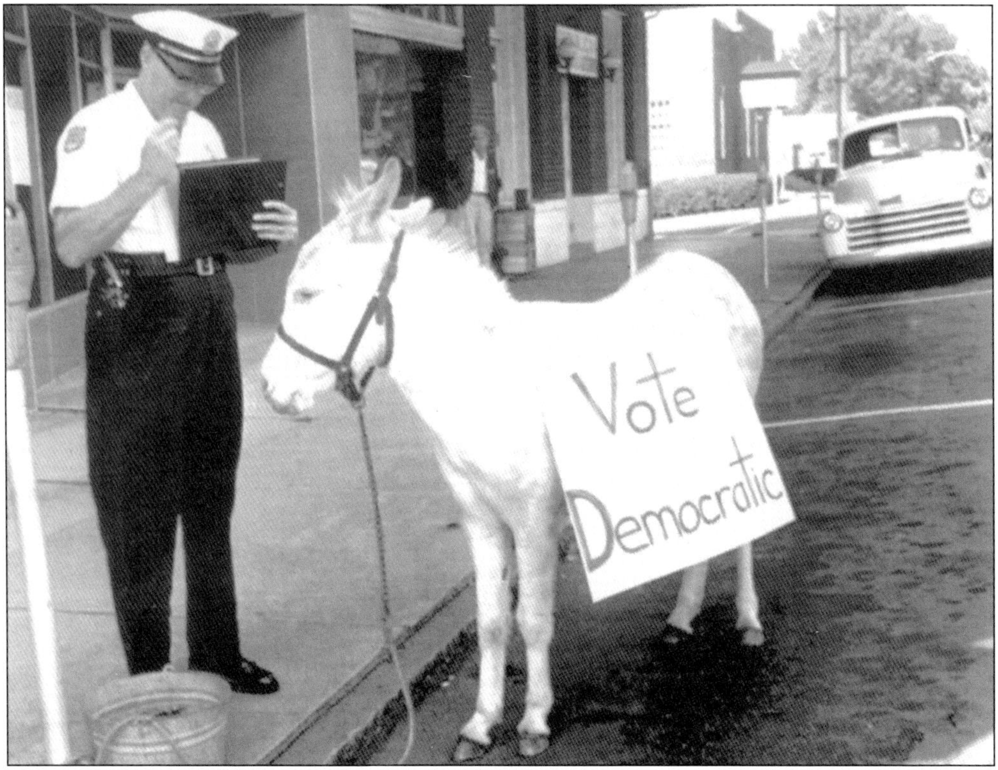

Two

LIFESTYLES

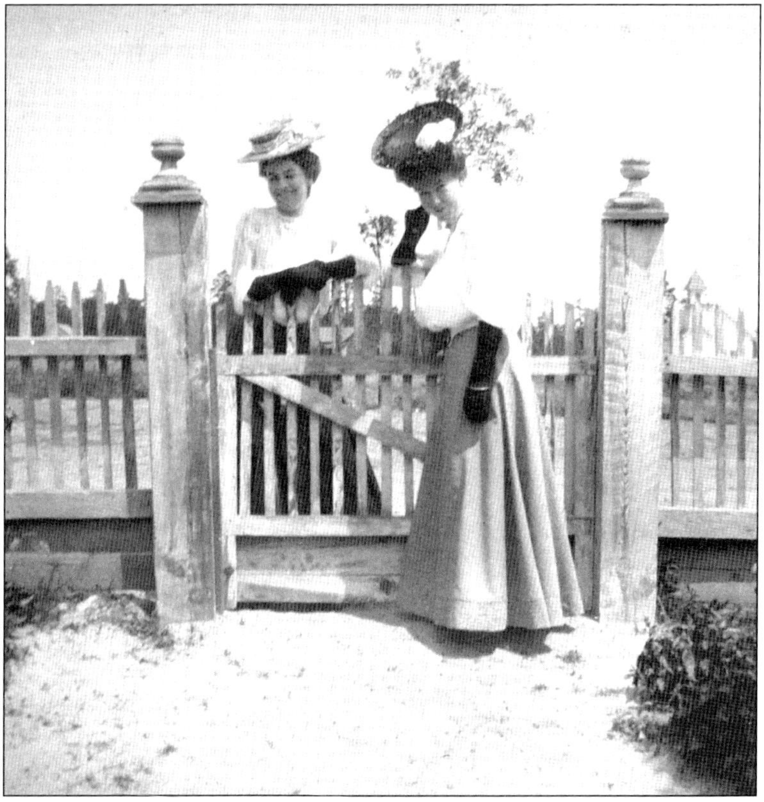

Lena Spinks and her unidentified friend stand by the gate discussing matters of mutual interest in the late 1800s. Spinks was the daughter of Henry W. Spinks, who started Spinks Academy, and she later married Dr. Laton. (Courtesy of the Stanly County Museum.)

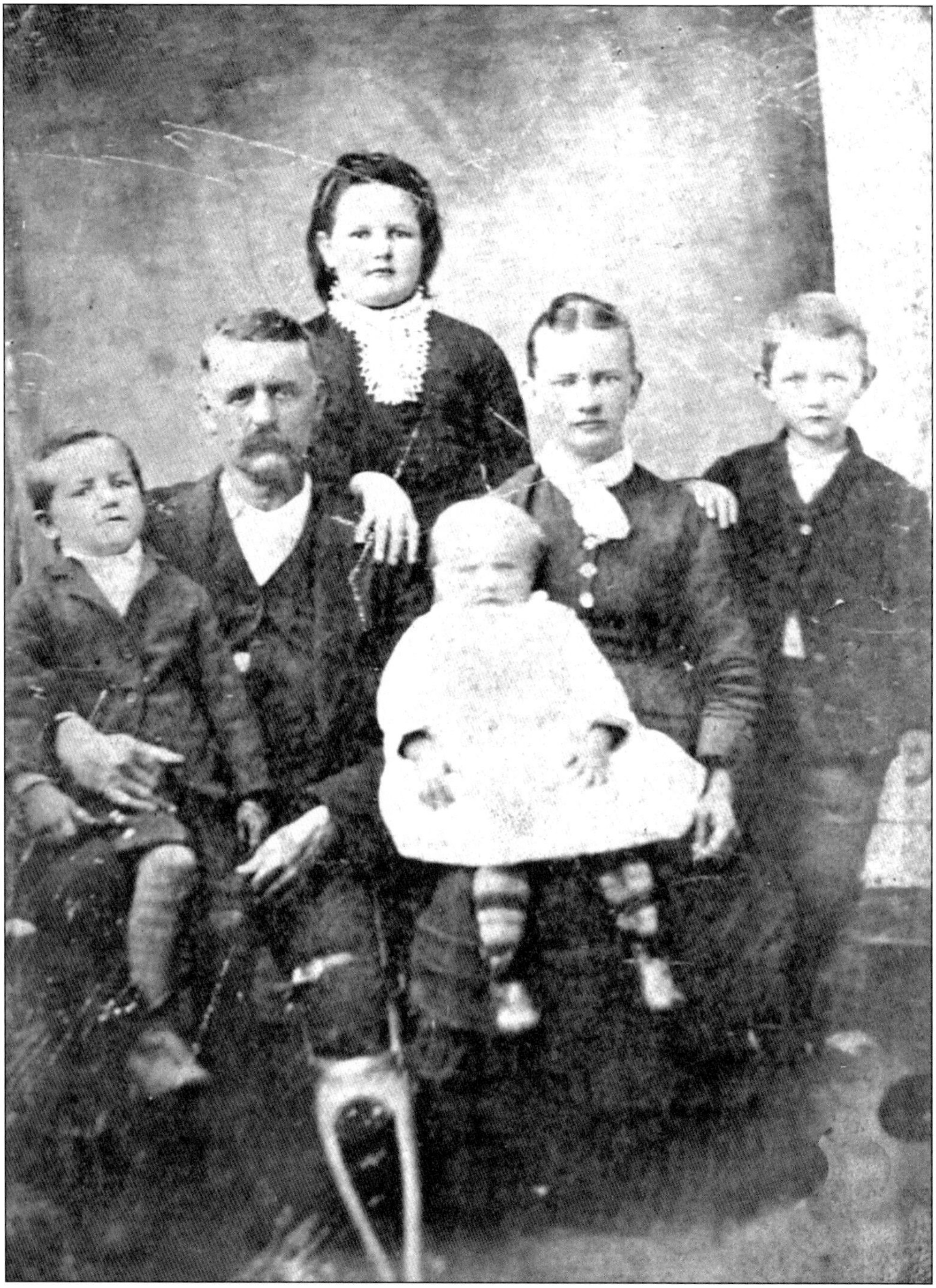

Isaiah W. "Buck" Snuggs sits with his family for a portrait in 1885. Snuggs, a Confederate soldier, lost his leg in the Battle of Spotsylvania Courthouse. He went on to become the ninth sheriff of Stanly County. His home is one of the historic properties owned by the Stanly County Museum. Pictured from left to right are his son Henry; Isaiah; his daughters Bertie and Mary; his wife, Ellen; and his son Ed. (Courtesy of the Stanly County Museum.)

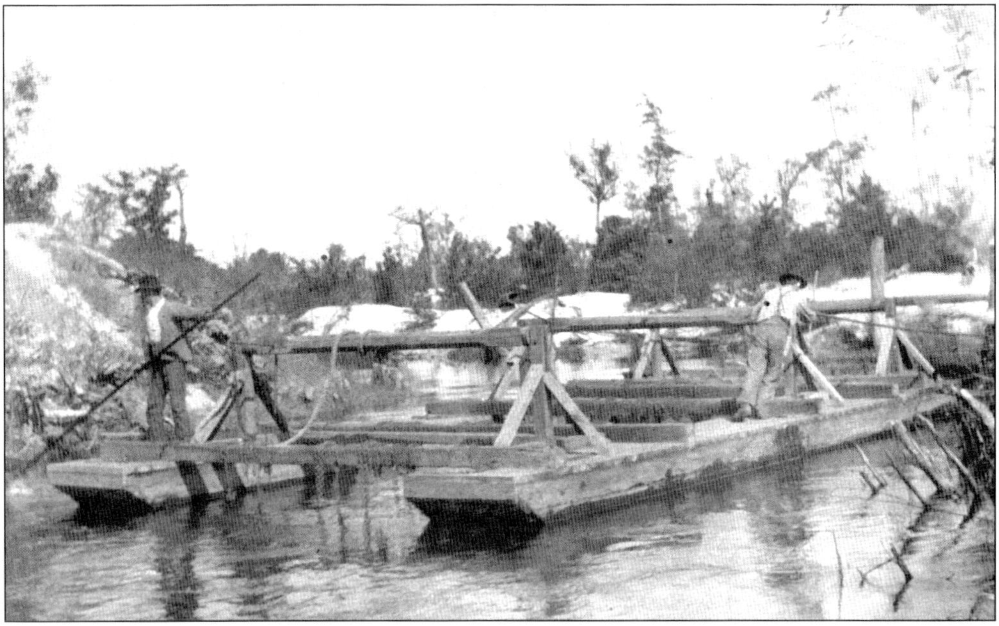

Ferries were often needed to cross the strong rivers. Prior to the formation of Stanly County, citizens on the west side of the river had to travel to Montgomery County Courthouse via ferry. Citizens living in the area that is now Albemarle could have crossed the river by the following ferries: Colson in 1770, Robert Lane in 1775, Tindalesville in 1808, Cupples in 1808, McLendon in 1808, Clarks in 1861, Swift Island in 1861, and Lowder's in 1910. (Courtesy of Dent Turner.)

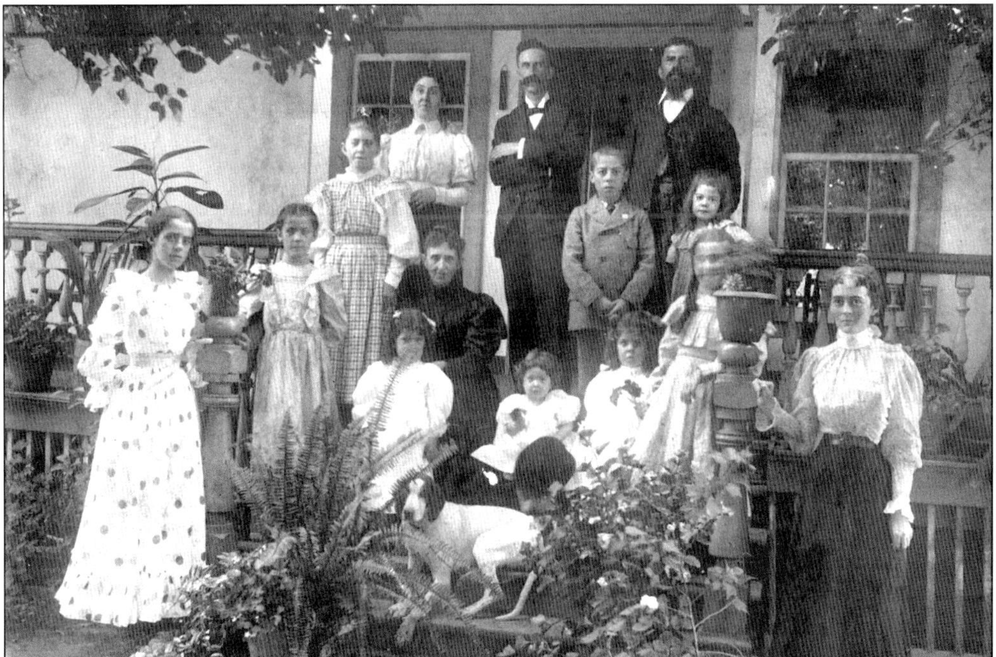

Sidney Hannibal Hearne's family gathers together at home on Albemarle's South First Street for a portrait in 1896. (Courtesy of the Stanly County Museum.)

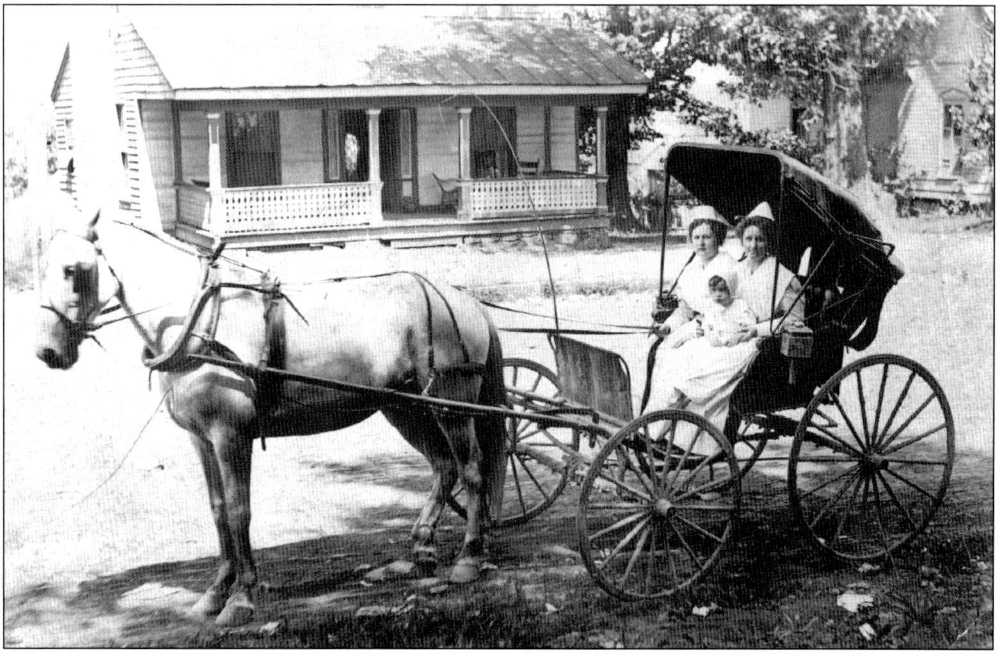

In 1910, nurses Jonah Ross of Wadesboro and Miss Stribling hold George A. "Buck" Morrow in a buggy parked in front of the John R. Ross House. The location is currently occupied by the Alameda Theater. (Courtesy of the Stanly County Museum.)

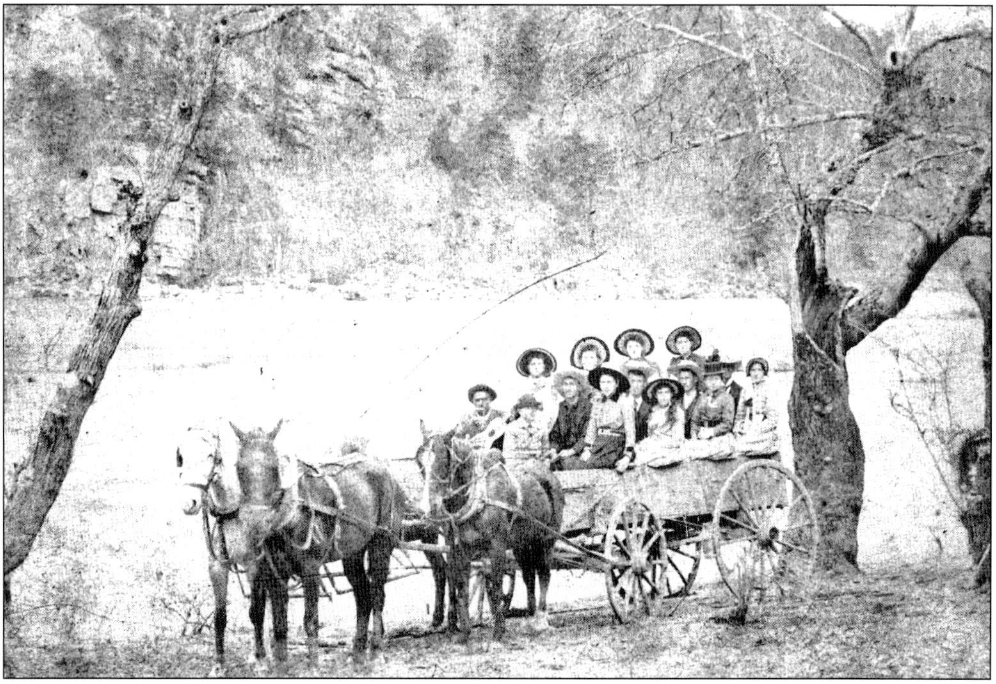

Lizzie and Pattie Ross with a group of children are out for a ride in a wagon pulled by four horses. They are going on a picnic for Easter Monday. (Courtesy of Dent Turner.)

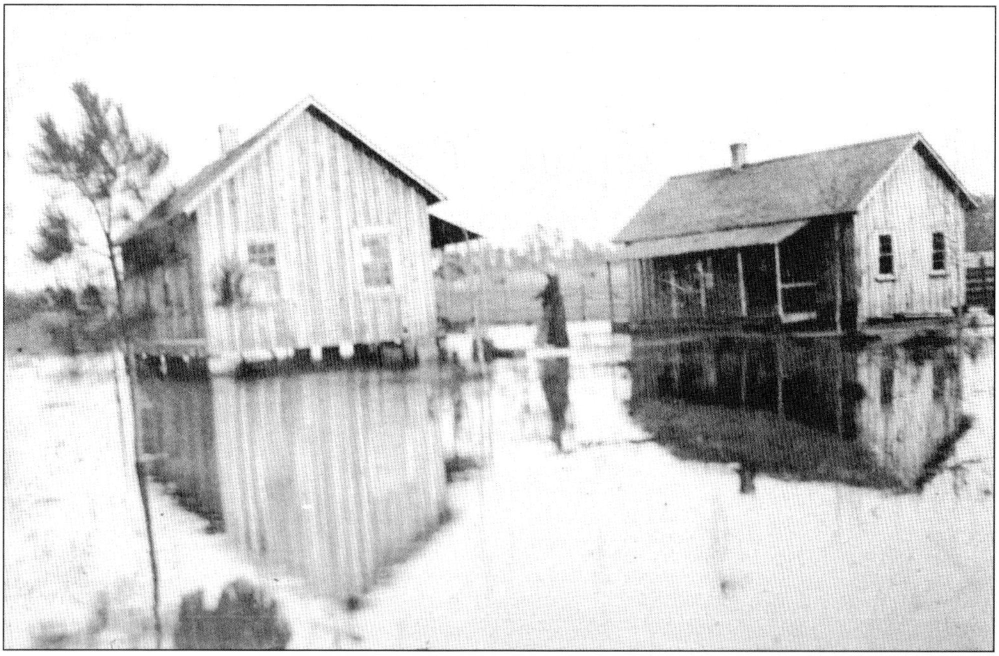

Strong rains often caused detrimental flooding. An unknown woman wades between two structures. (Courtesy of Dent Turner.)

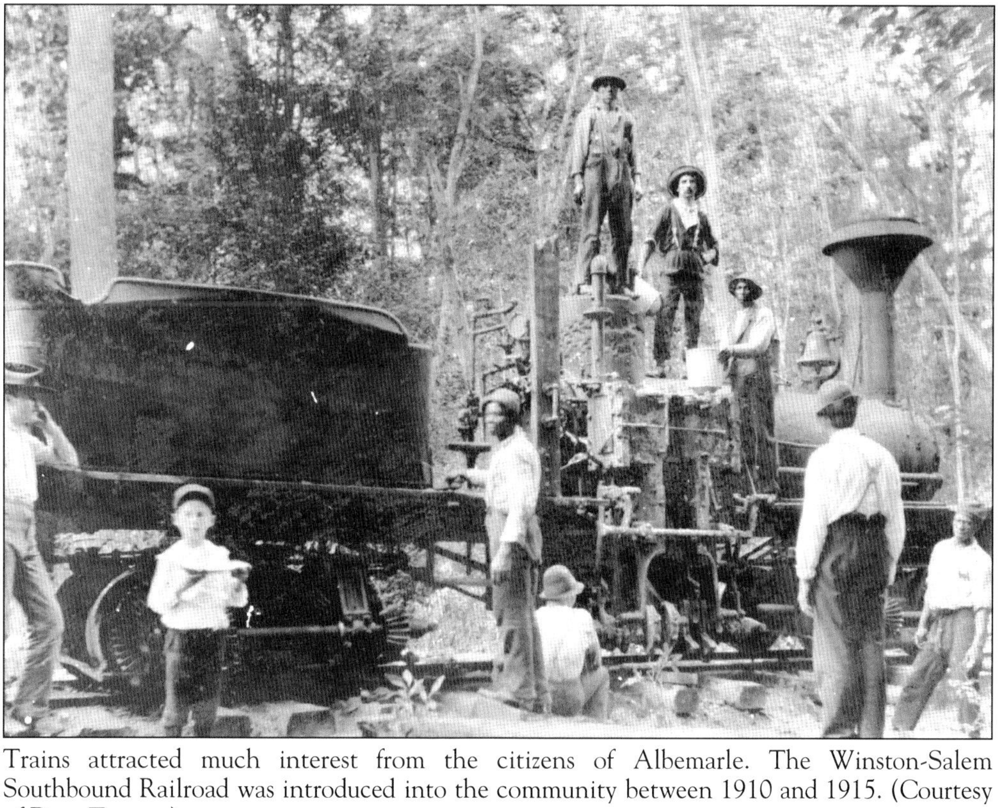

Trains attracted much interest from the citizens of Albemarle. The Winston-Salem Southbound Railroad was introduced into the community between 1910 and 1915. (Courtesy of Dent Turner.)

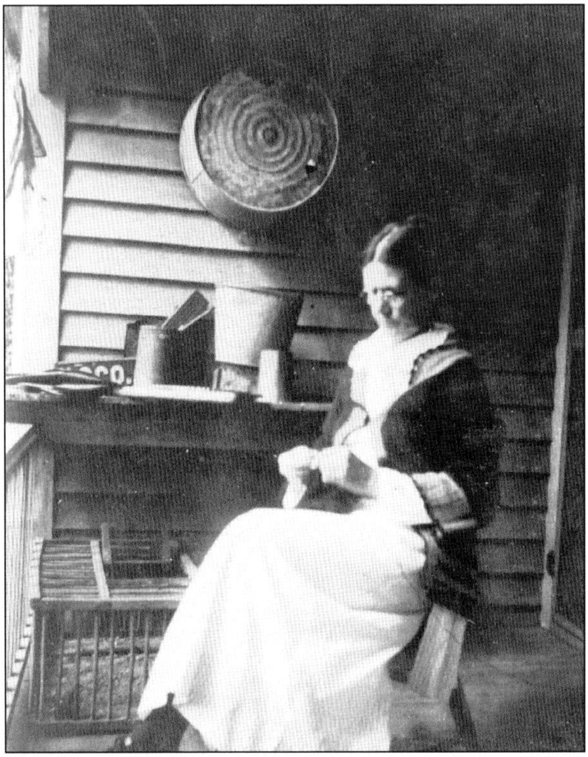

Mrs. Watkins sits on the back porch of her home at 232 North Second Street. A wash pan hangs on the wall behind her. (Courtesy of the Stanly County Museum.)

Wagons were loaded with produce to take to market. (Courtesy of Dent Turner.)

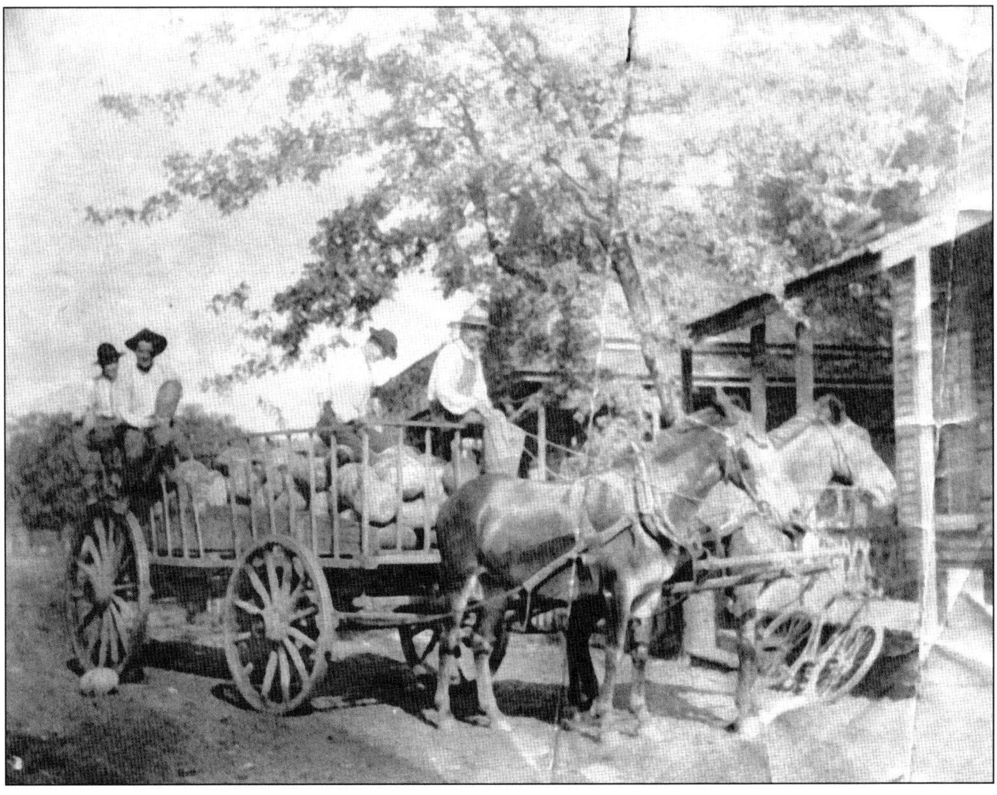

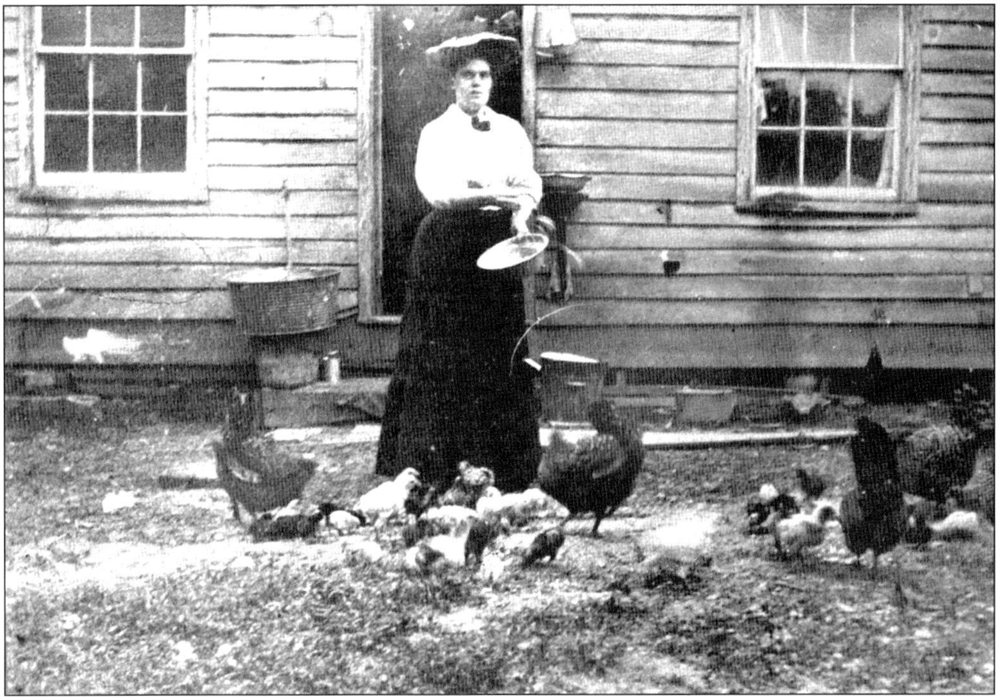

A woman feeds chickens roaming outside the Kluttz house. (Courtesy of the Stanly County Museum.)

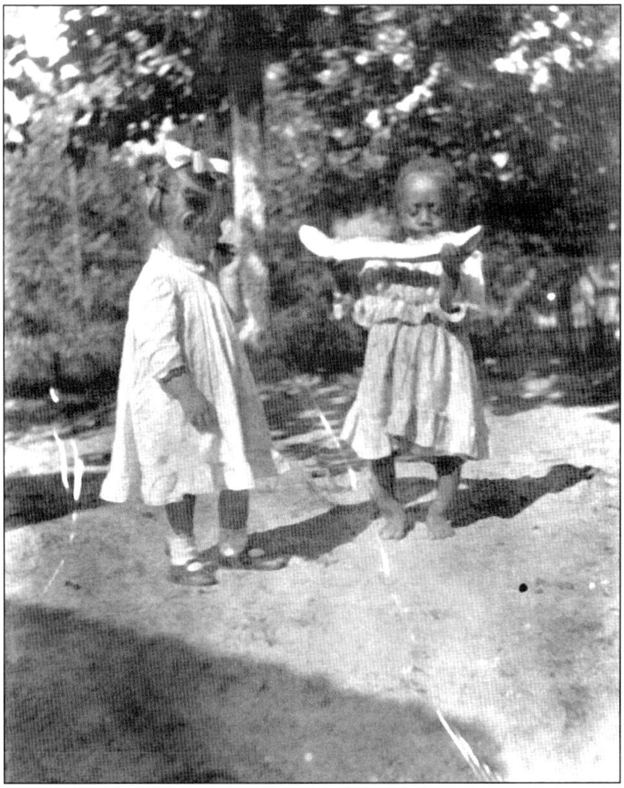

Two girls stand outside on a hot summer day. (Courtesy of Dent Turner.)

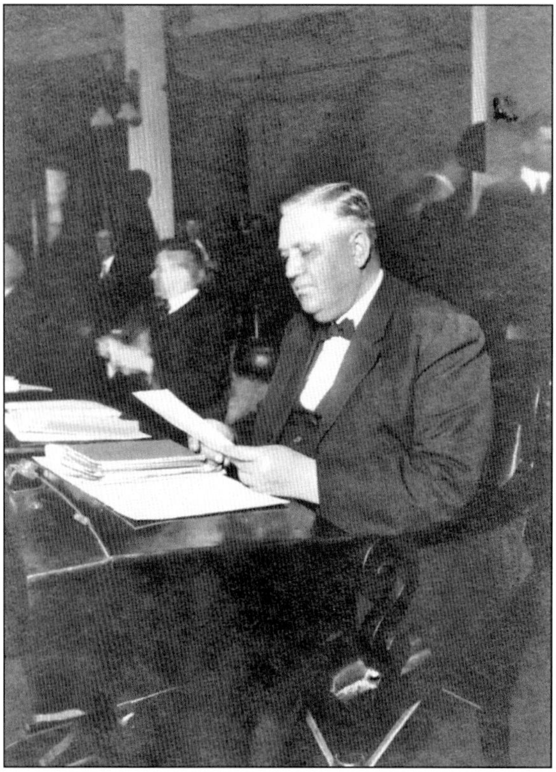

John S. Efird of Albemarle worked in the North Carolina Senate from 1896 to 1927. He founded Efird Manufacturing Company in conjunction with his father. John S. Efird's second wife was Bertha Snuggs, daughter of Buck Snuggs. (Courtesy of Jane Rogers.)

A family relaxes together on the front porch. (Courtesy of the Stanly County Museum.)

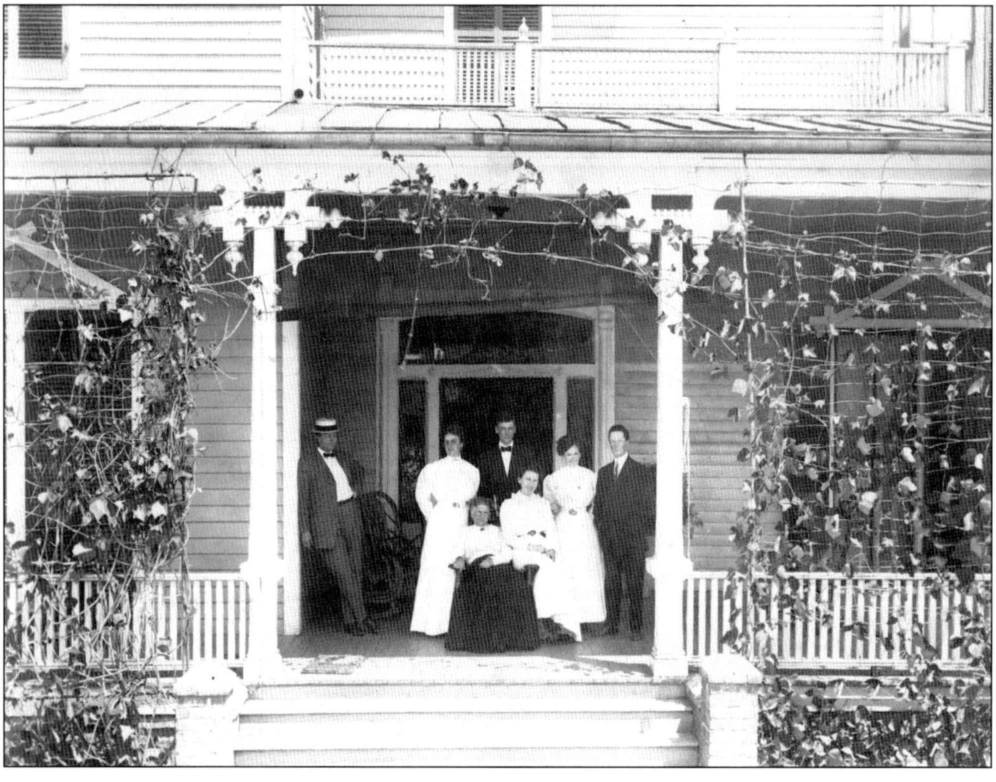

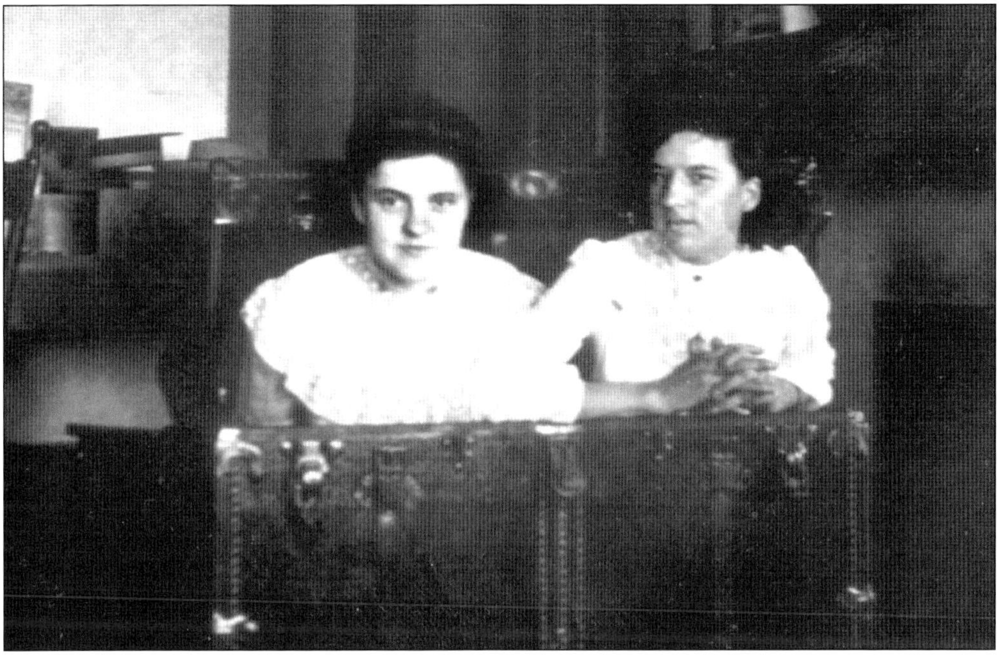

Mary Mabry and her unidentified friend play in a trunk inside the Maralise Hotel. The Mabrys owned the Maralise Hotel, which opened in 1908 and closed in the 1960s. Former President Theodore Roosevelt Jr. and Jimmy Stewart were both guests. (Courtesy of the Stanly County Museum.)

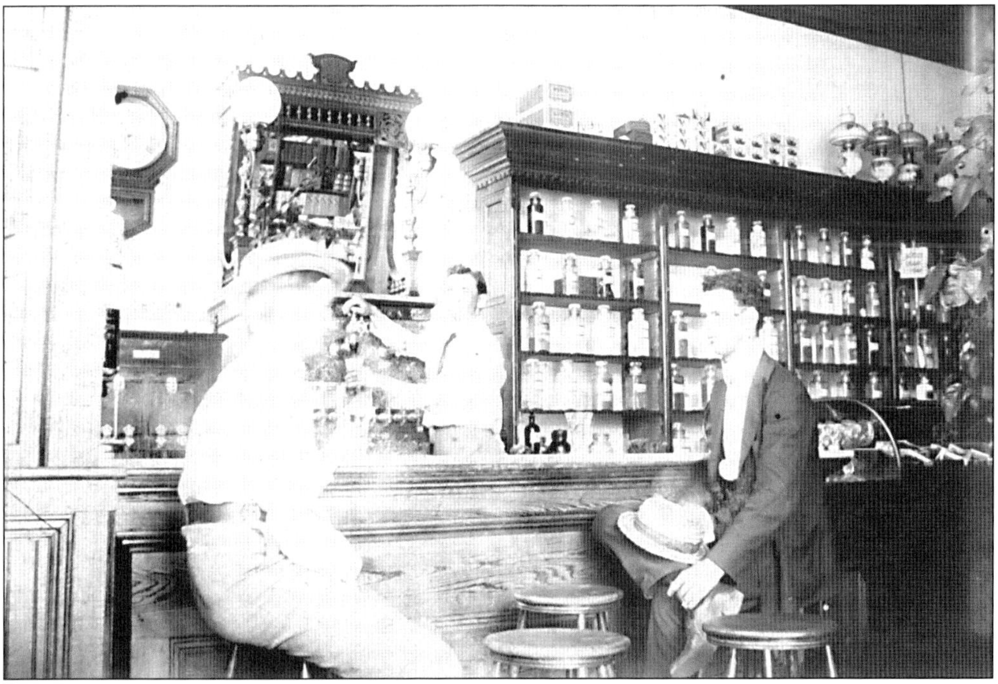

These men take a break at the soda fountain around 1918 to 1920. Pictured are, from left to right, Ed Snuggs, Hoyle Kluttz, and Henry Milton. The manager of the soda fountain was named J.C. Bradly. (Courtesy of the Stanly County Museum.)

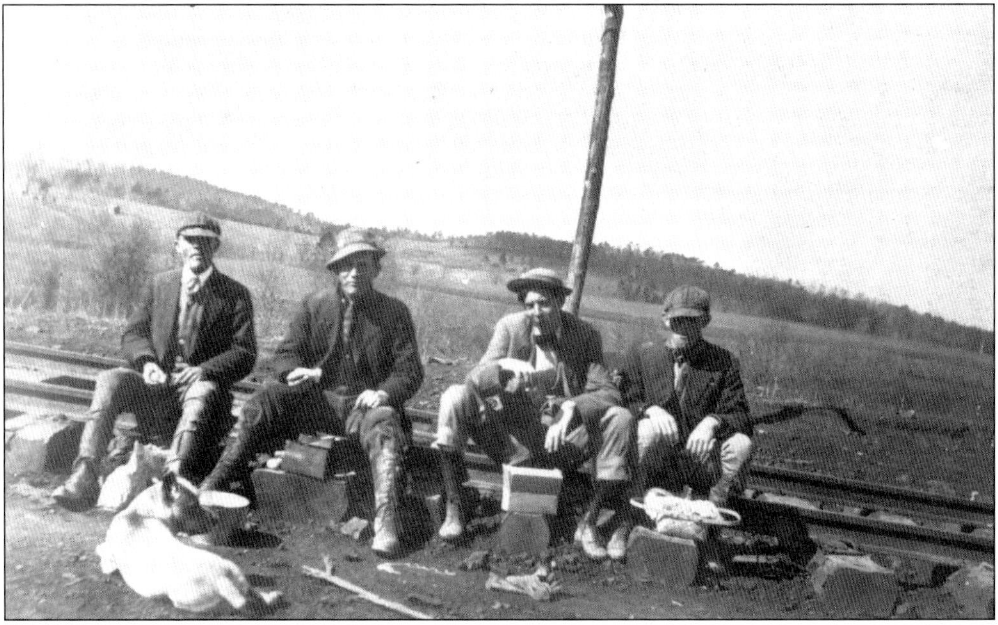

Four men and a dog eat lunch while sitting on the railroad track. (Courtesy of Dotty Plyler.)

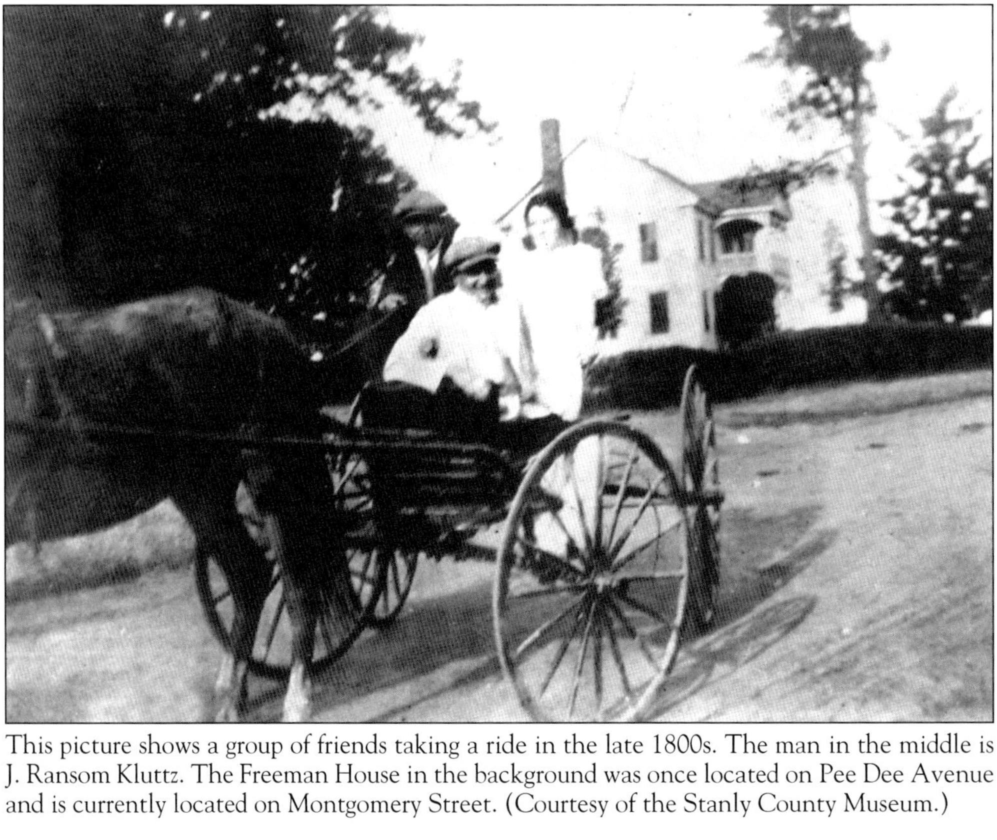

This picture shows a group of friends taking a ride in the late 1800s. The man in the middle is J. Ransom Kluttz. The Freeman House in the background was once located on Pee Dee Avenue and is currently located on Montgomery Street. (Courtesy of the Stanly County Museum.)

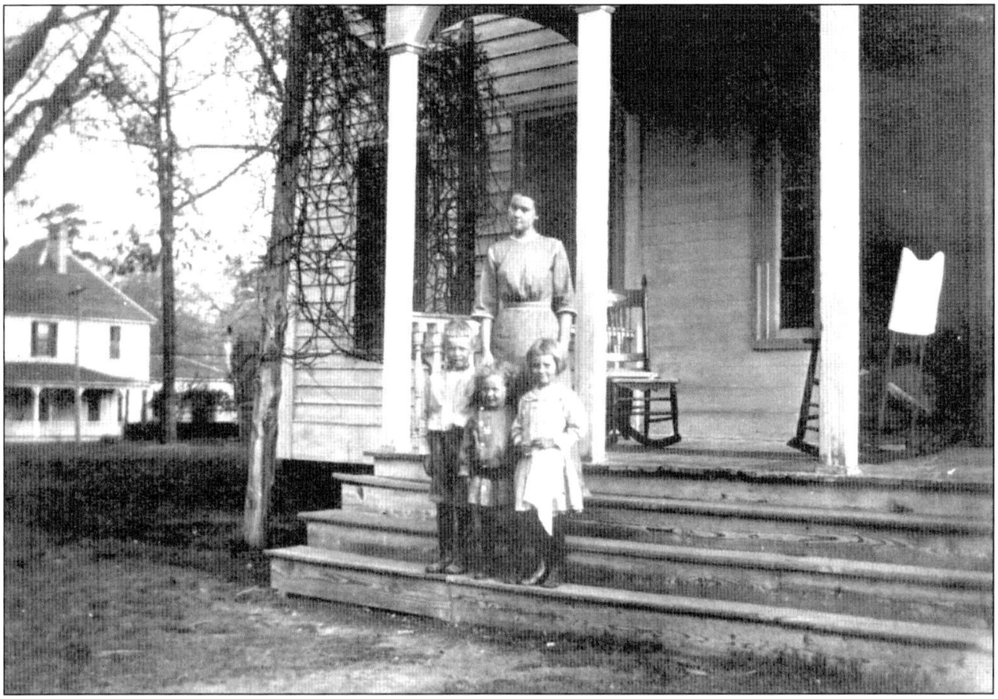

The Kluttz family gathers on the front porch of the Freeman House on Pee Dee Avenue in 1912. From left to right are the following: (front row) Heath, Joe, and Lewis Kluttz; (back row) Sara Kluttz. The R.L. Smith house can be seen in the background. (Courtesy of Joe Kluttz Jr.)

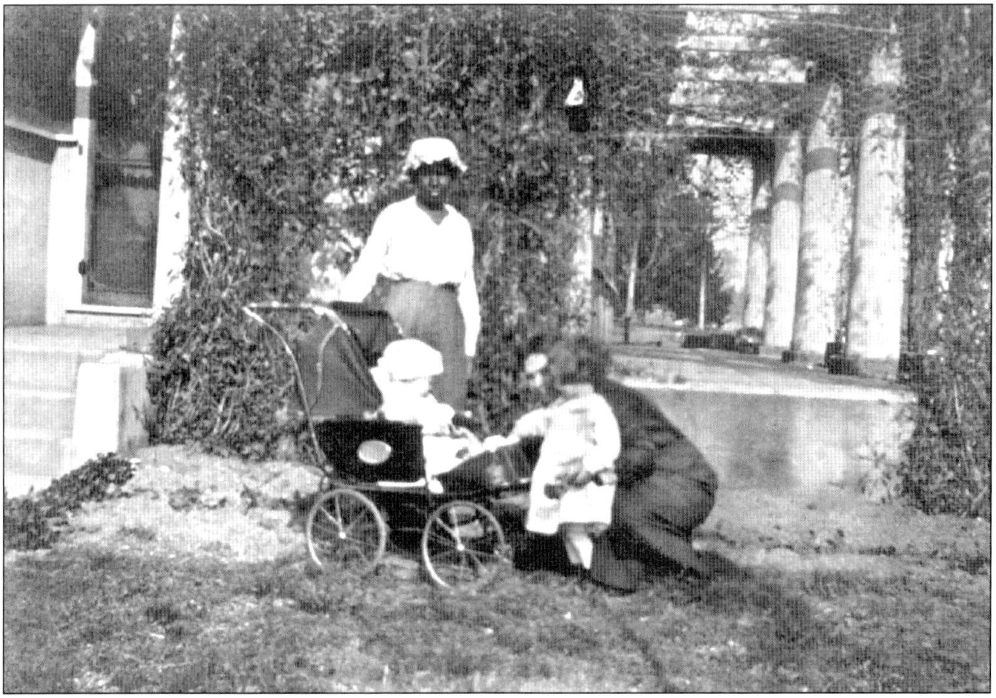

Sidney Hearne sits in a stroller while Elmina and Laura Hearne peer at him in 1912. An unidentified woman stands in the background. (Courtesy of the Stanly County Museum.)

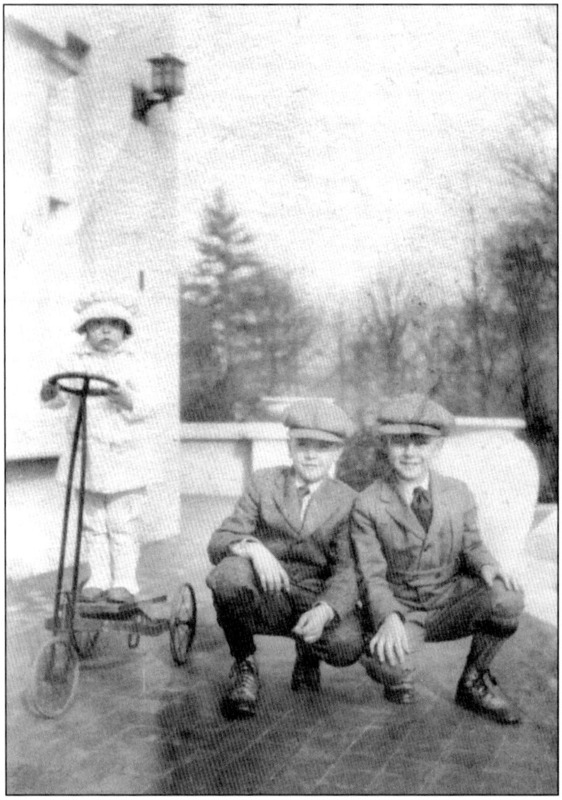

Two friends in matching suits, Sidney Hearne (center) and Brainerd Ronson (right), kneel together in the 1920s. They are watched by an unidentified child to the left who is perched on a toy. (Courtesy of the Stanly County Museum.)

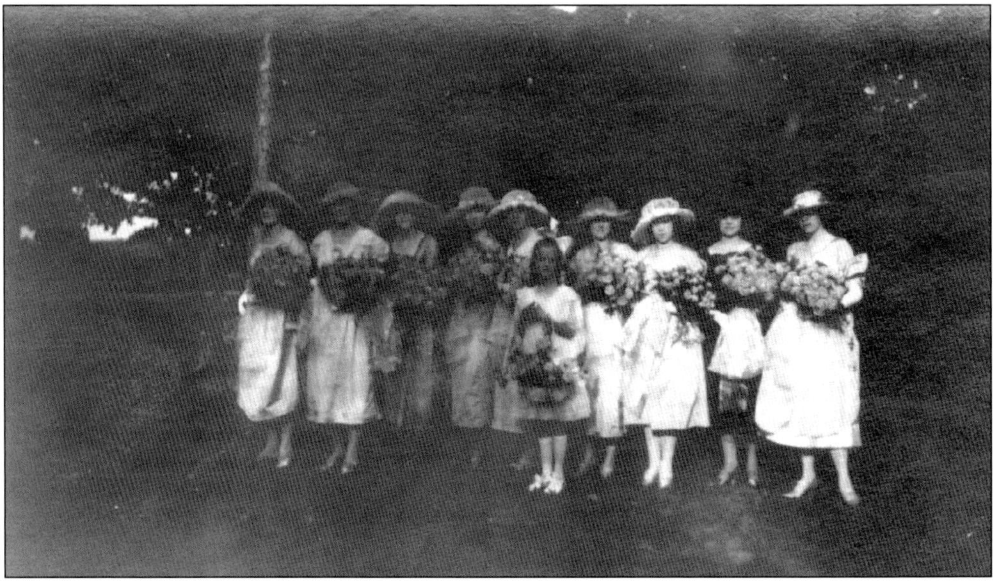

Velma Morrow married Gaines Whitley at the Morrow House, known as "Oakmarle," in 1921. The bridal party poses on the lawn. (Courtesy of Dotty Plyler.)

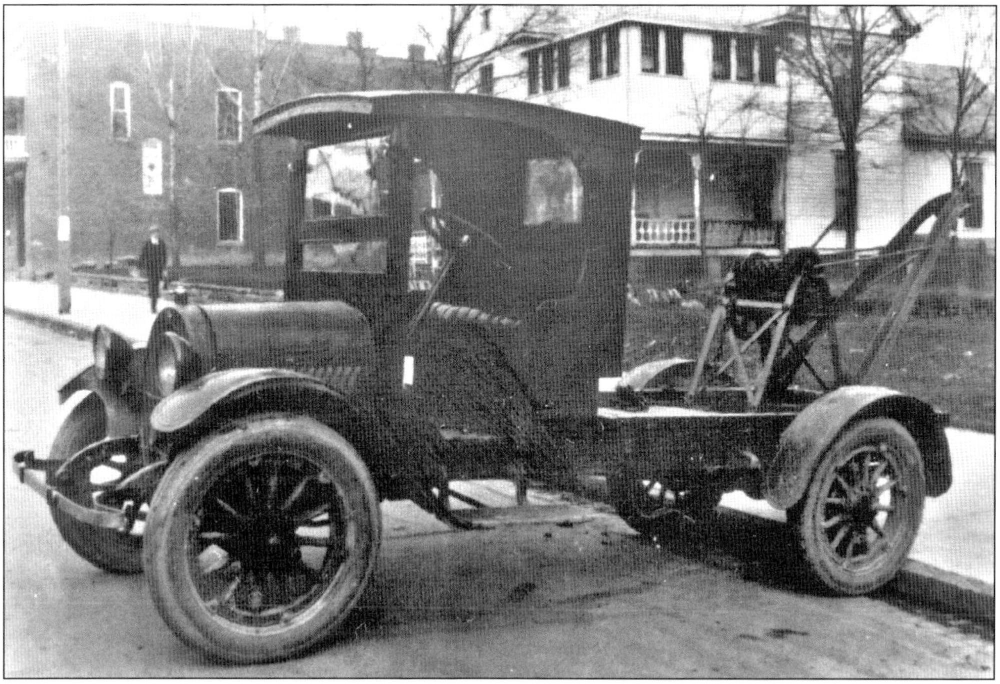

A Redwine tow truck pauses on South Second Street in the 1920s. J.C. Redwine's nearby shop built many of the county's earliest trucks and buses. (Courtesy of the Stanly County Museum.)

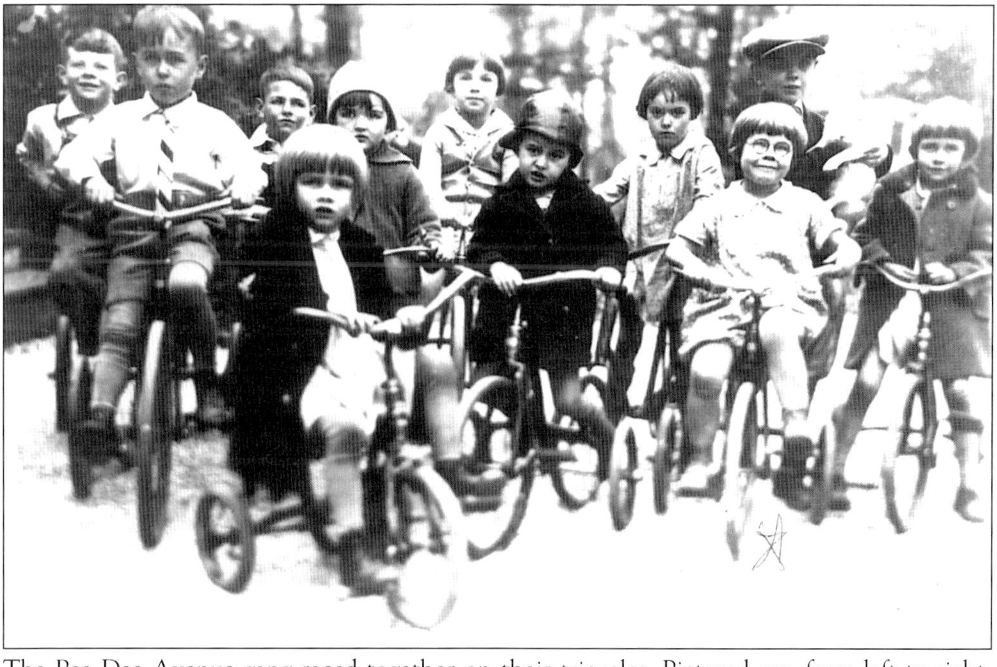

The Pee Dee Avenue gang raced together on their tricycles. Pictured are, from left to right, (front row) Tommy Rabe, Martha Ivey (Tiller), Margaret Patterson, Tommy Moore, Dotty Whitley Plyler, and Betsy Ivey (Sawyer); (back row) Gaines Whitley Jr., John B. Little Jr., Barbara Crowell (Bishop), Dora Alice Moore, and Jimmy Crowell (who is holding a rabbit). (Courtesy of Dotty Plyler.)

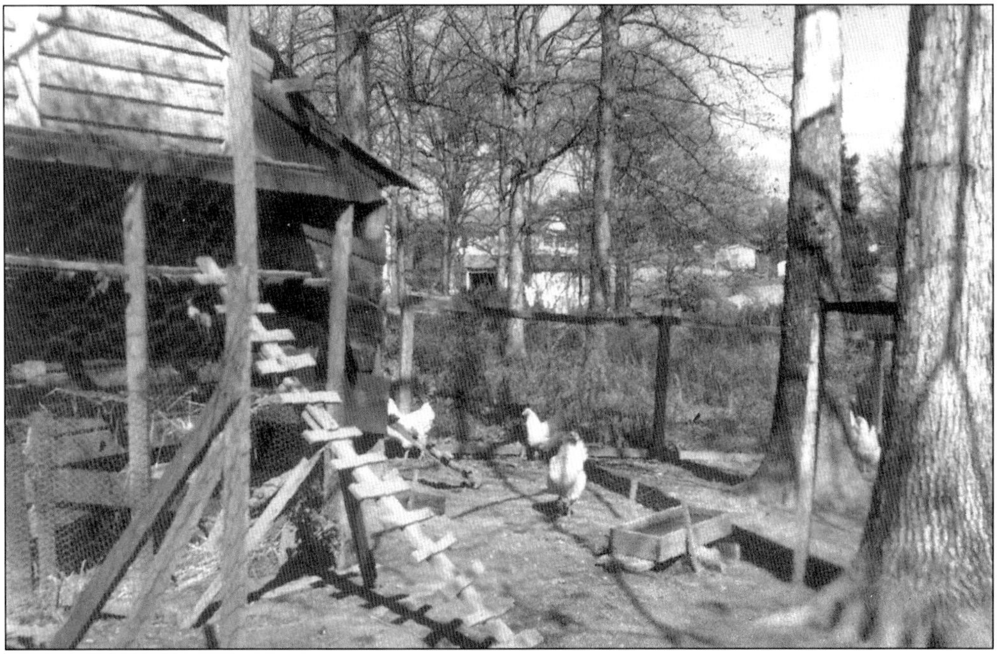

The yard of the Morrow house, located on Pee Dee Avenue, was filled with chickens and a chicken coop during World War II. (Courtesy of Dotty Plyler.)

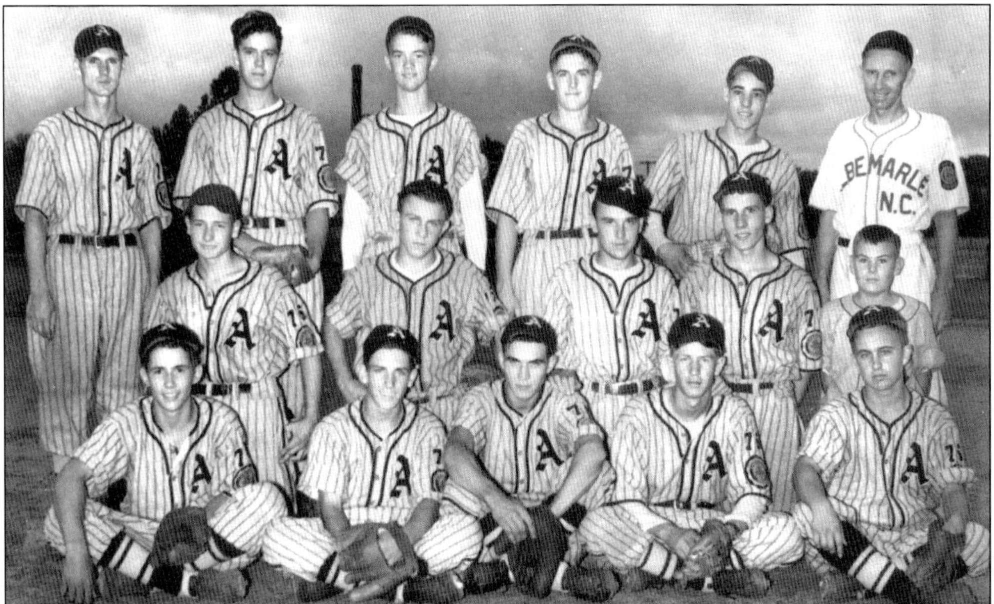

The Albemarle American Legion Junior Baseball team was the national champion in 1940. Albemarle played San Diego, California, September 3–7, 1940, in the American Legion Junior World Series. Pictured from left to right are (front row) Sherrill Cranford, Tommy Swanner, Clyde Hartsell, Craig Lisk, and Tommy Rabe; (middle row) James McCarnes, Hoyle Boger, Bill Long, J.W. "Lefty" Lisk, and Frank Little; (back row) Coach Porter Sheppard, Clyde Dick, Sam Andrew, John Little, Junior Holt, and Frank Marbry. Lee Moir is not pictured. (Courtesy of the Stanly County Museum.)

Three

EDUCATION AND ATHLETICS

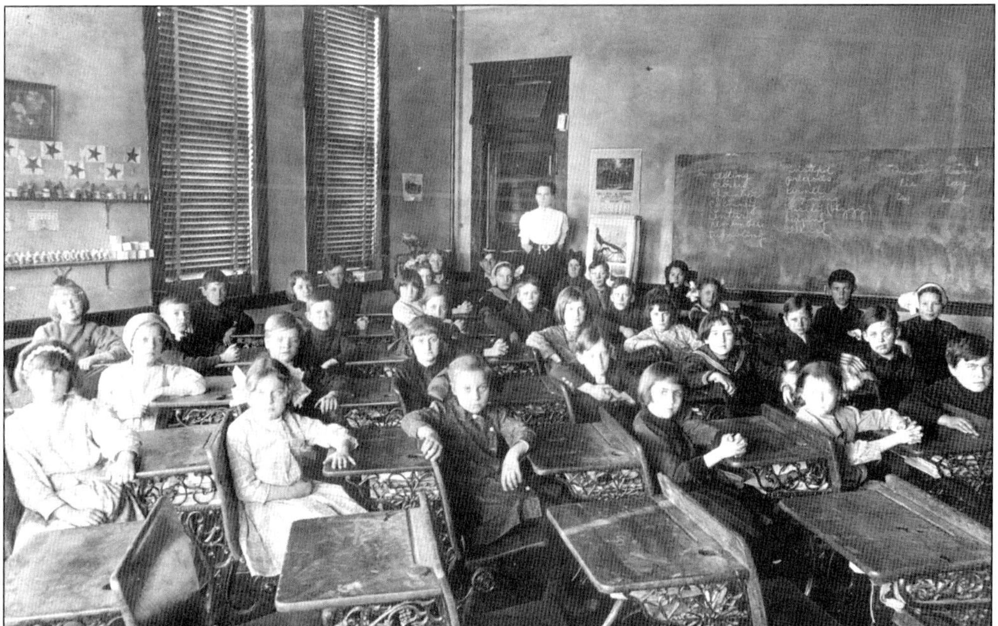

Pattie Marks instructs her class in grammar and pronunciation in 1910. She began teaching in Oklahoma before teaching in several Albemarle schools. (Courtesy of the Stanly County Museum.)

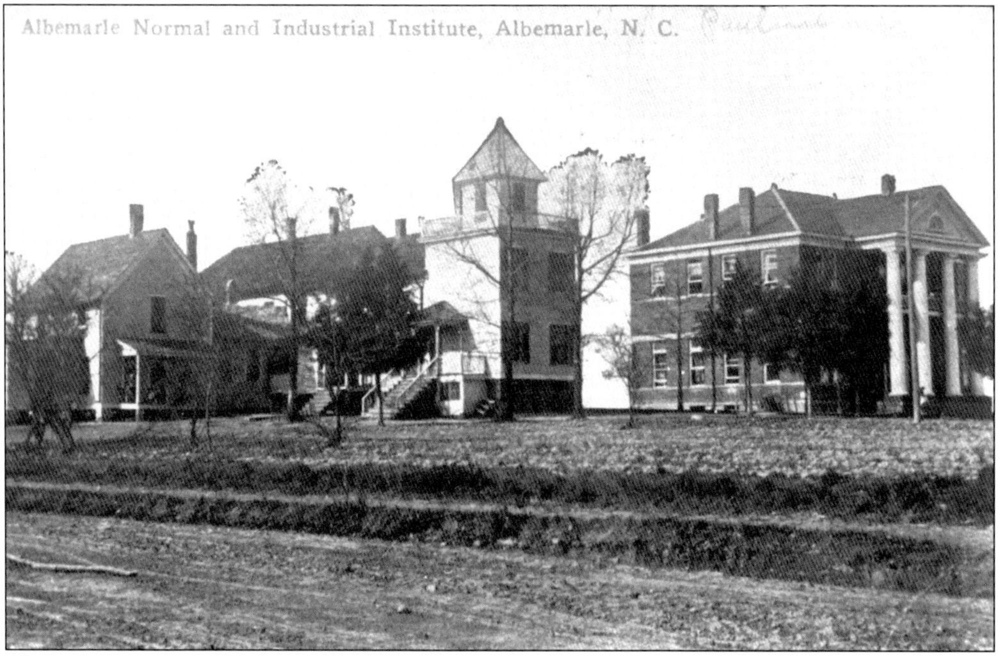

The Albemarle Normal and Industrial Institute, founded in 1894 by Francis Ufford and Helen Northrup, was located between South Third Street and South Fourth Street. The school was originally called Englewood. (Courtesy of the Stanly County Museum.)

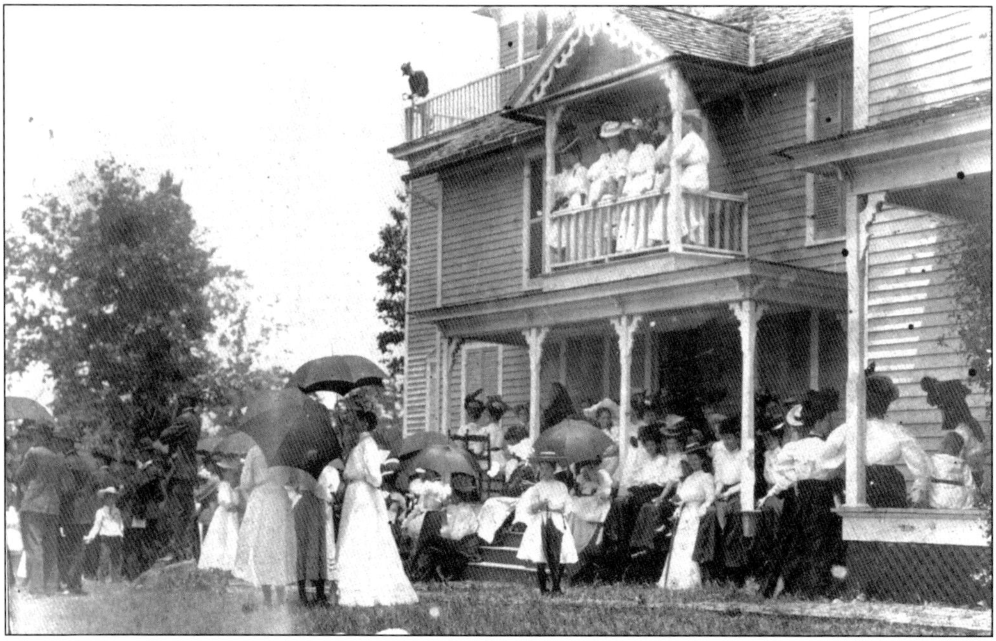

The Albemarle Normal and Industrial Institute was a boarding school for women. In this image, crowds congregate outside the house where the ladies stayed, possibly for graduation or the dedication of a new building. The school existed from the late 1800s until the late 1920s. (Courtesy of the Stanly County Museum.)

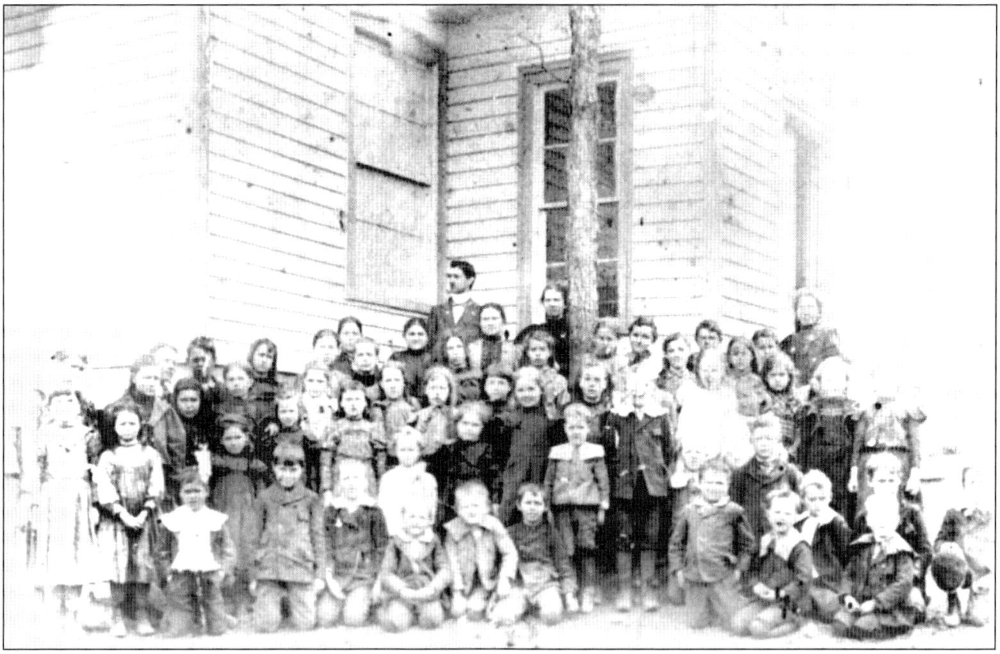

Shown here in 1893 or 1894 are students assembled outside of the Hillside School, which was located on the south side of East Main Street and South Fifth Street beyond Five Points. Frances Ufford operated the school. (Courtesy of the Stanly County Museum.)

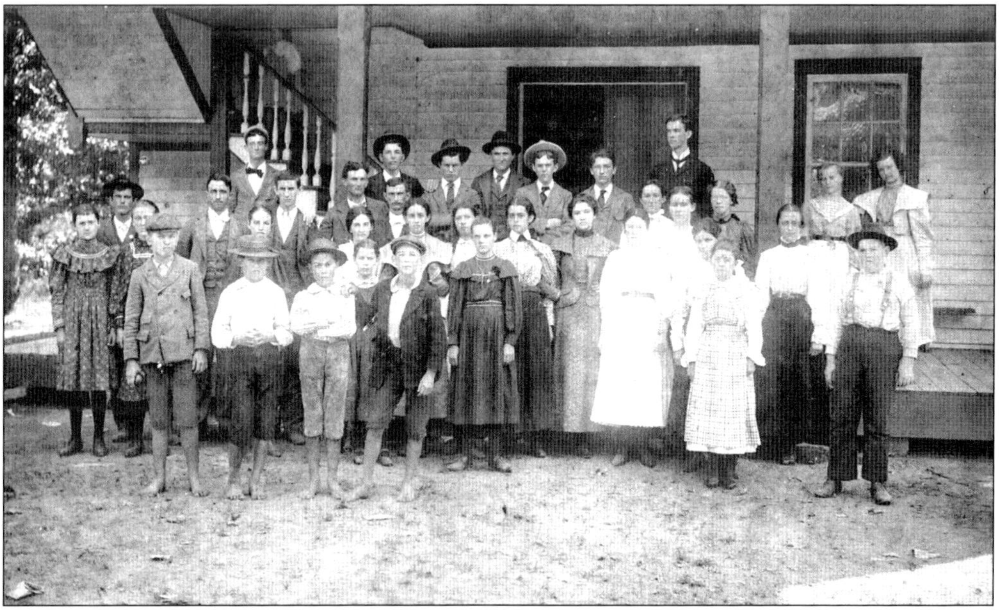

In this picture from 1900, students gather outside of the Spinks School. The Spinks School was located on the corner of East North Street and North Third Street. Built in 1875 as the Albemarle Academy, it was sold to Henry W. Spinks in 1882. The Reverend C.M. Gentry bought the school in 1894. He then sold it to the Albemarle school commissioner five years later. (Courtesy of the Stanly County Museum.)

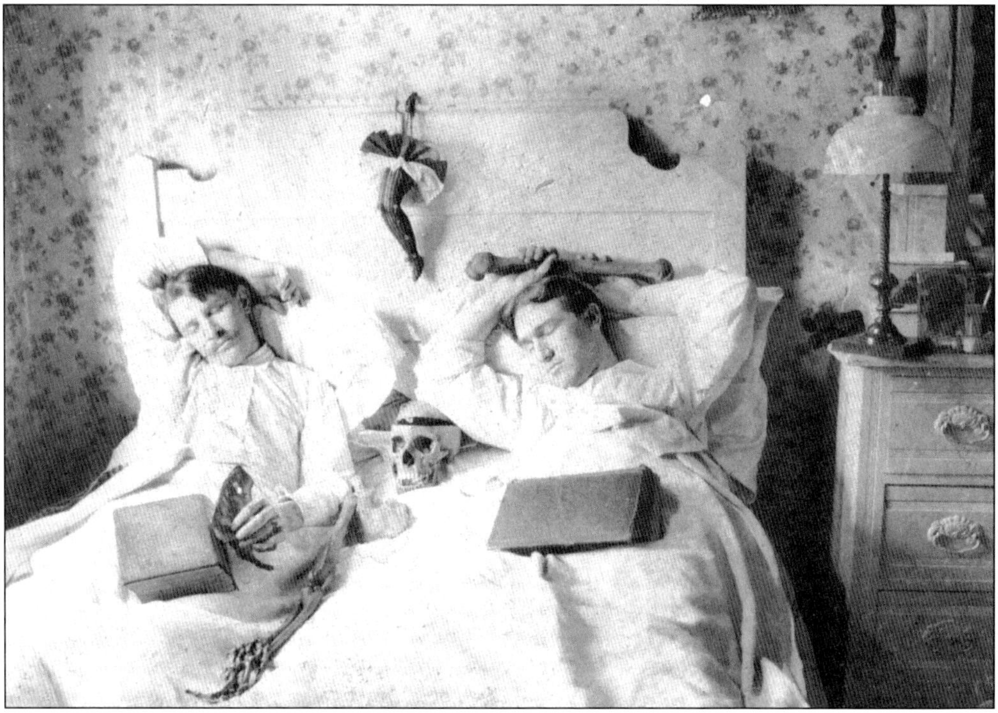

Dr. W.C. Fitzgerald and his roommate L.C. Bell have bones on the brain as they study for their medical exams in April of 1903. (Courtesy of the Patterson family.)

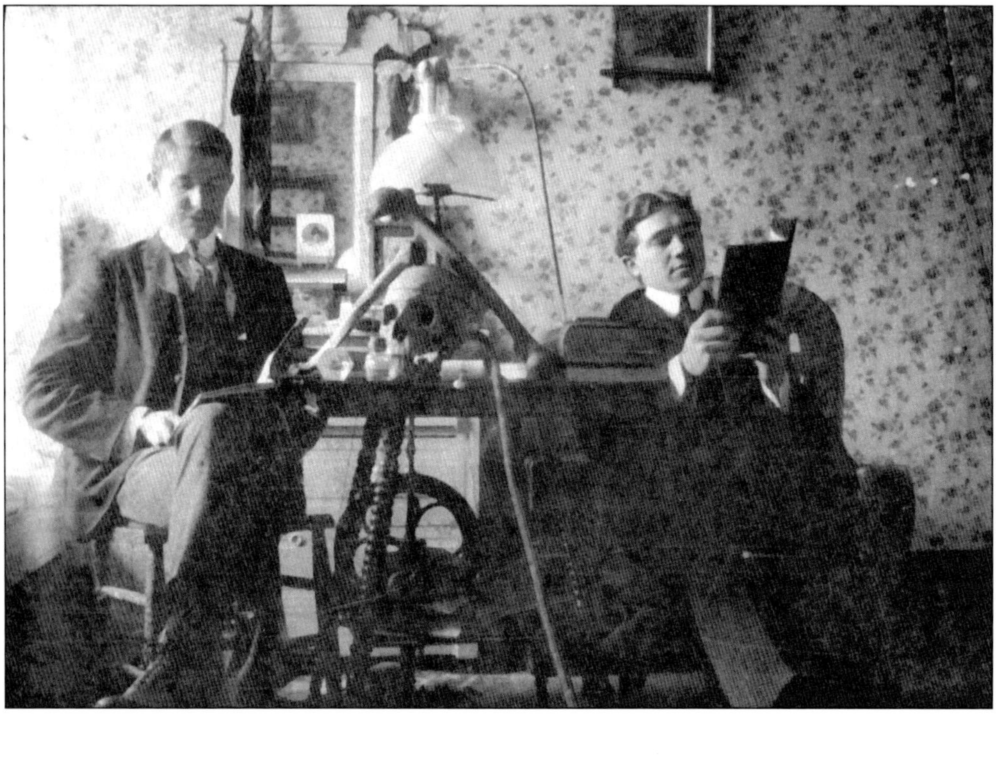

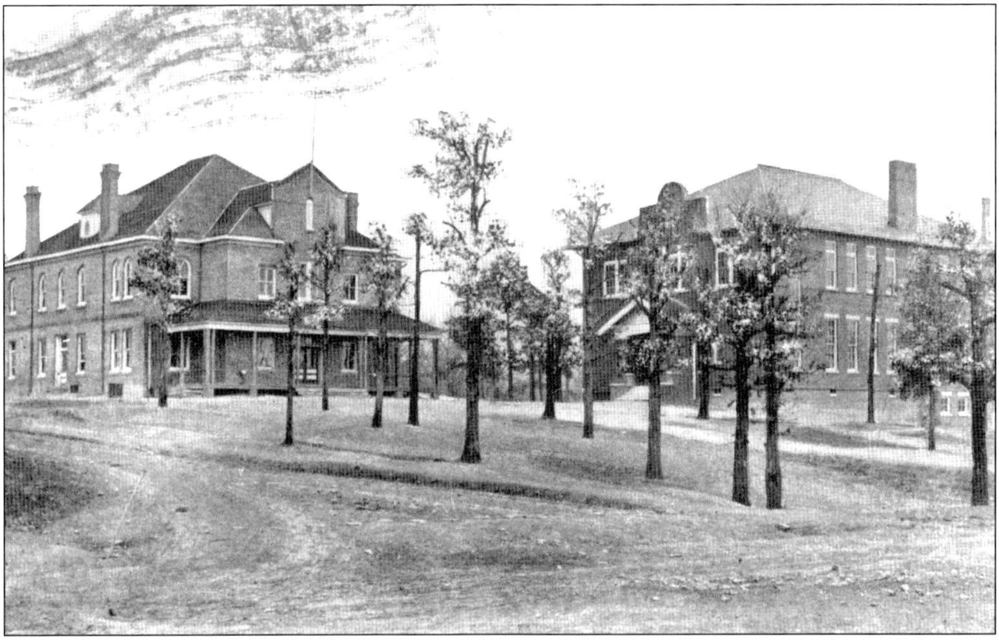

The Albemarle Graded School was an elementary and high school complex that had two buildings on East North Street. The building on the left was built in 1900 but was damaged by fire in 1920. It was restored by 1923. The building on the right was built in 1915, but it was torn down c. 1965. (Courtesy of the Stanly County Museum.)

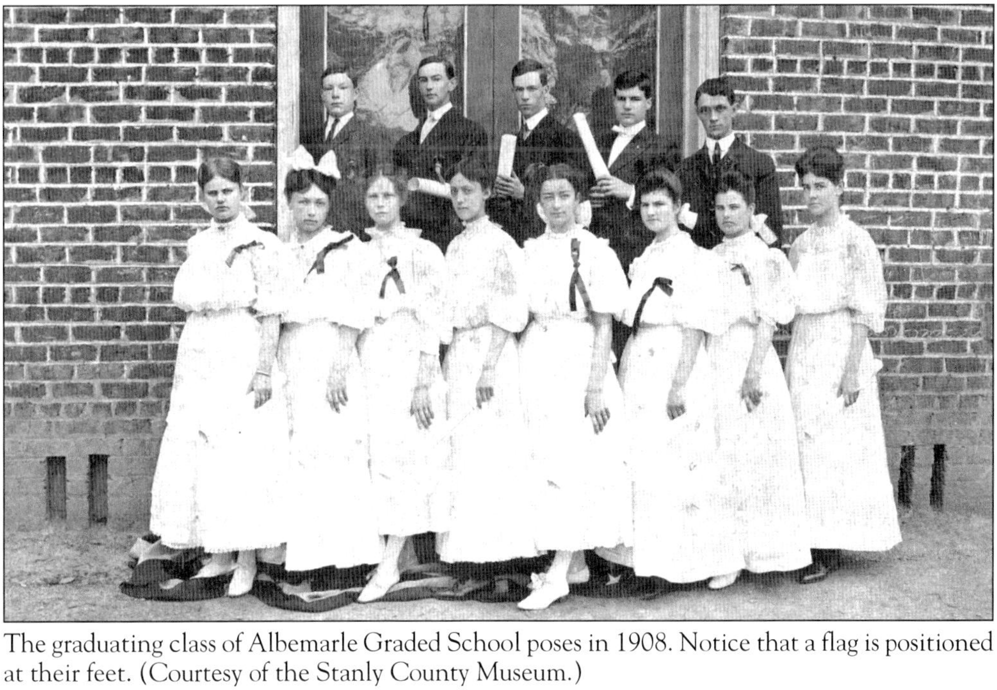

The graduating class of Albemarle Graded School poses in 1908. Notice that a flag is positioned at their feet. (Courtesy of the Stanly County Museum.)

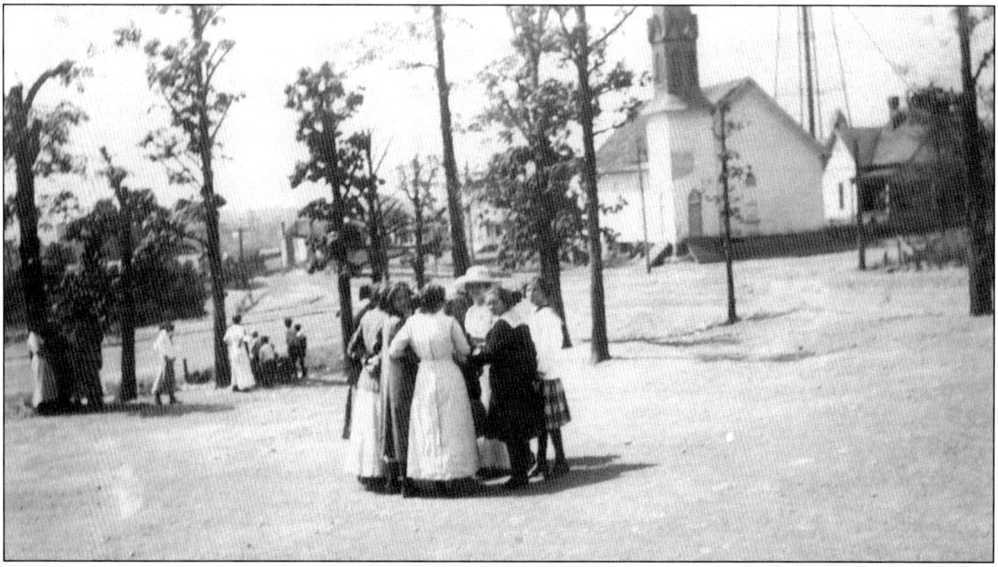

In this early 1900s photograph, teachers watch as children play during recess at the Albemarle Graded School. The First Baptist Church can be seen in the background. (Courtesy of Frank Patterson.)

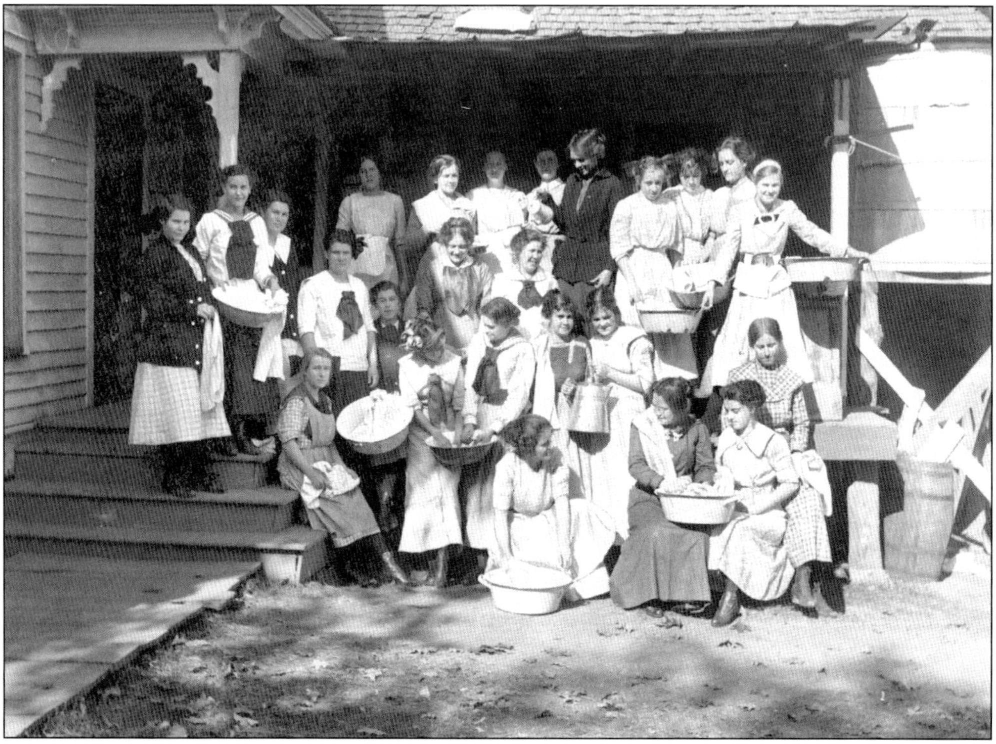

Members of the 1913 dishwashing class of Albemarle Normal and Industrial Institute display classroom supplies. (Courtesy of Gene Starnes.)

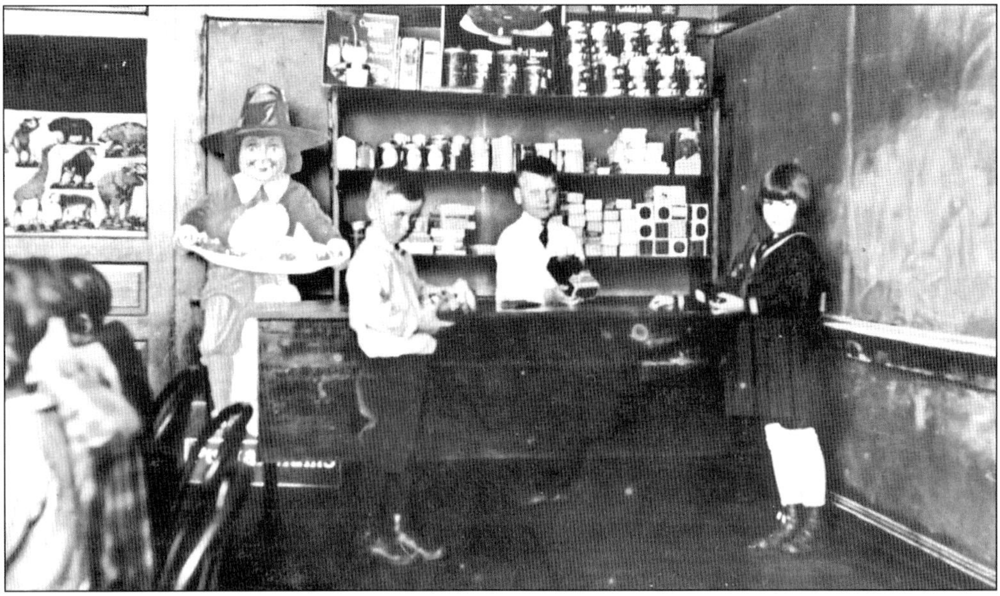

In this image from the 1900s, students in an elementary school classroom celebrate the Thanksgiving season. Stockpiles of food fill shelves behind the students. (Courtesy of the Stanly County Museum.)

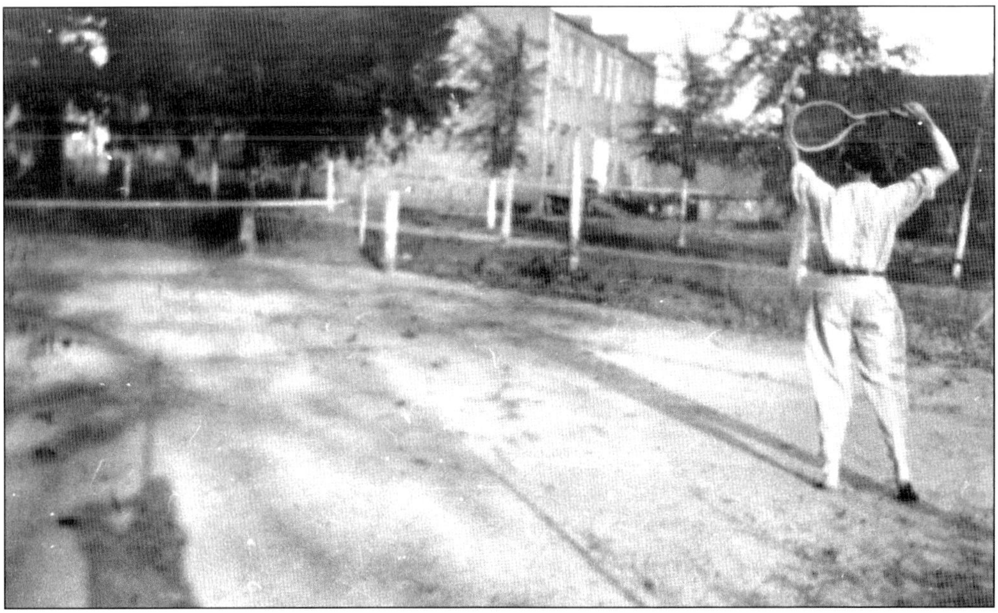

An unidentified tennis player practices behind Albemarle Graded School, c. 1914. (Courtesy of the Stanly County Museum.)

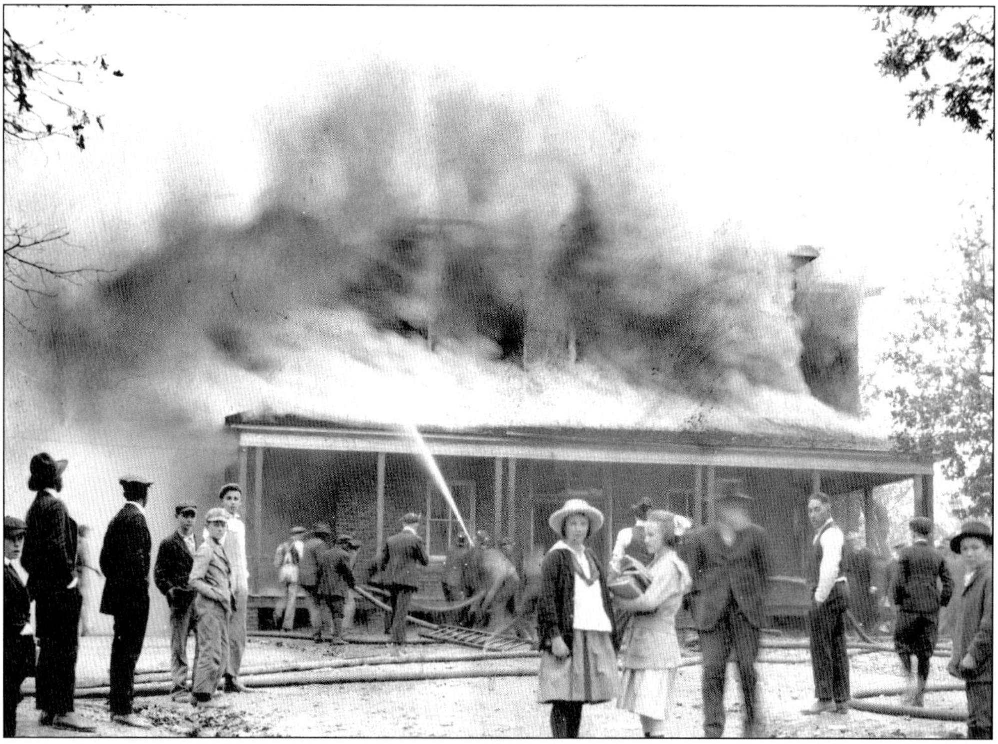

People gather around Albemarle Graded School during a fire in November of 1920. Despite extensive damage, the building was restored by 1923. Albemarle Graded School is now called Central Elementary School. (Courtesy of the Stanly County Museum.)

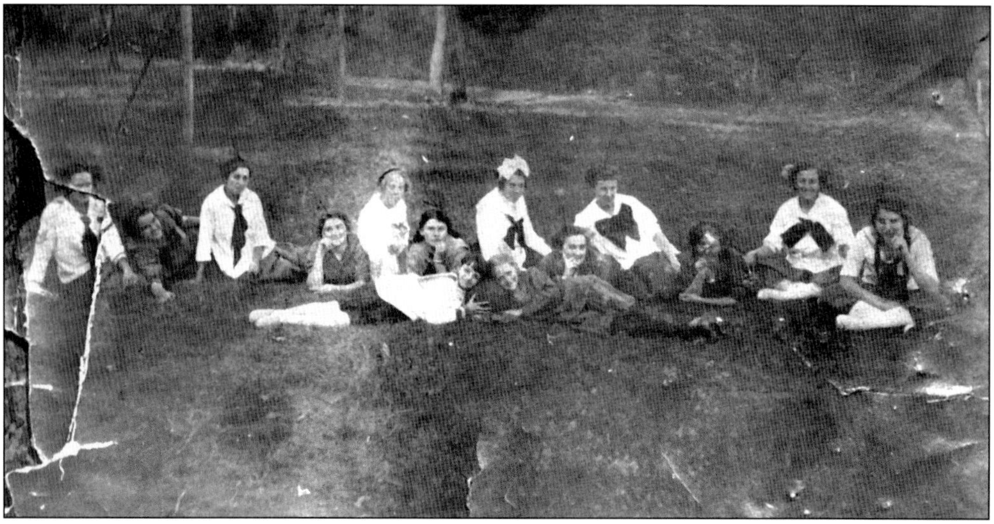

An Albemarle girls' basketball team takes a break from practice in 1920. (Courtesy of the Stanly County Museum.)

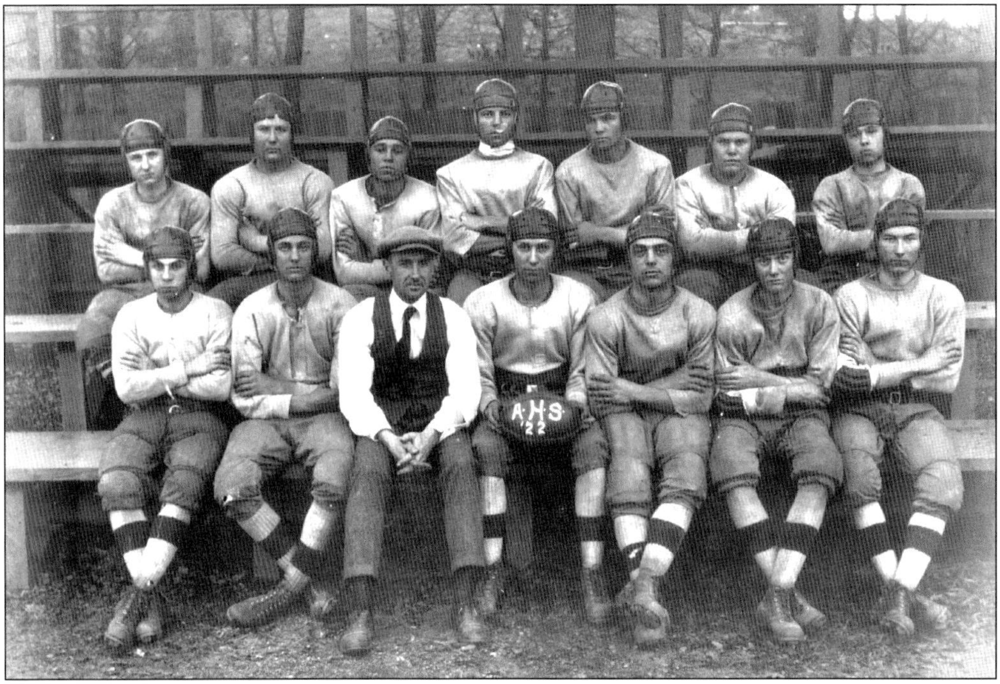

The Albemarle Bulldogs await the start of the 1922 season. The members of the team are, from left to right, (front row) Virhil Whitley, Hoyle Efird, Lee Morrow, Frank Marbry, Ralph Fagan, Steve Davis, and Eddie Crisco; (back row) Dan Boger, Tom Kimrey, Travis Coggins, Reen Burleson, Glenn Lowder, Edward Hinson, and Robert Cranford. Team members David Hinson and Marvin Huneycutt missed the picture. (Courtesy of the Stanly County Museum.)

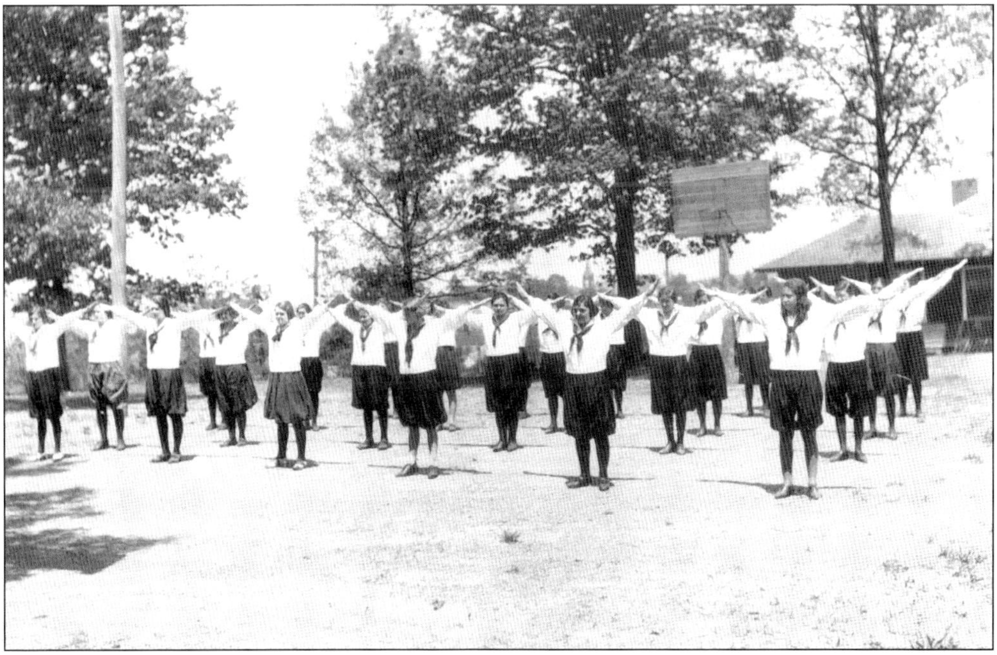

This photograph depicts girls exercising in a physical education class at Albemarle Normal and Industrial Institute *c.* 1922. (Courtesy of the Stanly County Museum.)

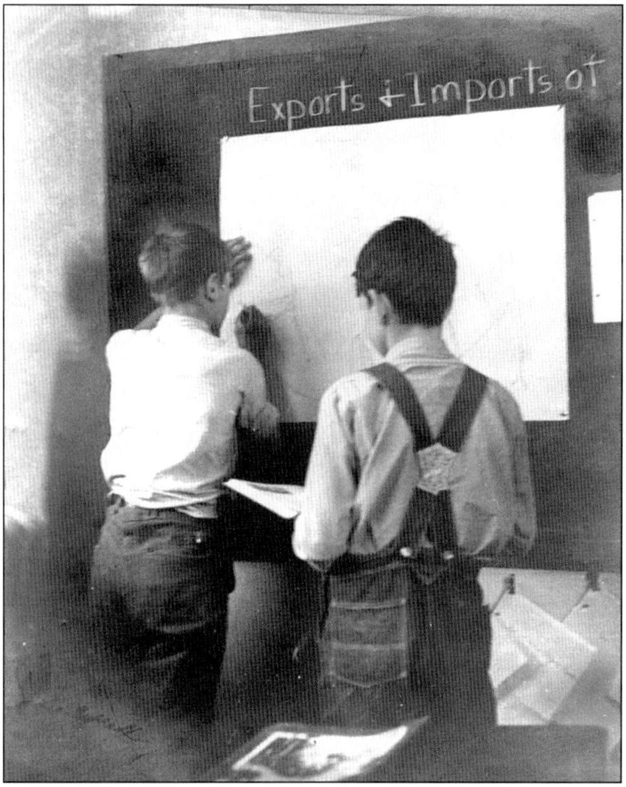

Two boys standing at the blackboard answer an economics question in a 1920s schoolroom. (Courtesy of the Stanly County Museum.)

The 1923 Albemarle High School baseball team sits on the steps of the school. Pictured are, from left to right, (front row) Boyd Hatley, Ralph Fagan, and unidentified; (middle row) Robert Sides, Marvin Huneycutt, and unidentified; (back row) Frank Marbry, Marvin Carter, and Dewy Fesperman. Ray Lowder stands to the left. The boy in the foreground is unidentified. (Courtesy of the Stanly County Museum.)

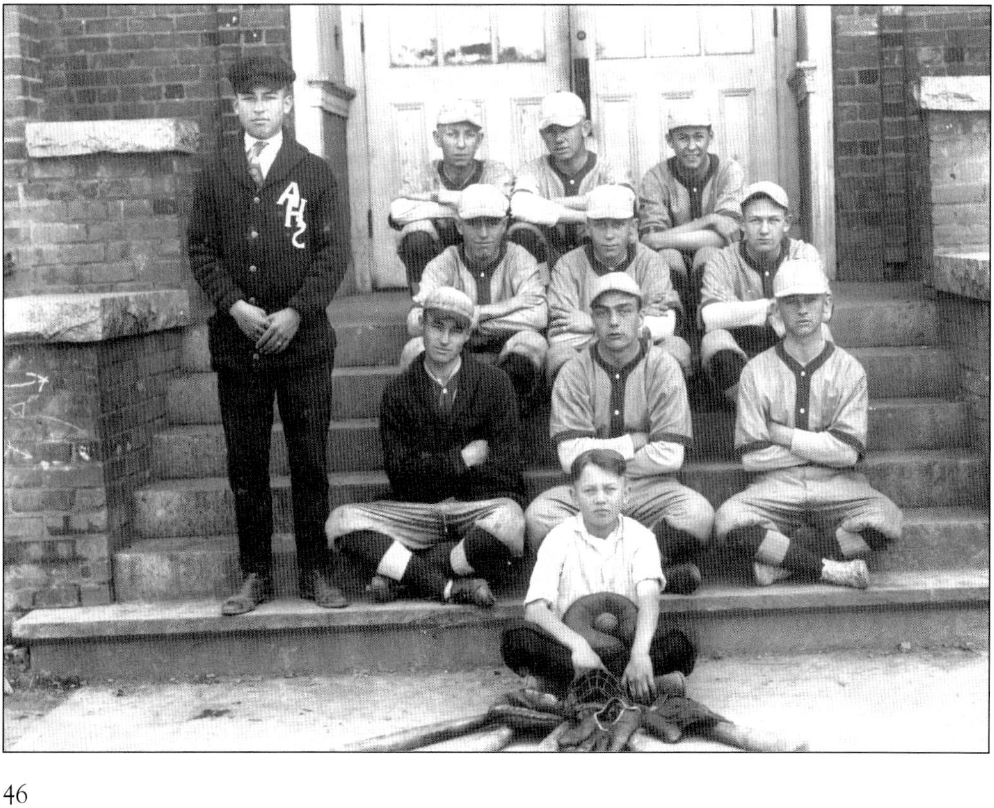

The members of the 1929 girls' varsity basketball team from Albemarle Senior High pose on the steps of the school. Pictured are, from left to right, (front row) Lucille Neal, Margaret Kennedy, and Margaret Casper; (back row) Loretta Moose, Coach Meadow, ? Aderholt, and Lydia Lentz. (Courtesy of the Stanly County Museum.)

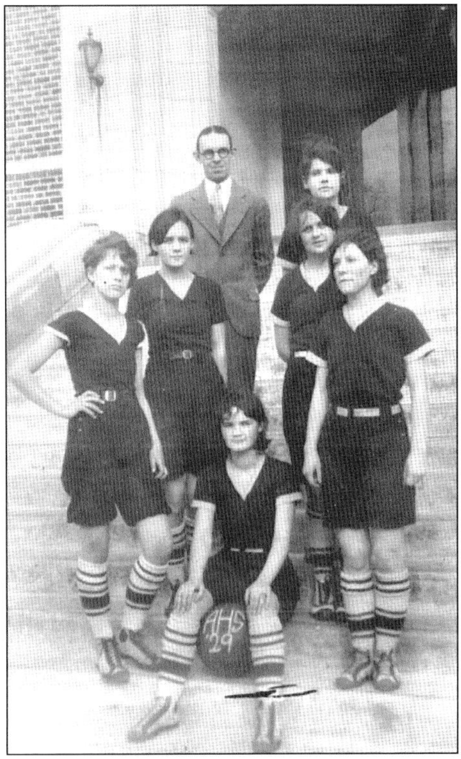

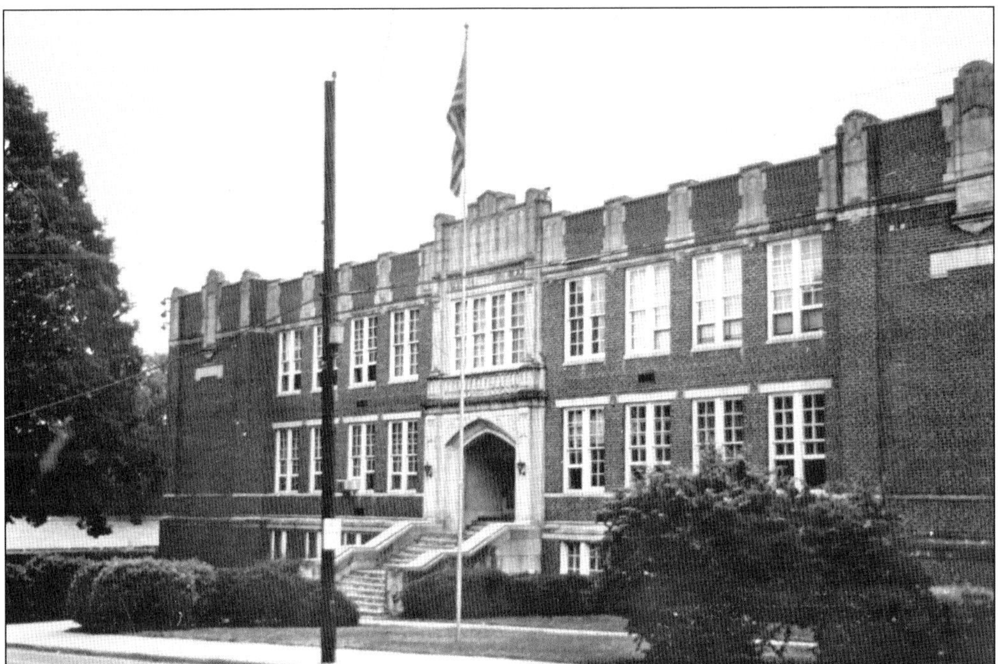

Albemarle High School was built in 1924 then converted to a junior high school in 1960. C.C. Hook was the architect, and E.C. Derby was the builder. It is currently being converted to Central Elementary School. (Courtesy of the Stanly County Museum.)

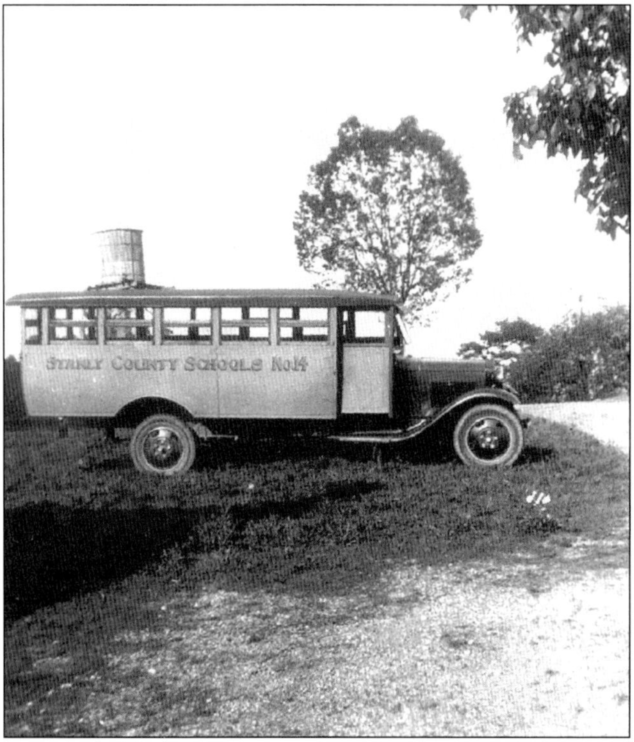

June Shaver of Badin Road was proud of Stanly County School Bus #14, which he drove for East Albemarle School students in 1932. He recalled how he ran a wire from his bus battery to the radio in his house each night because his house was not equipped with electricity. (Courtesy of the Stanly County Museum.)

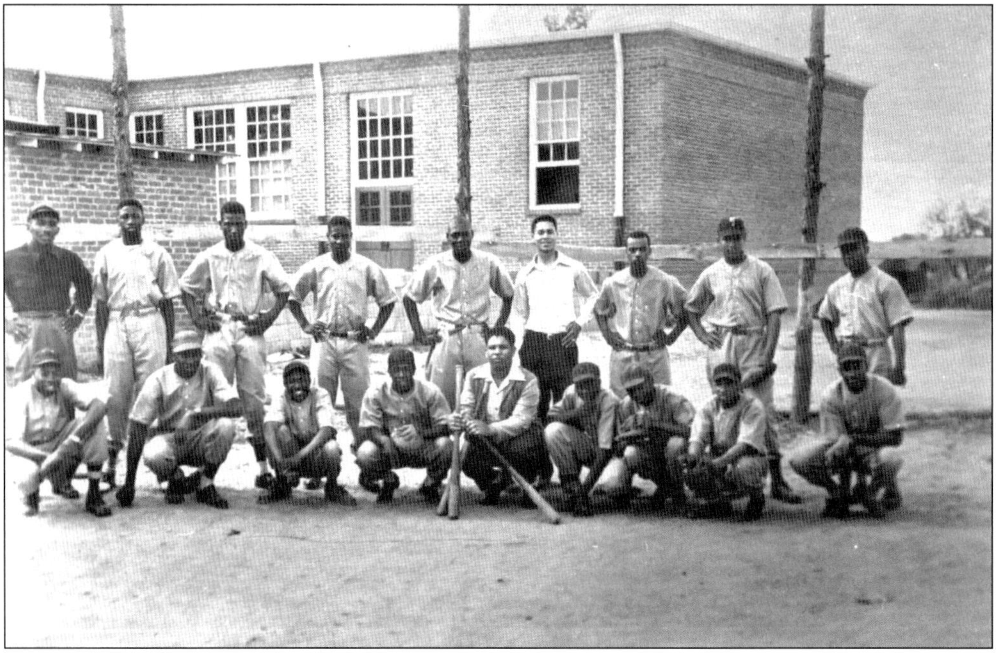

The Kingville High School baseball team poses in front of Kingville High School in the mid-1940s. Pictured are, from left to right, (front row) Bo Ingram, Gene Willoughby, "Bunk" Ingram, Mack Bruton, Stanly Cambell, Phenlo Ellis, Earl Colston, Troy Waddell, and Howard Colson; (back row) Bill Stanton, Tommy Richardson, Odell Lilly, Thomas Smith, Fisher Wall, E.E. Waddell, Arnold Flake, Owen Nance, and J.C. River. (Courtesy of the Stanly County Museum.)

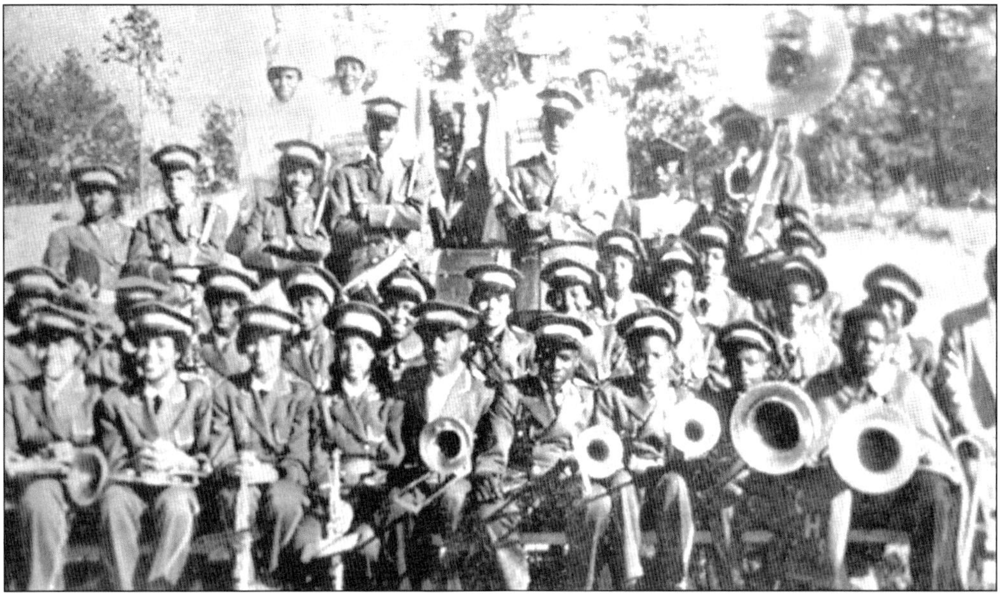

The members of the Kingville High School's marching band pose together. Kingville High School was built in 1920. It was a segregated school located at Wall Street. In 1940, Kingville had 31 teachers and 1,000 students. (Courtesy of the Stanly County Museum.)

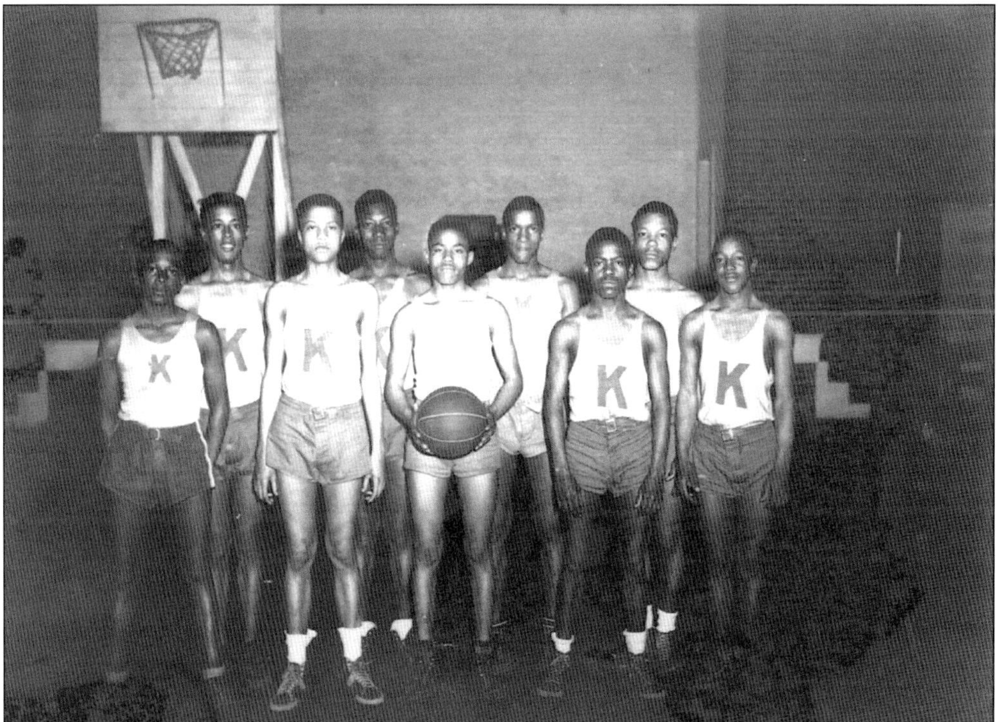

The Kingville High School basketball team poses in the auditorium in the 1950s. Kingville High School closed soon after the county schools were desegregated in 1965. (Courtesy of the Stanly County Museum.)

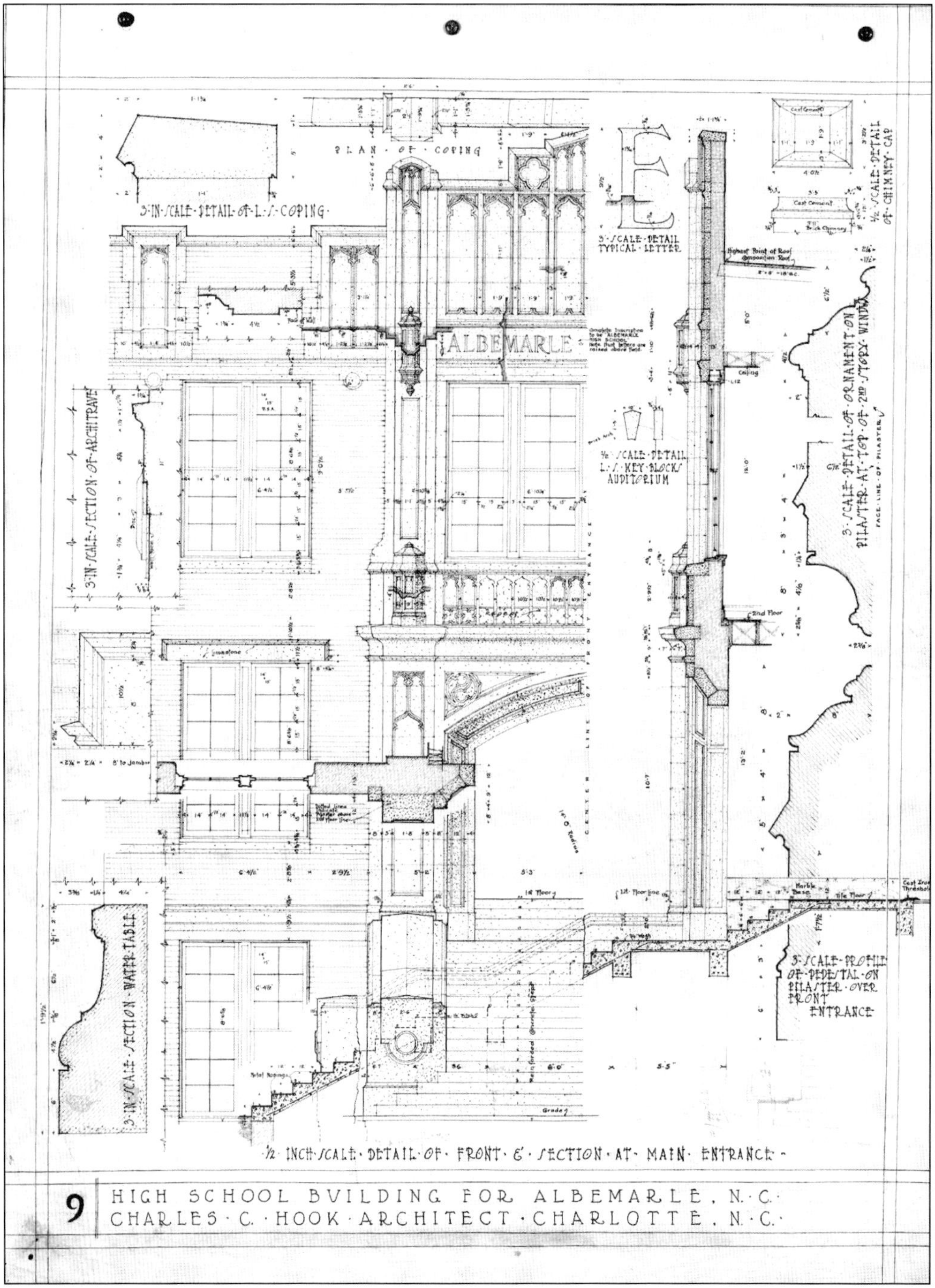

The architect of Albemarle High School, Charles C. Hook (1870–1938), drew the plans for the building on linen in the early 1920s. He also designed buildings at Trinity College (Duke) and the Mill building in Albemarle. (Courtesy of John T. Williams Jr.)

Four

Culture and Entertainment

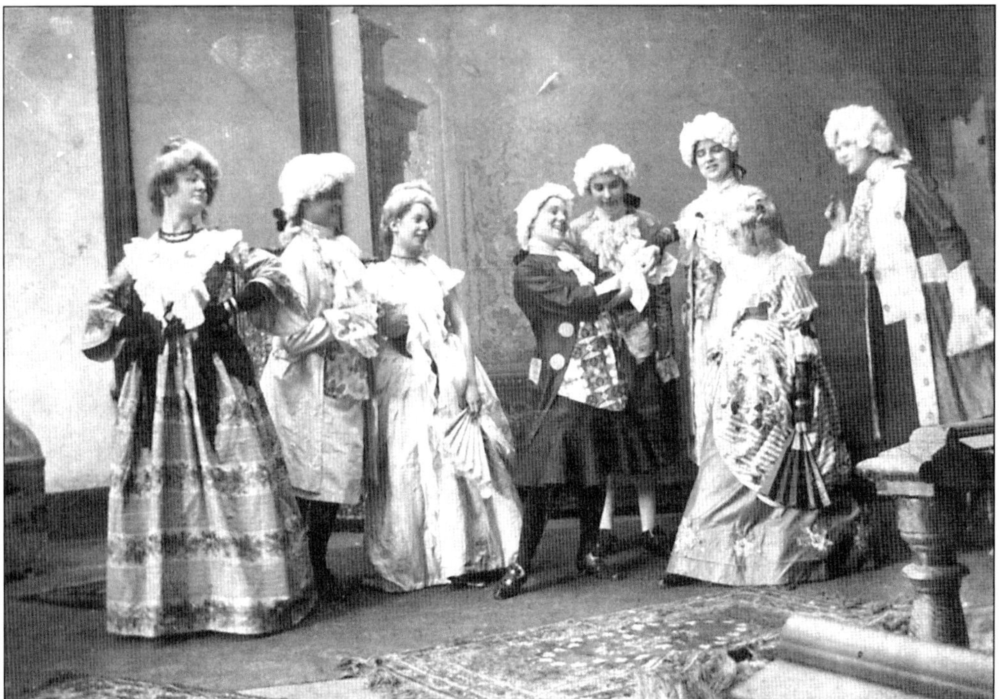

Actors perform in a period play during March of 1903. They are, from left to right, Ruth Stone, Will King, Eunice Tennent, Lexa Woodruff, Mildred Gould, Jessie Thrash, Rosa Crook, and Inez McRae. (Courtesy of the Stanly County Museum.)

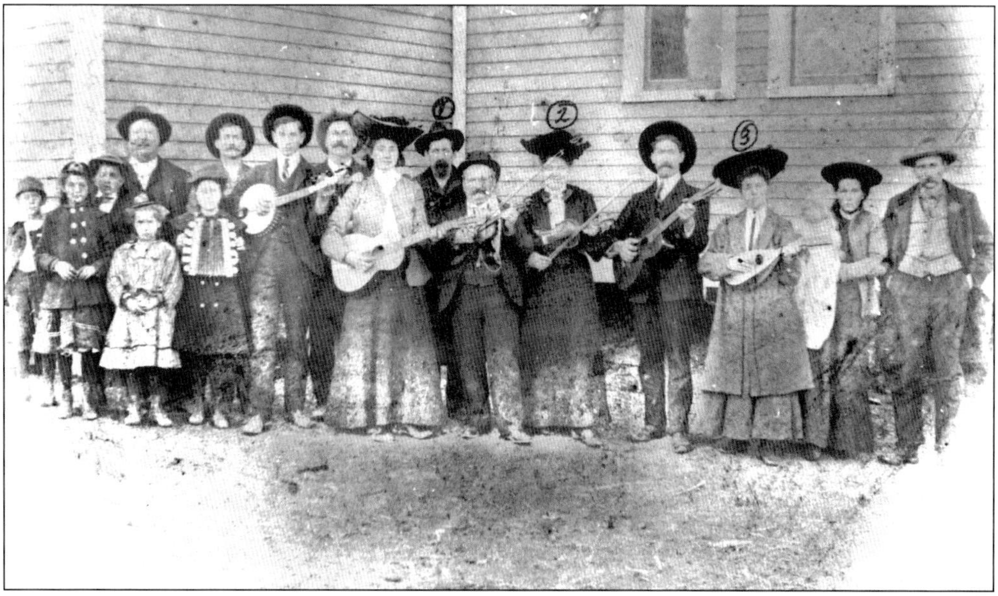

Noah J. Pennington's family assembles for a group portrait in the early 1900s with their musical instruments. The Pennington family lived on the corner of North Second and East North Street. The original First Baptist Church, on Third and North Street, can be seen in the background. (Courtesy of the Stanly County Museum.)

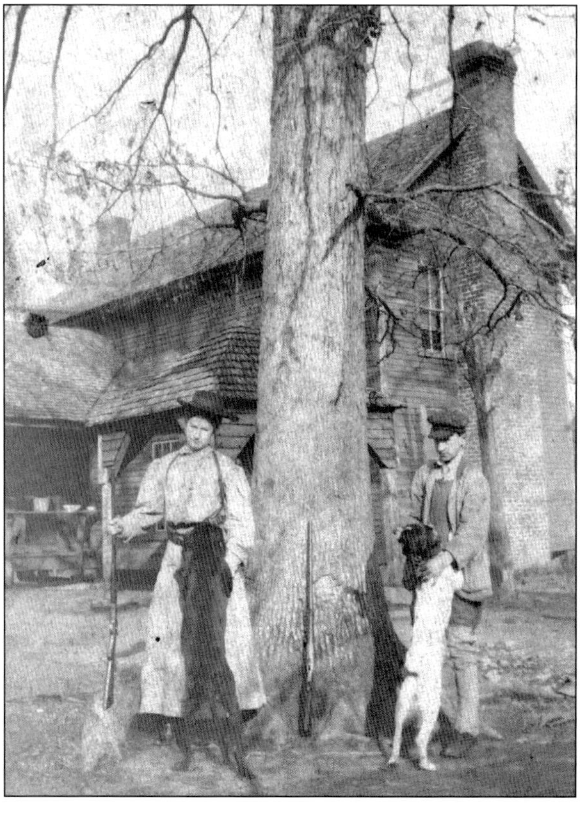

Sally Lilly, Grady Lilly, and "Old Bob" go hunting in the early 1900s. (Courtesy of Dr. and Mrs. Whitman.)

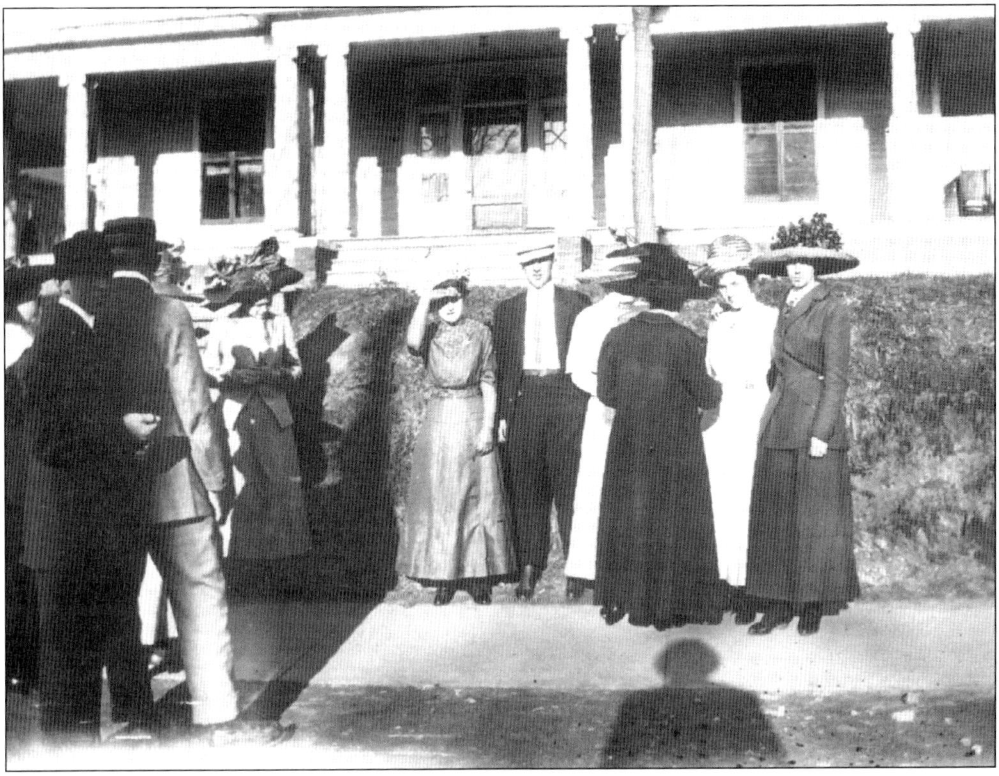

A party congregates in front of the W.T. Huckabee house on North Second Street in 1905. House parties were a popular form of entertainment in the early 1900s and are still enjoyed today. (Courtesy of the Stanly County Museum.)

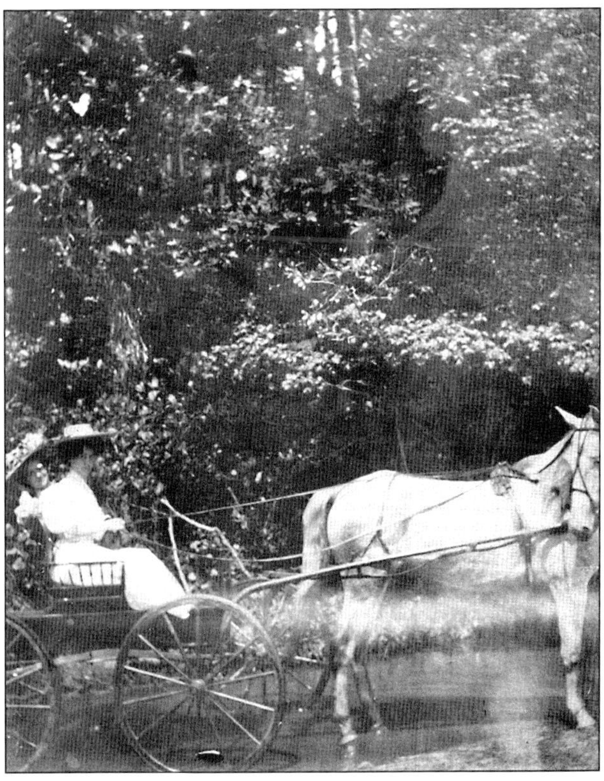

Mary Ellen Patterson peeps out from behind Estelle Morrow in the early 1900s. Both women were teachers at Albemarle Graded School. (Courtesy of the Stanly County Museum.)

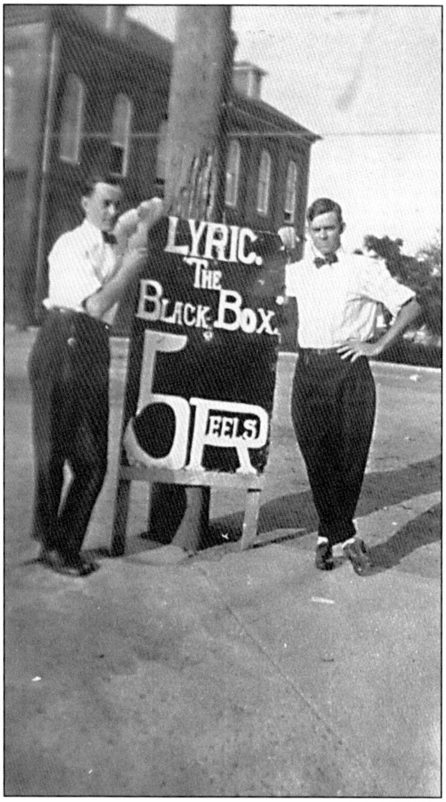

Gaines Whitley Sr. and another young man stand beside a movie theatre sign, *c*. 1914. The Lyric Theater was located at 123 South Second Street. (Courtesy of the Stanly County Museum.)

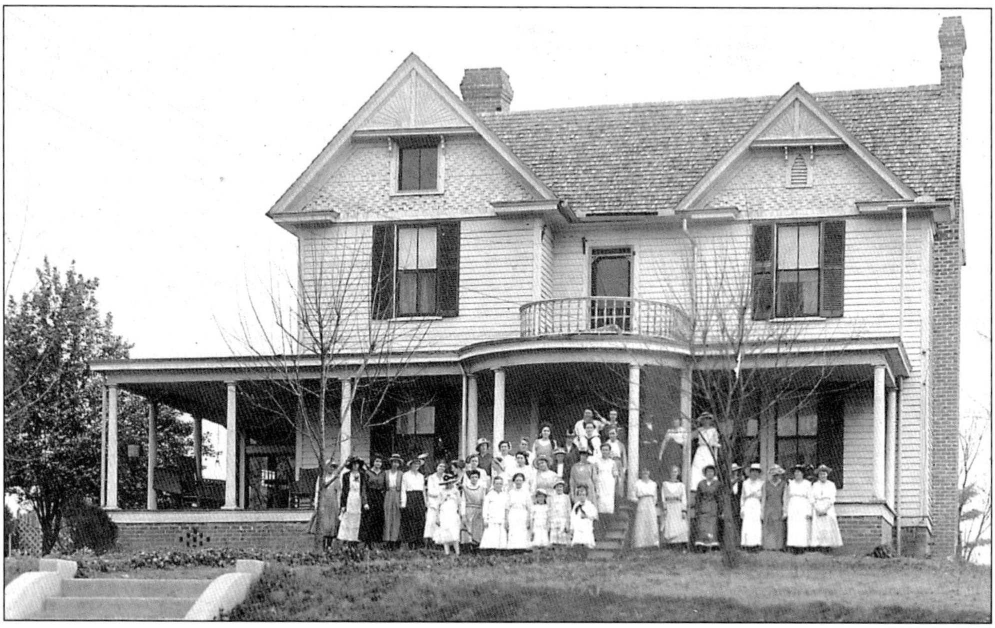

Friends and family gather in front of the Reynolds house on East Main Street. The house was built between 1910 and 1915. (Courtesy of the Stanly County Museum.)

Uncle Kirk and Miss Colson enjoy refreshments in the early 1900s. (Courtesy of the Patterson family.)

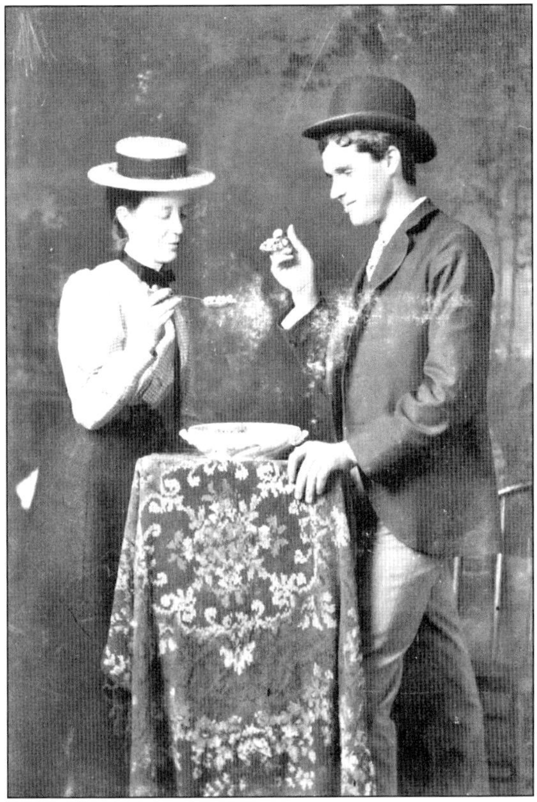

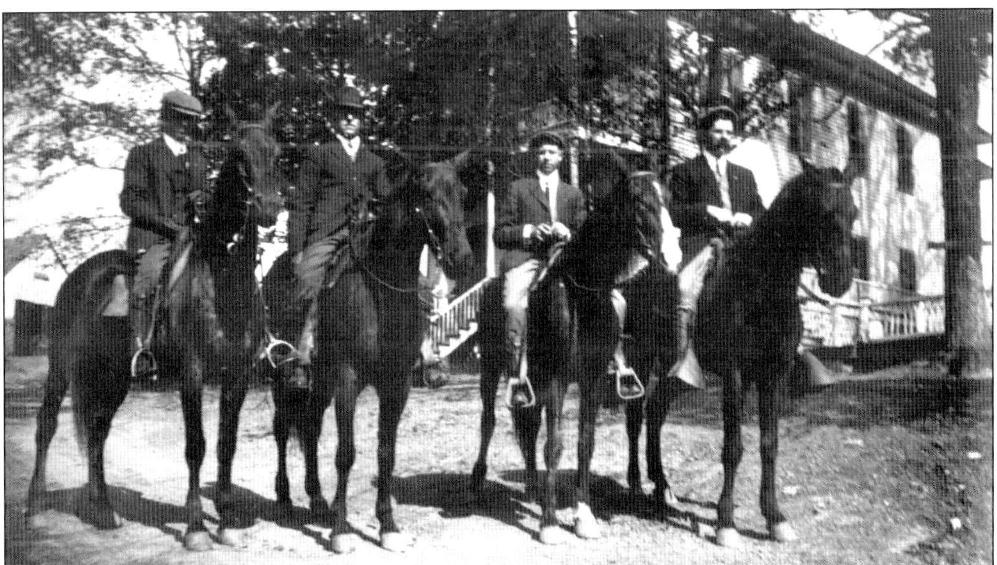

W.E. Smith and four other riders enjoy a nice day *c.* 1913. W.E. Smith was born in 1896. He was a North Carolina senator and served multiple terms from the 1920s to 1939. (Courtesy of Dr. and Mrs. Whitman.)

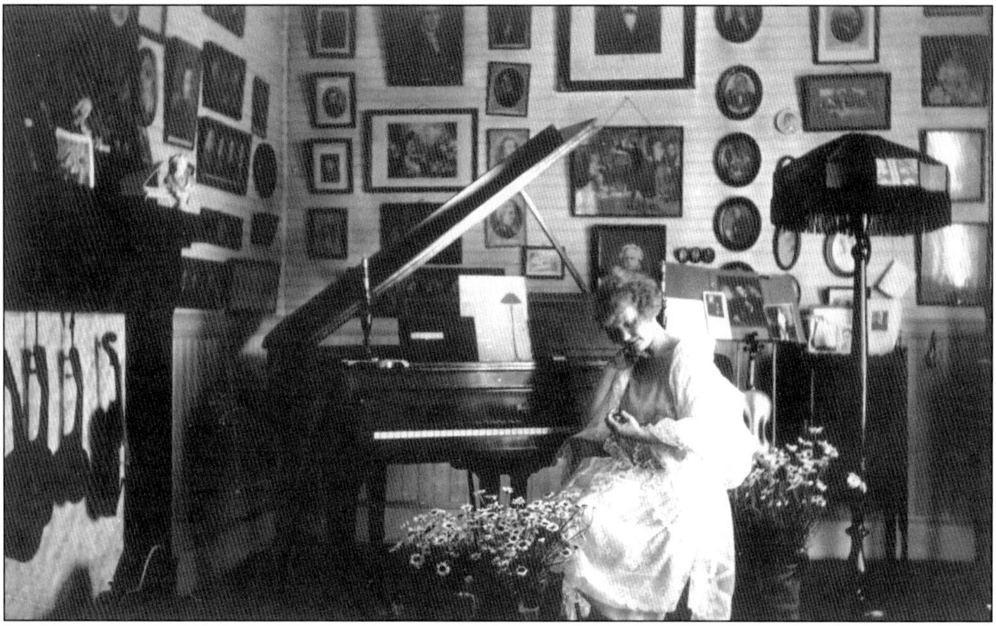

Seated at her piano, Margie Mauney strikes a thoughtful pose. She was the organist at the Central Methodist Church from 1921 to 1953. (Courtesy of the Stanly County Museum.)

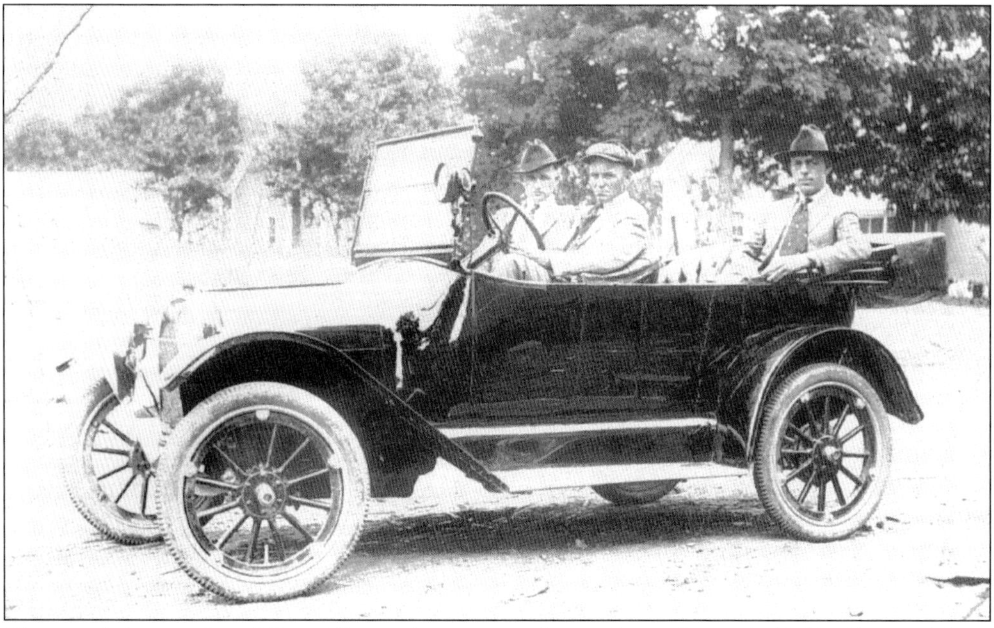

These stylish men from West Albemarle were out for a ride in the early 1900s. Pictured from left to right are Jim Green, Arthur Furr, and Fred C. Efird. Furr was the driver for Mr. Canon of Canon Mills. (Courtesy of Zelma Eudy.)

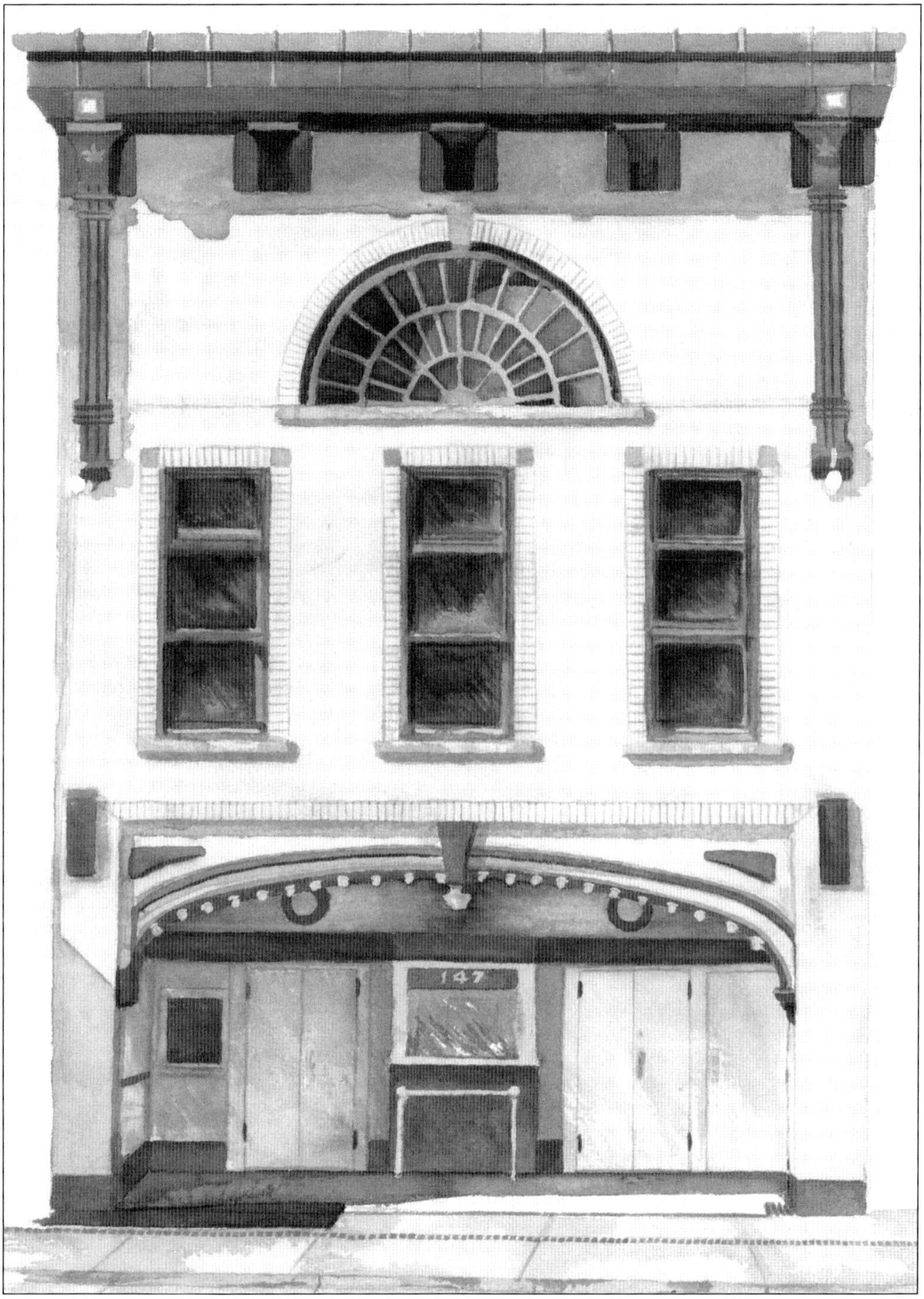

Terry Armstrong Hamra painted this image of the Alameda Theater, which was built in 1916. The painting is titled *The Old Picture Show*. Eben L. Hearne was the manager. The marquis was added in 1938. (Courtesy of Terry Hamra.)

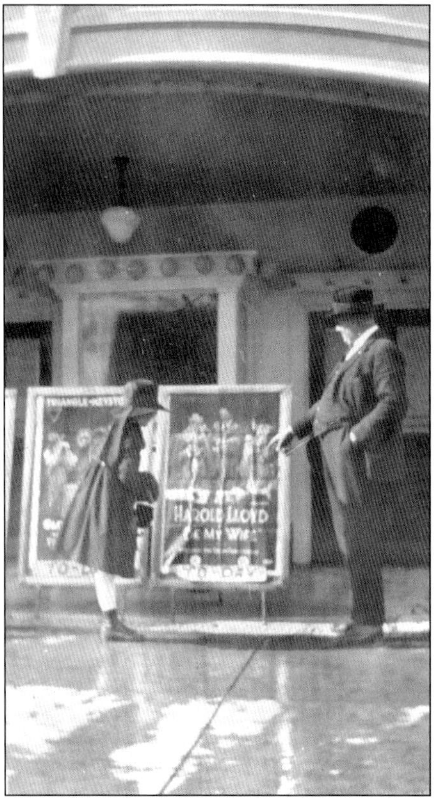

Nell Whitworth inspects the playbill for shows at the Alameda Theater. (Courtesy of the Stanly County Museum.)

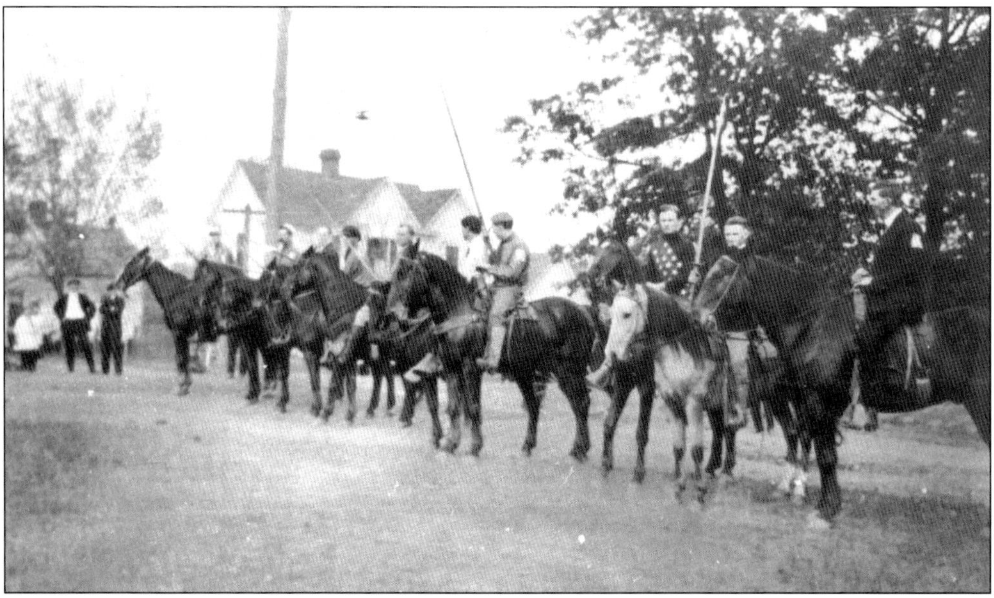

Men on horses line up in 1914. They all have numbers on their sleeves to identify them as contestants. Some of the men are holding lances in preparation for a jousting tournament. (Courtesy of the Stanly County Museum.)

Nell Whitworth serves tea at Margie Mauney's house, located on North First Street. (Courtesy of the Stanly County Museum.)

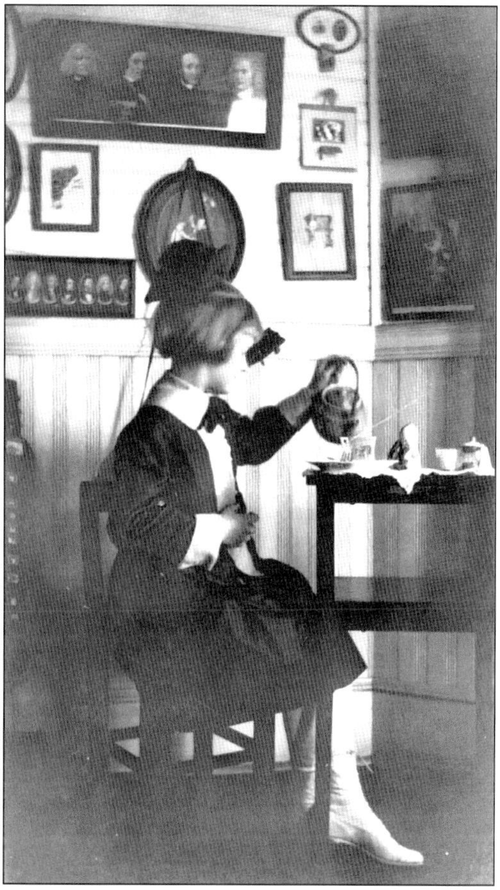

A child sits in a cart that is being drawn by a large horned goat, *c.* 1920. (Courtesy of the Stanly County Museum.)

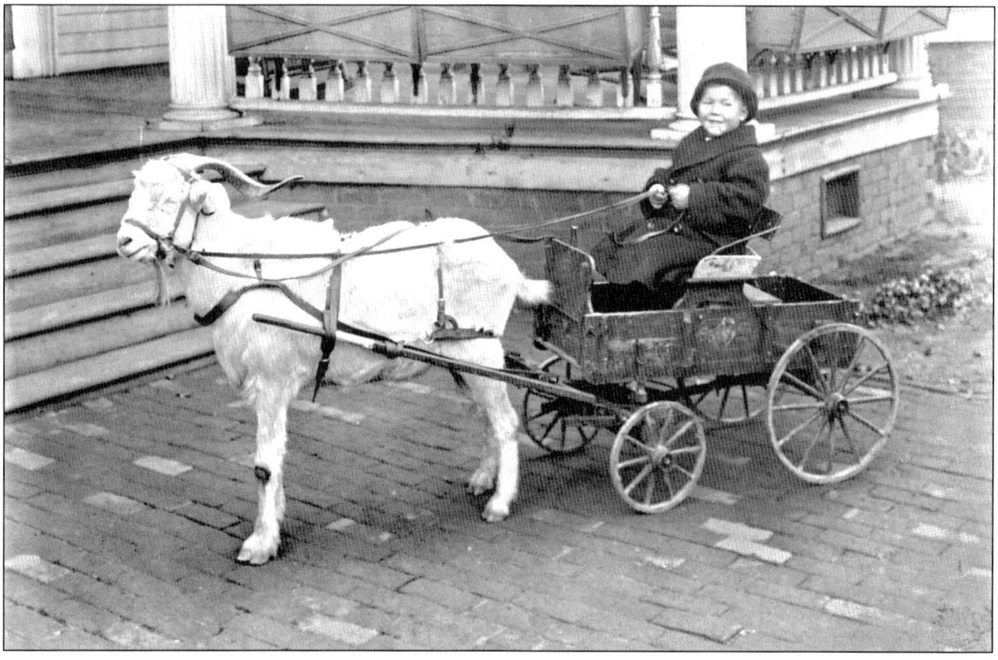

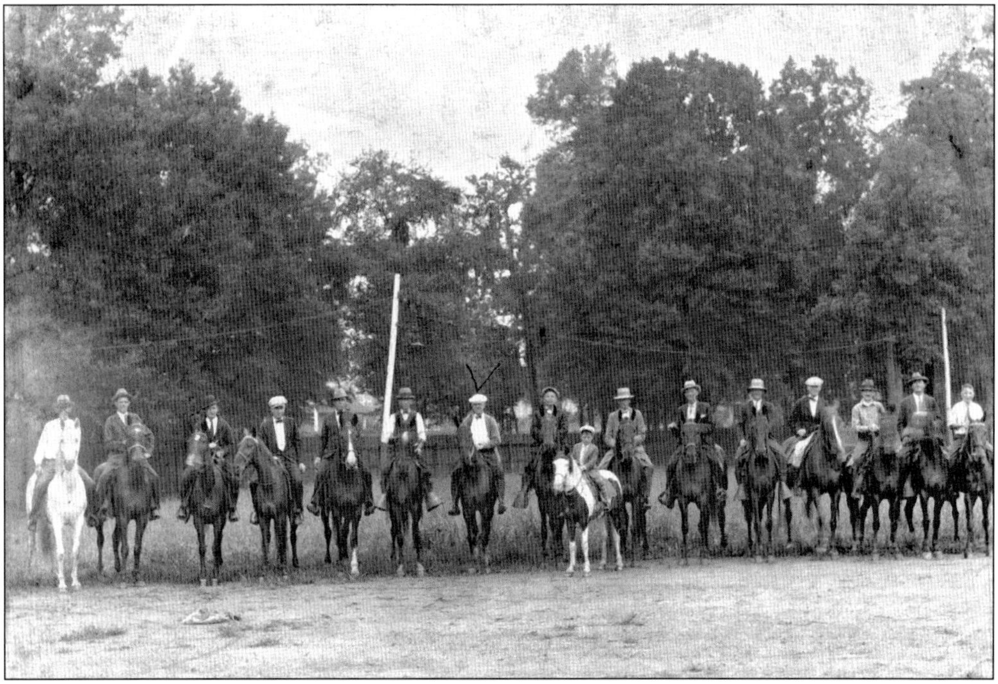

The Albemarle Riding Club is shown here lined up for an outing, *c.* 1918. The rider in the center is James A. Howard. (Courtesy of the Stanly County Museum.)

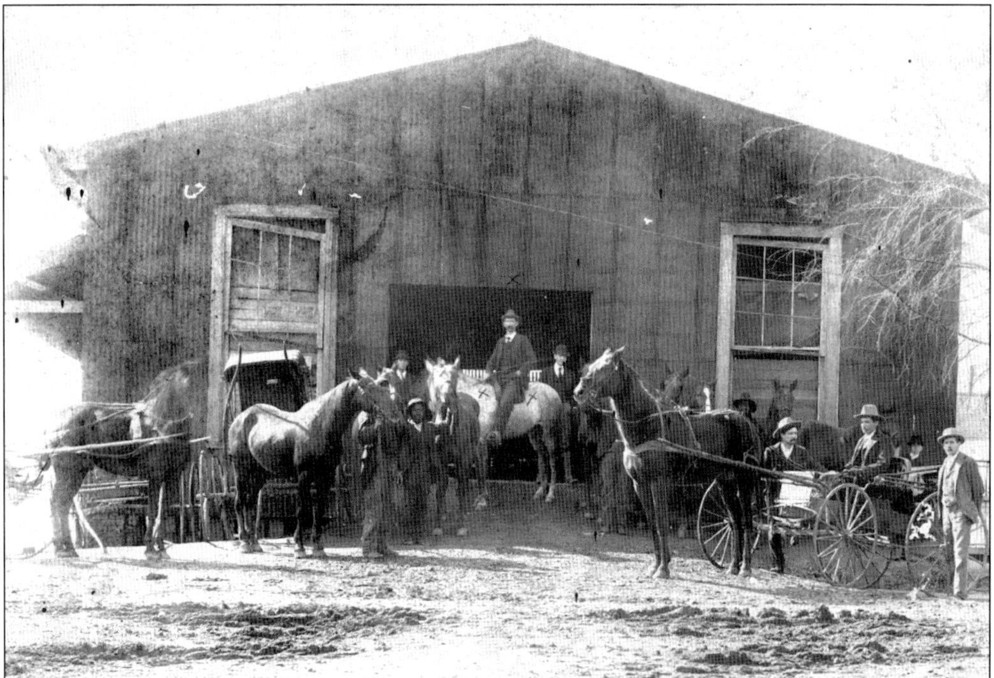

Dr. W.I. Hill sits astride a horse in the early 1900s outside stables that would later burn down. This location is now where the post office can be found. Dr. Hill was born on December 31, 1869. (Courtesy of the Dr. Hill family.)

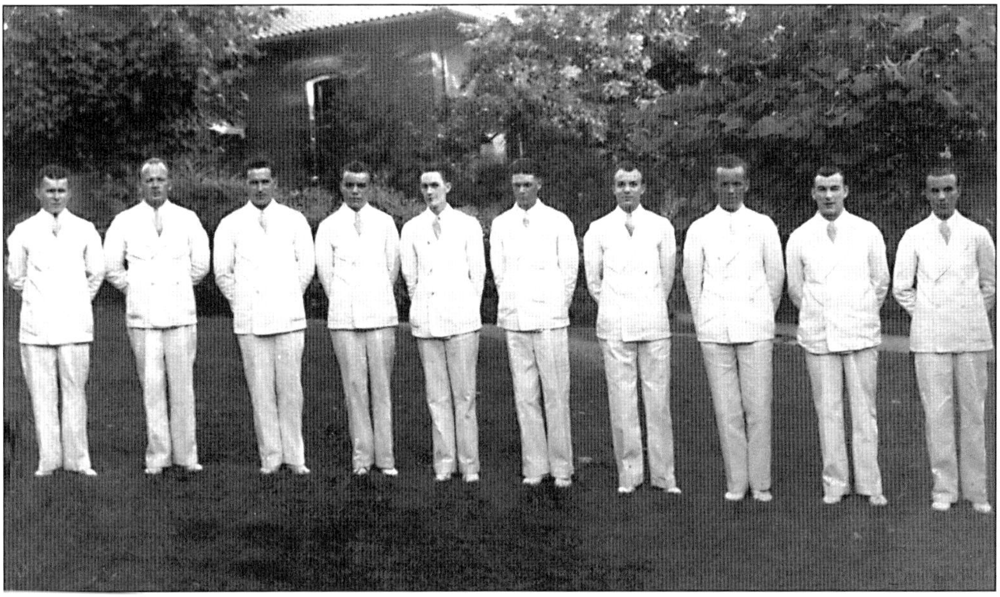

Pee Wee Furr and the Tar Hill Orchestra played at the Opera House. (Courtesy of the Stanly County Museum.)

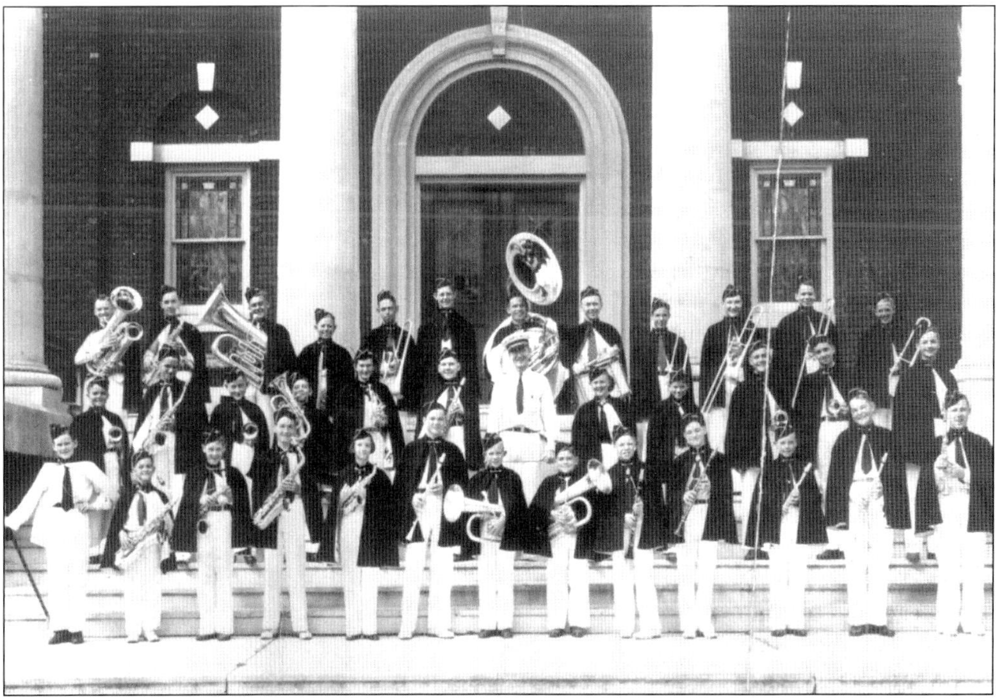

The members of the Albemarle band, directed by Pat Leonard, line up on the steps of the First Presbyterian Church in the 1930s. (Courtesy of the Stanly County Museum.)

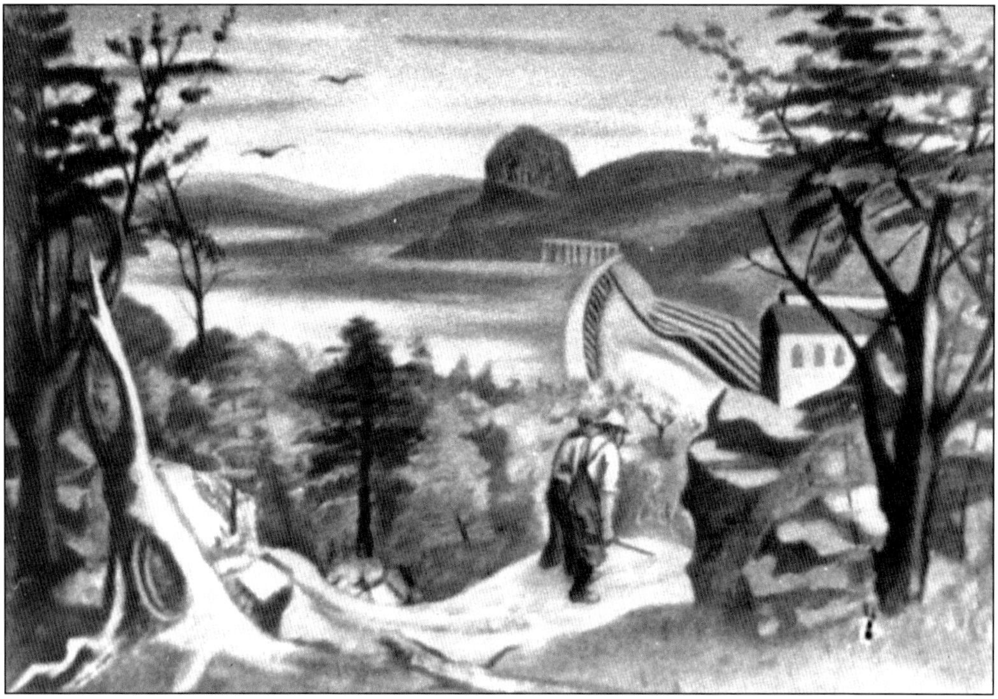

This mural, titled *View Near Albemarle*, was once located in the Albemarle post office. Louis Ribak completed the mural in the early 1940s for the Public Works of Art Project, part of President Roosevelt's New Deal. (Courtesy of the Stanly County Museum.)

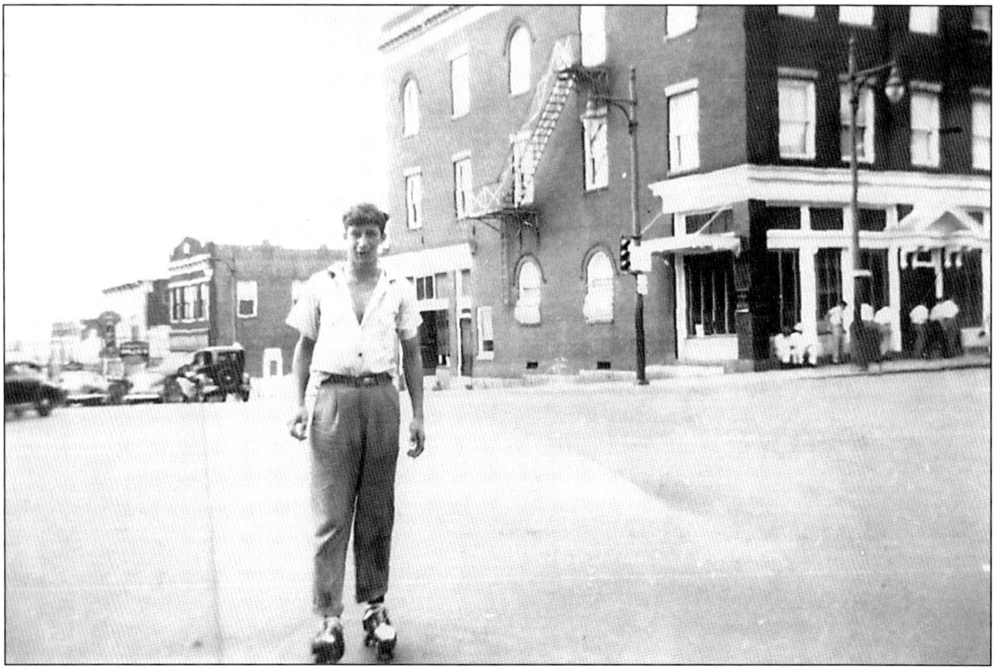

Bob Burleson roller skates in the town square, c. 1942. Albemarle Insurance Company and the First National Bank were located in the Trust Building in the background. Albemarle Insurance Company was founded in 1905. (Courtesy of the Stanly County Museum.)

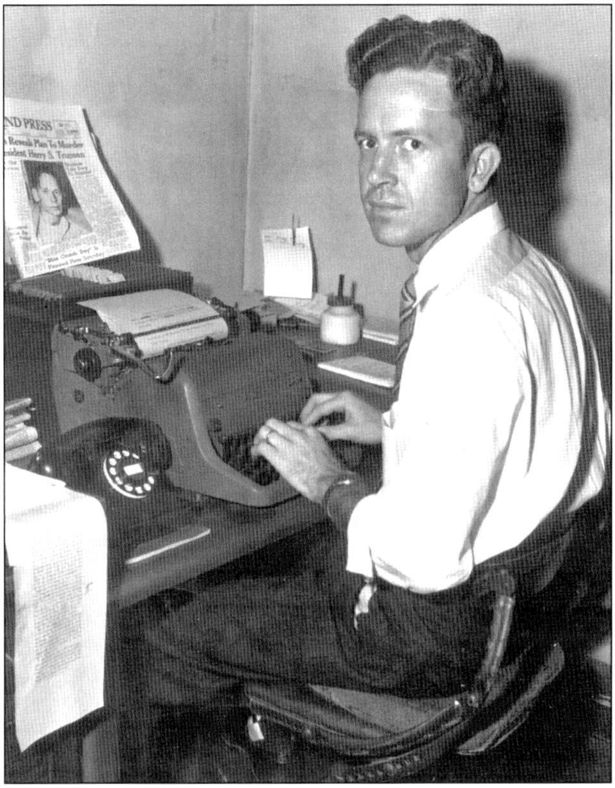

Fred T. Morgan writes at *The Stanly News & Press* in the 1950s. He is also the author of many ghost story books, including *Ghost Tales of Uwharries* (1968), *Haunted Uwharries* (1992), and *The Revolt and 28 More Original Uwharries Ghost Stories* (2004). (Courtesy of the Stanly County Museum.)

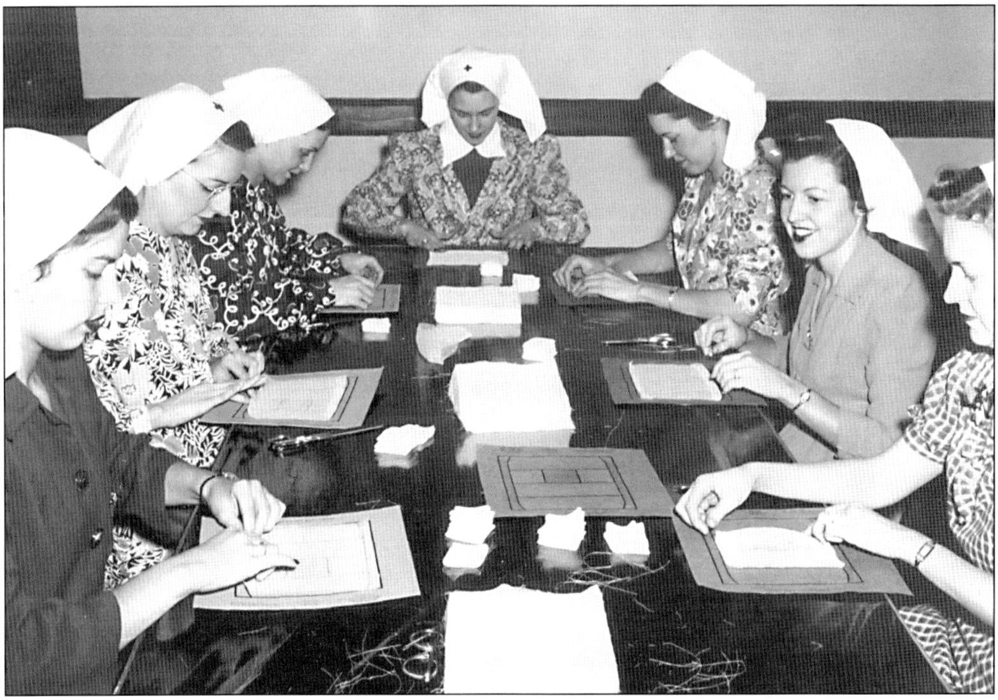

Members of the Albemarle Spinster's Club are shown here rolling bandages for the Red Cross in 1943. (Courtesy of the Stanly County Museum.)

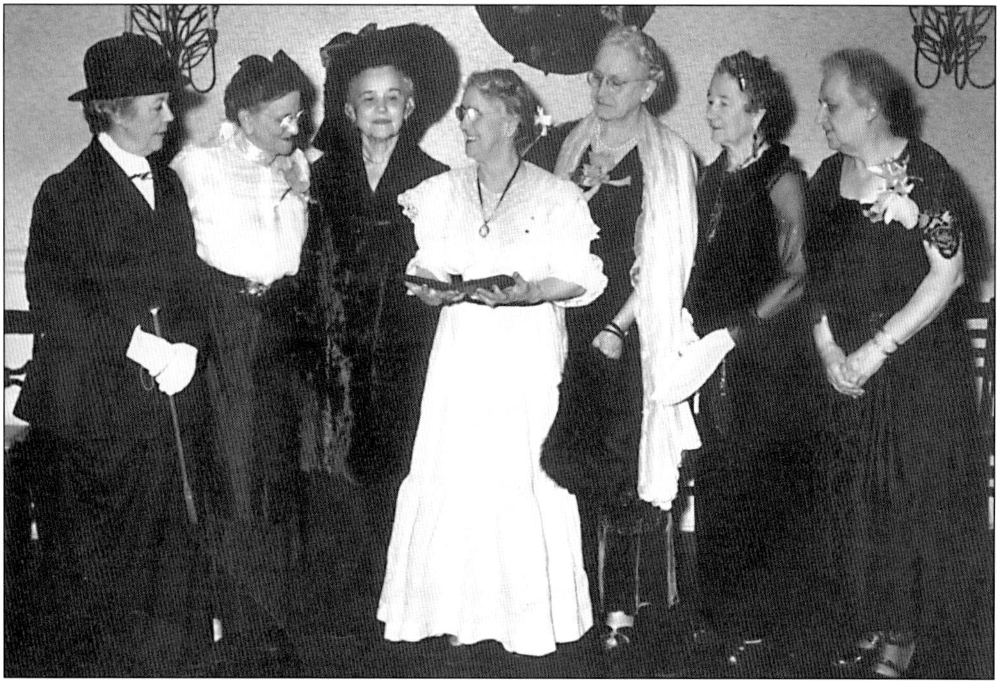

Charter members of the Tuesday Bridge Club celebrate their 50th anniversary in 1956. (Courtesy of the Stanly County Museum.)

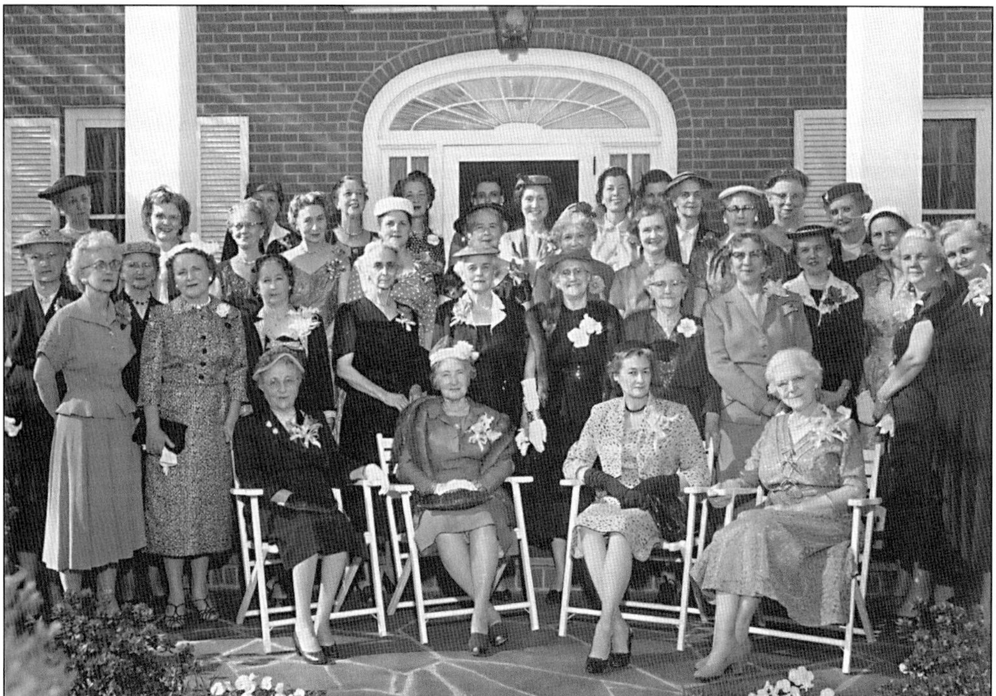

The Mamie Crowell Garden Club poses in front of the Denning House on Pee Dee Avenue in 1956 for their 25th anniversary celebration. The Freeman House was originally at this location until it was moved to Montgomery Avenue. (Courtesy of the Stanly County Museum.)

Five

FINANCE AND INDUSTRY

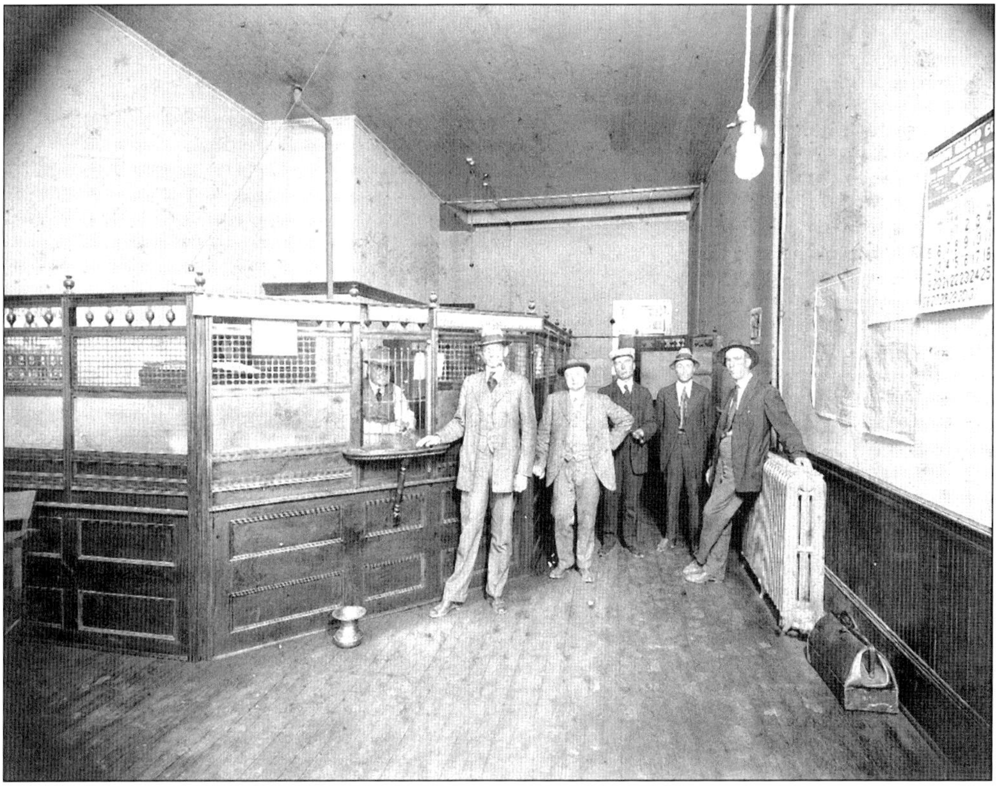

Cabarrus Bank started in 1897 at 160 West Main Street. In 1934, W.B. Beaver was made vice president of the bank. In this picture, "Governor" Groves stands to the immediate right of the cage with ? Patterson to his right. The Fitzgerald building is currently located at this site. (Courtesy of the Stanly County Museum.)

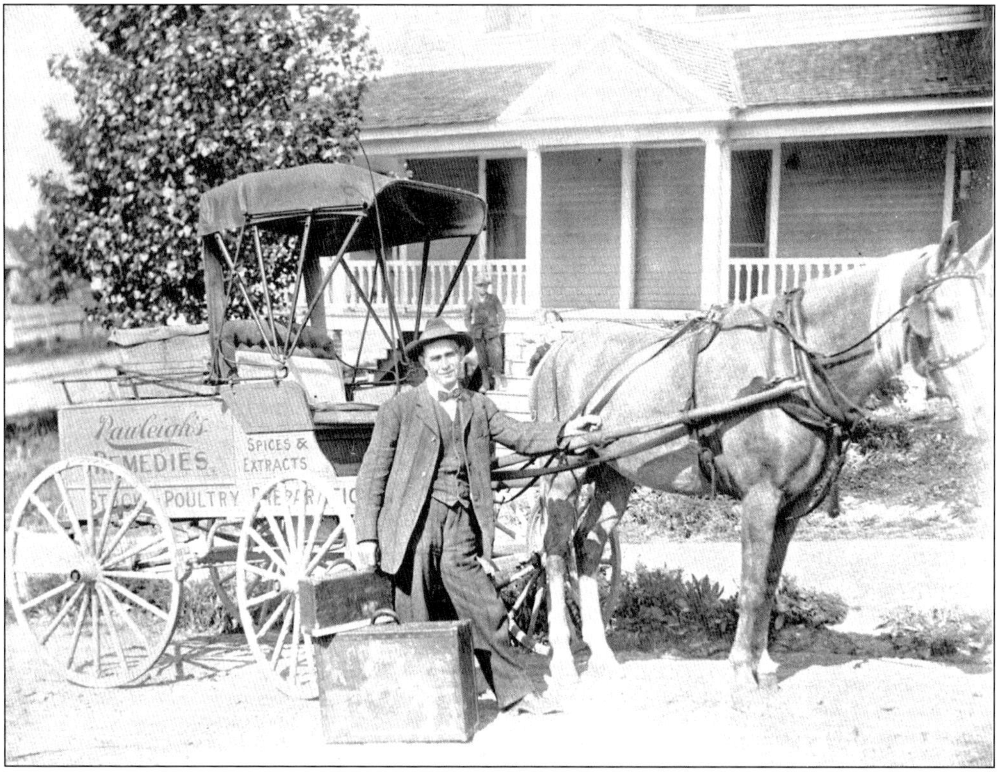

A traveling salesman sits cases filled with remedies beside his horse and buggy. "Rawleigh's Remedies" is painted on the side of the buggy. (Courtesy of the Stanly County Museum.)

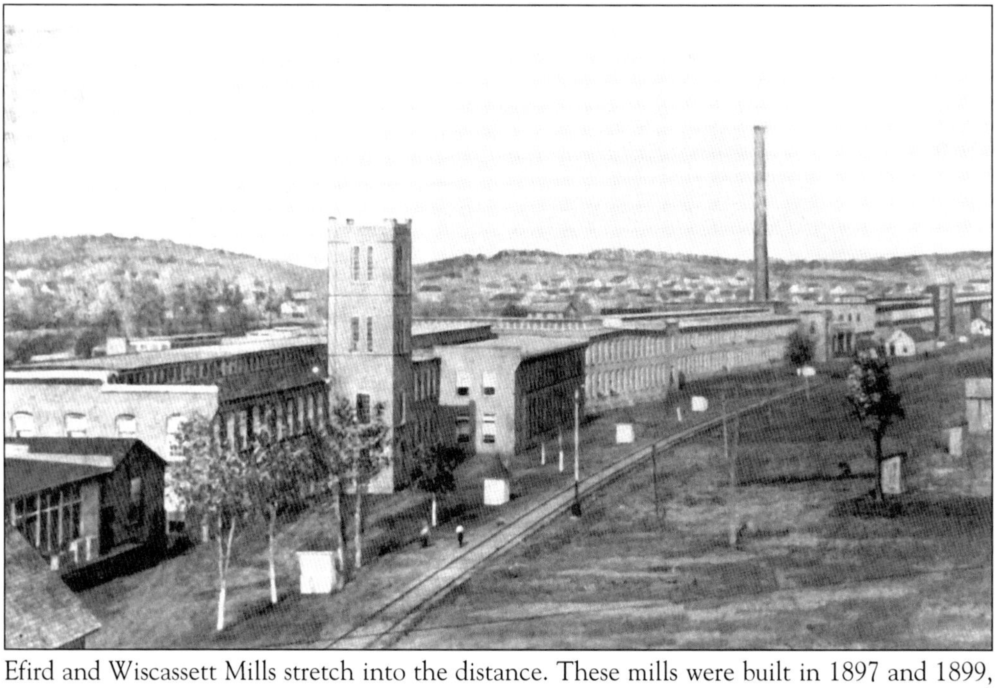

Efird and Wiscassett Mills stretch into the distance. These mills were built in 1897 and 1899, respectively. (Courtesy of the Stanly County Museum.)

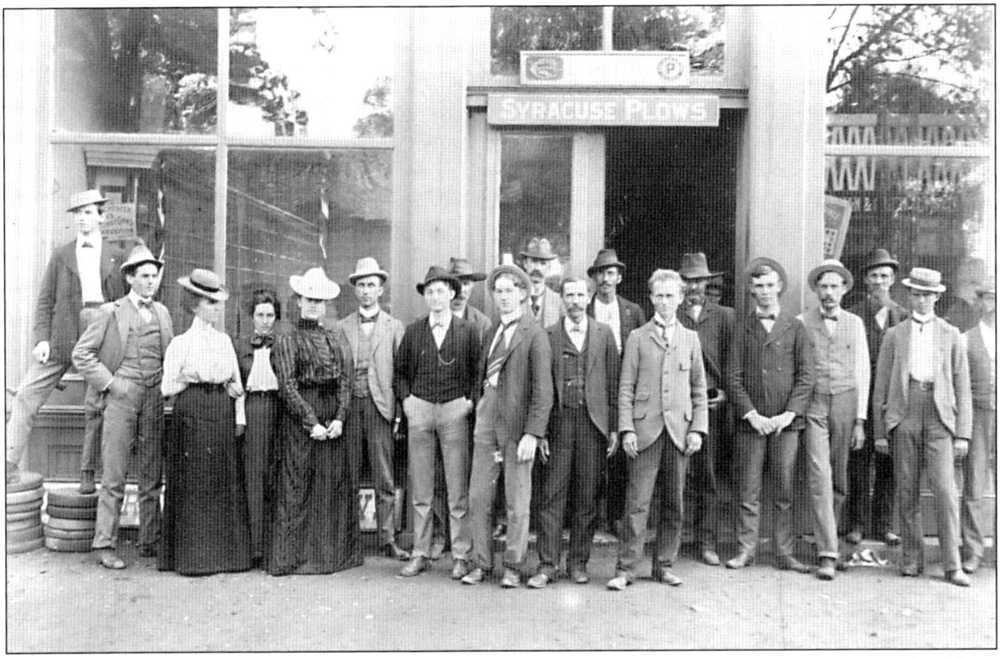

A group assembles in front of the first Morrow Brothers and Heath Company building on South Street in 1900 for a big sale. The Morrow Brothers building was the first brick building in town. J.M. Morrow was president, W.E. Milton was vice-president, and J. Heath Morrow was secretary, treasurer, and general manager in the 1940s. (Courtesy of the Stanly County Museum.)

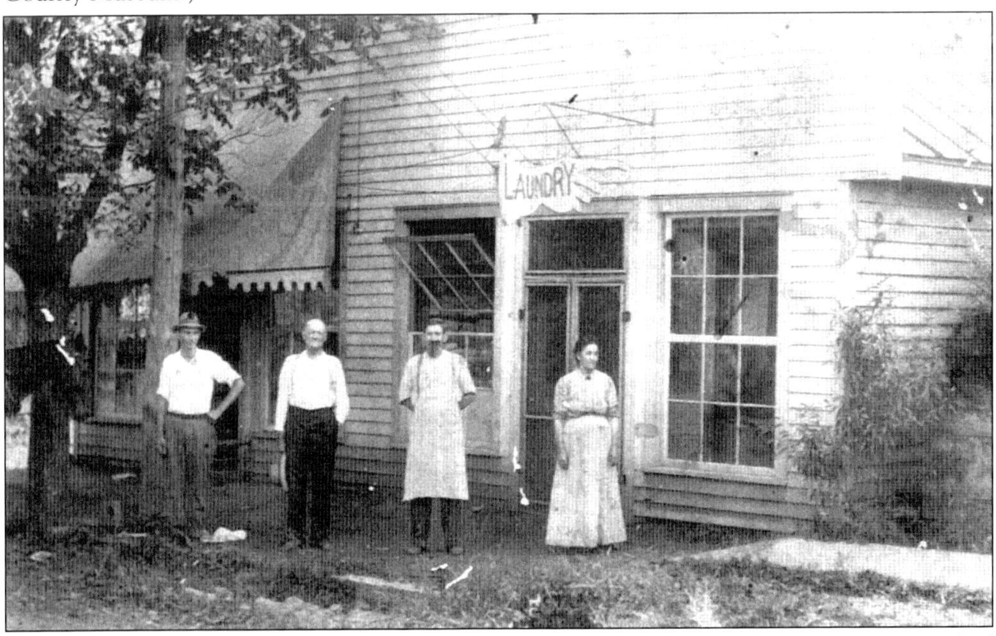

The Laundry and Harness Shop was located on Second Street in the early 1900s. A sign crafted in the shape of a hand with "LAUNDRY" painted on it indicates the entrance. The owner of the shop, Noah J. Pennington, stands second from the right in this photograph. (Courtesy of the Stanly County Museum.)

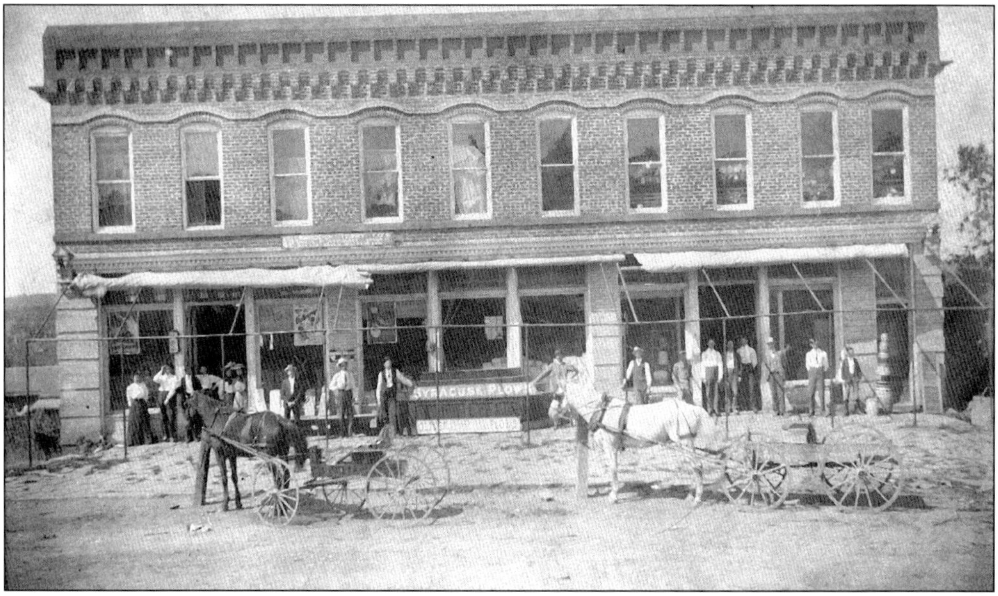

The second Morrow Brothers and Heath Company was located at the corner of First Street and Main Street. They moved into this building in 1903. The building was constructed in 1898 and was originally named the Big Store. (Courtesy of the Stanly County Museum.)

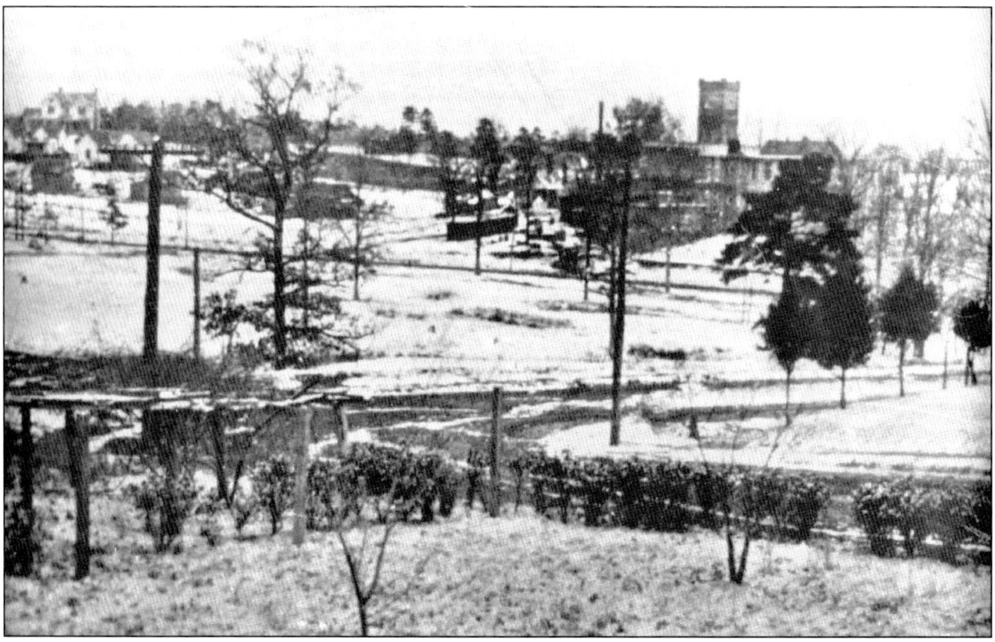

The Lillian Textile Mill, built in 1905, was named for the wife of founder Arthur Patterson. This view is from Fourth and North Streets. (Courtesy of the Stanly County Museum.)

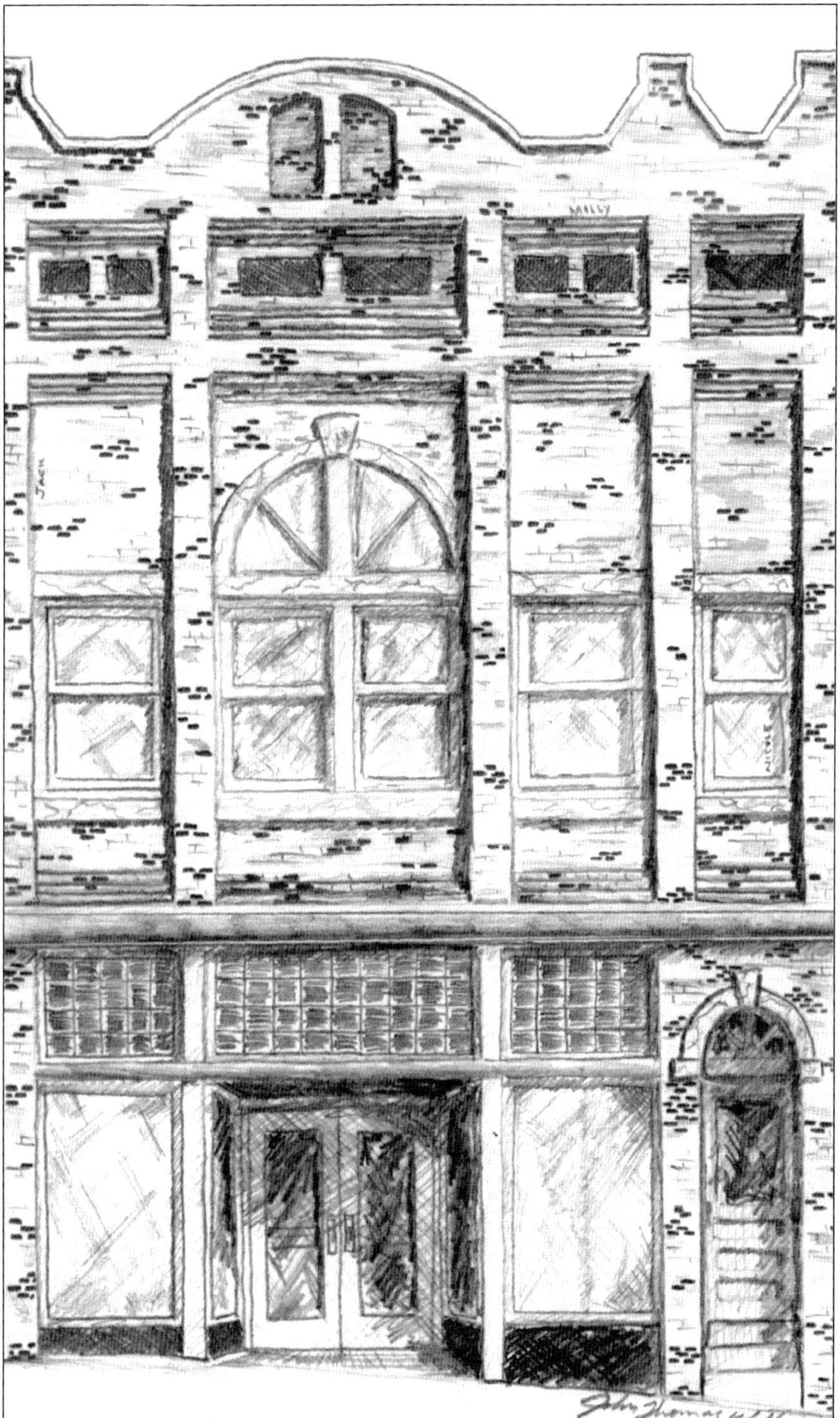

G.M. Dry once operated out of this building located at 139 West Main Street. The Boardroom Bar and Bistro currently occupies this building. John T. Williams Jr., a local artist, drew this rendition of the building's original appearance. (Courtesy of John T. Williams Jr.)

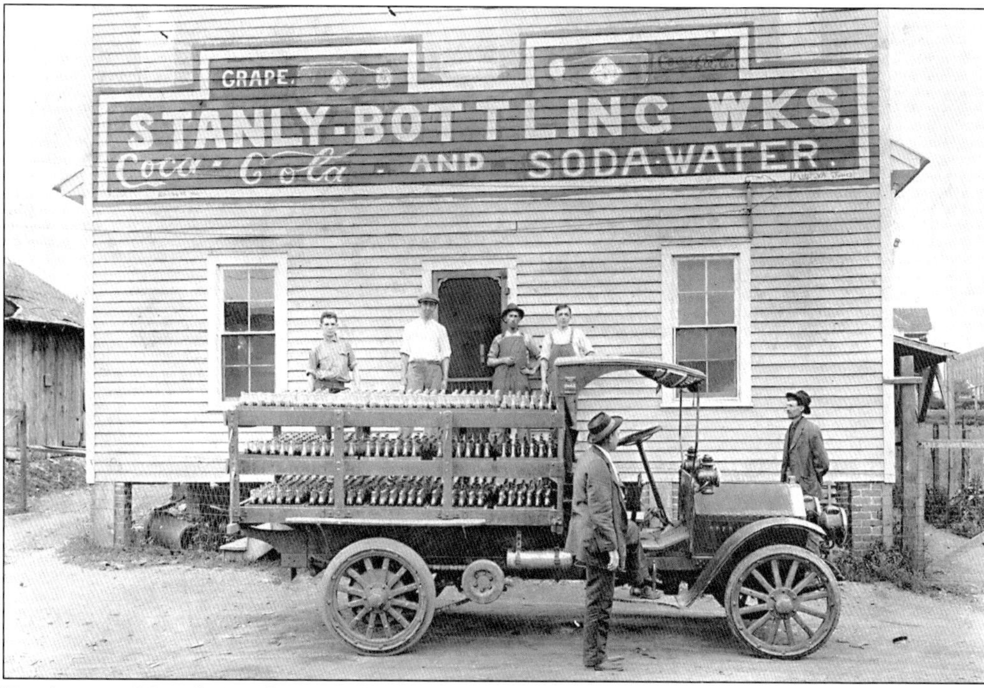

Employees of Stanly-Bottling Works pose with their chain-driven delivery truck, *c.* 1905. The building in the background is the Morrow Brothers and Heath Company on South Street. (Courtesy of the Stanly County Museum.)

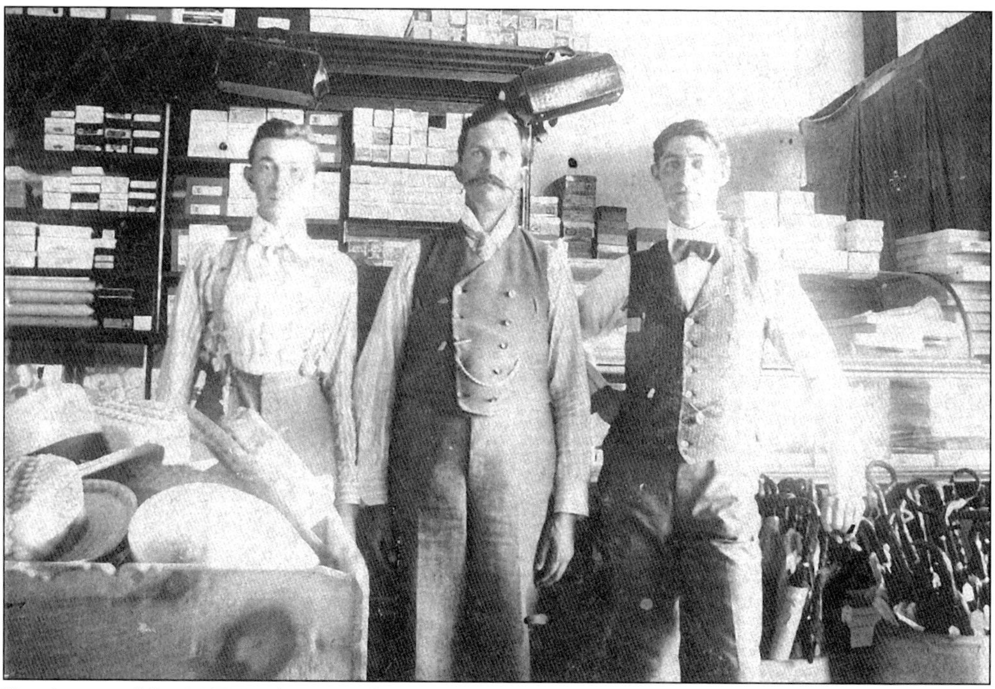

Employees of the M.F. Little Store, located at 143 North Second Street, pose between hats and umbrellas, *c.* 1906. Pictured are, from left to right, Frank Ross, Tom Forrest (former sheriff), and W. Frank Snuggs. (Courtesy of the Stanly County Museum.)

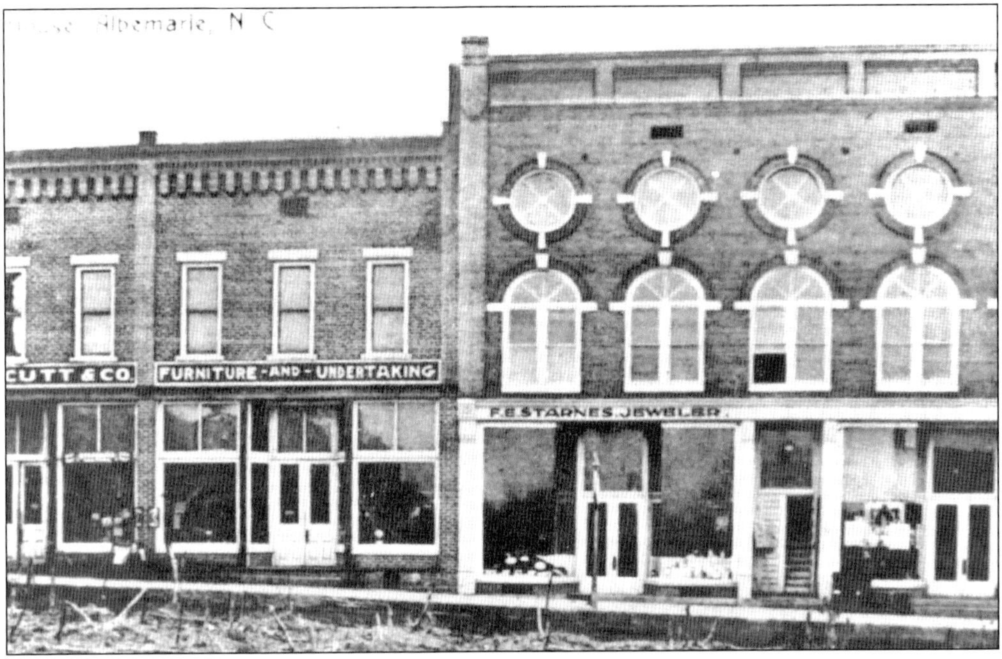

After 1907, Starnes Jewelry and Huneycutt Furniture and Undertaking were located side by side on West Main Street. Directly to the right of Starnes Jewelry, one can see the entrance to the Albemarle Opera House, located on the second floor over Starnes Jewelry. Thomas Edison's moving pictures were shown at this location. Later, a doorway was created between the second floor of Huneycutt Furniture and Undertaking and Albemarle Opera House to store caskets. (Courtesy of Gene Starnes.)

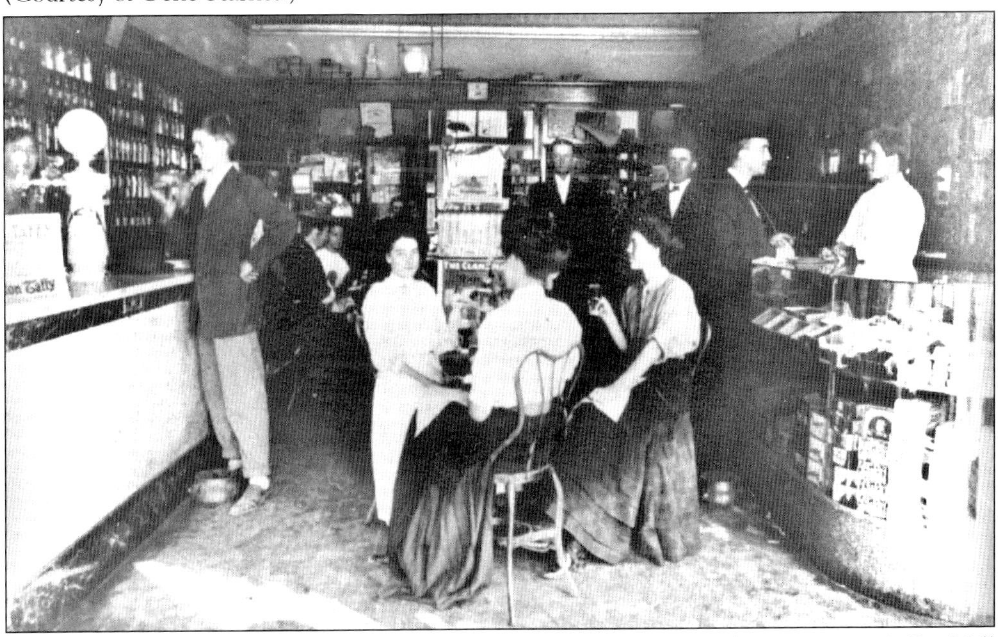

Dr. Julius Clegg Hall's second store was located at 120 North Second Street in 1910. Dr. Hall was born November 23, 1874, and died October 1929. He practiced medicine in Albemarle between 1906 and 1929. (Courtesy of the Patterson family.)

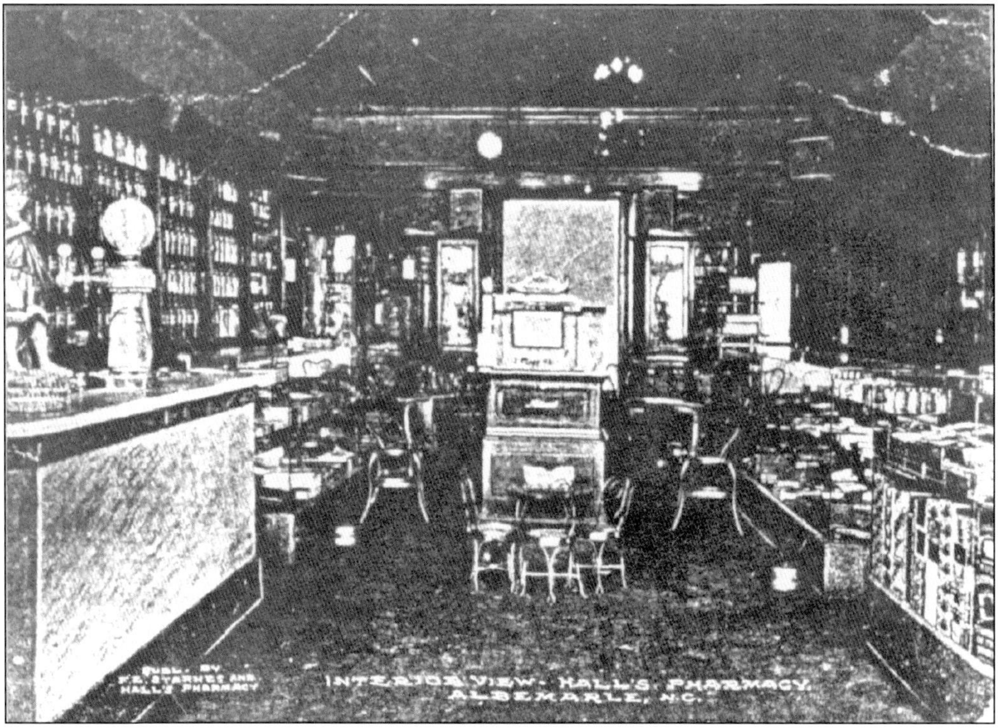

In 1910, Dr. Hall celebrated the opening of his second store with a grand opening. His first store was located at West Main Street. (Courtesy of the Patterson family.)

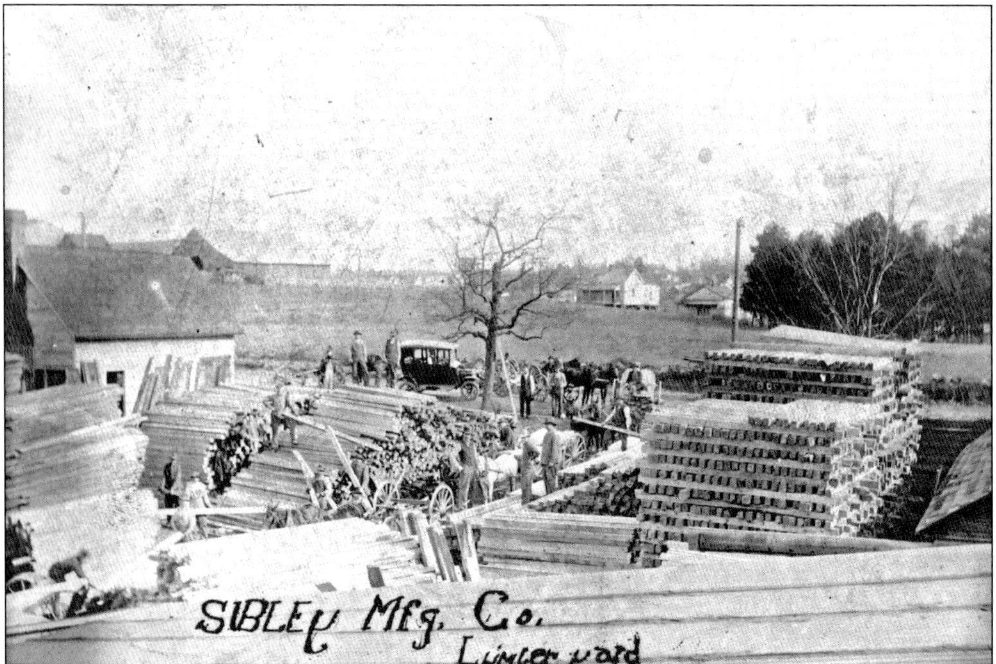

Sibley Manufacturing Company's lumberyard began operation in 1900 and was located on South First Street. It later became Builder Mart. (Courtesy of the Stanly County Museum.)

In this picture from 1911, surveyors from Winston-Salem Southbound Railway pause with their equipment. Notice Wiscassett Mill in the background. O.G. Whitley Sr. stands second from left. He attended State College and later became an Albemarle city engineer. (Courtesy of the Stanly County Museum.)

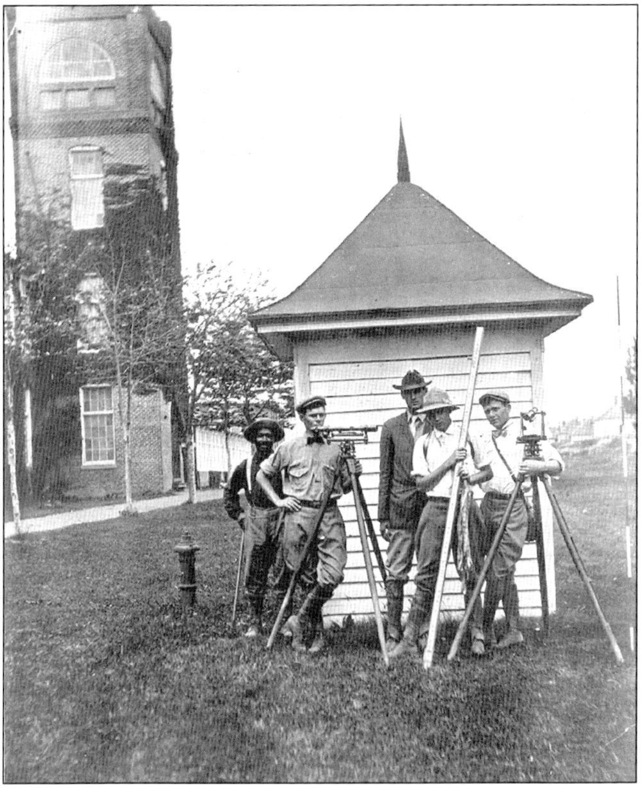

"Albemarle Plumbing Co." is printed across a Redwine truck in the early 1920s. The truck was parked on North Third Street in front of an early hospital. Note the phone number printed on the side of the truck. The number (234) only had three digits. (Courtesy of the Stanly County Museum.)

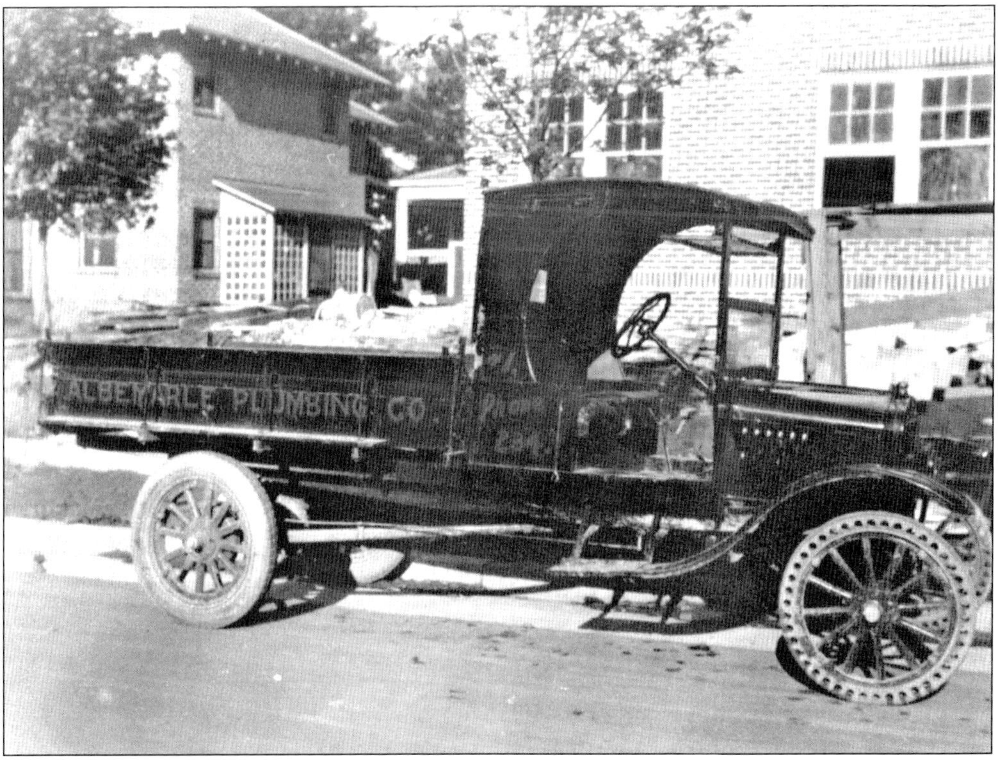

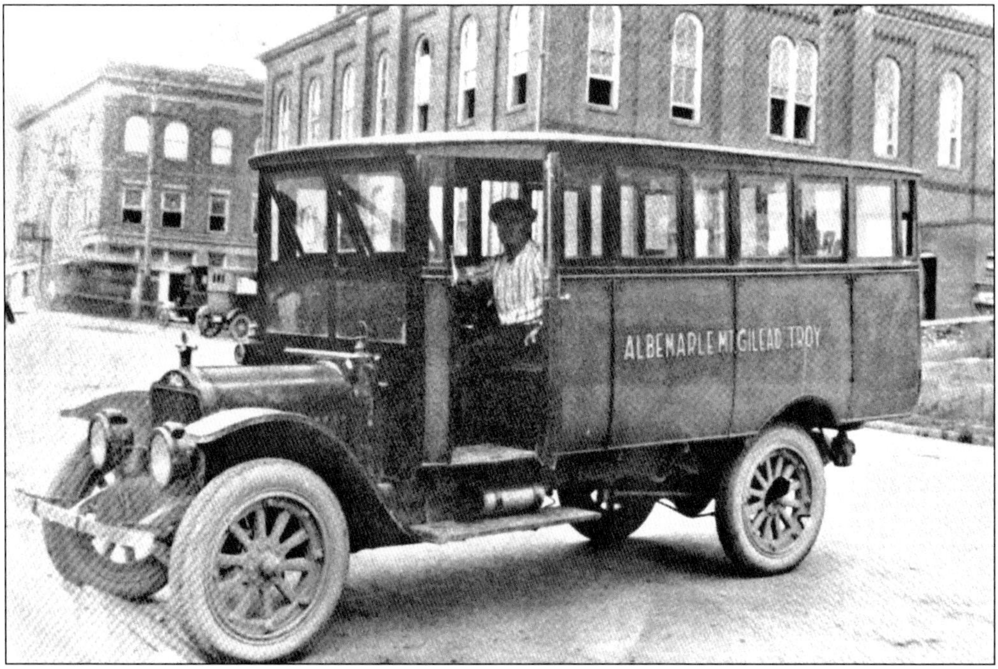

A man drives a Redwine bus between Albemarle, Mt. Gilead, and Troy in the early 1920s. The second courthouse is visible in the background. J.E. Redwine's nearby shop built many of the county's earliest trucks and buses. (Courtesy of the Stanly County Museum.)

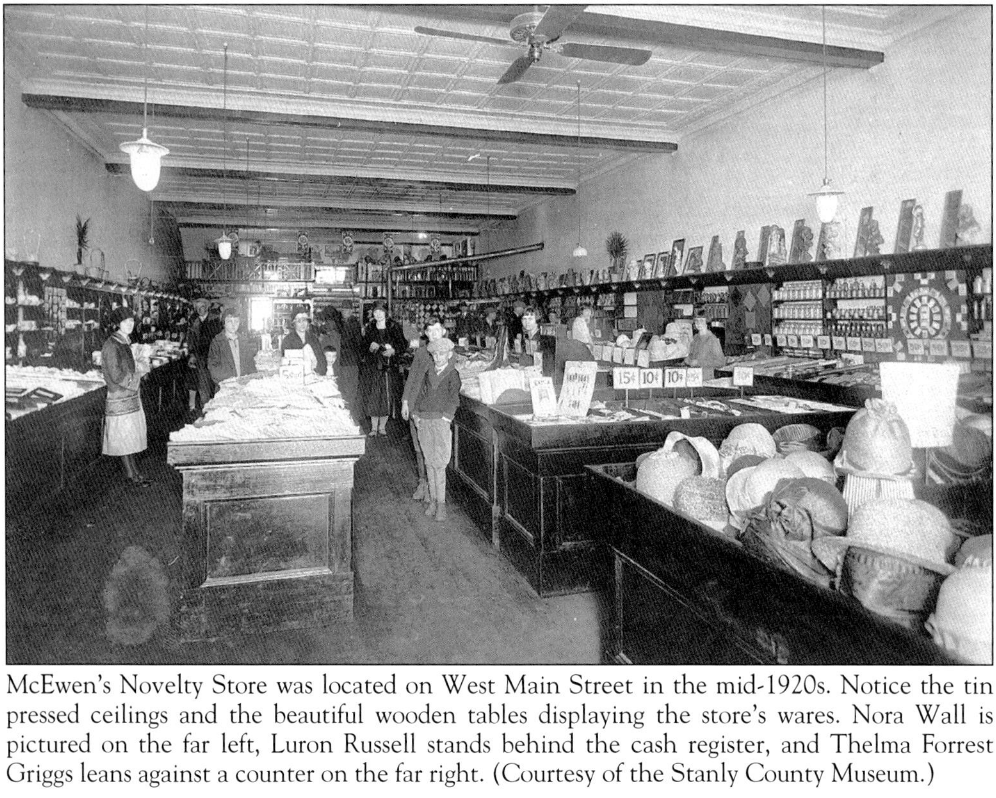

McEwen's Novelty Store was located on West Main Street in the mid-1920s. Notice the tin pressed ceilings and the beautiful wooden tables displaying the store's wares. Nora Wall is pictured on the far left, Luron Russell stands behind the cash register, and Thelma Forrest Griggs leans against a counter on the far right. (Courtesy of the Stanly County Museum.)

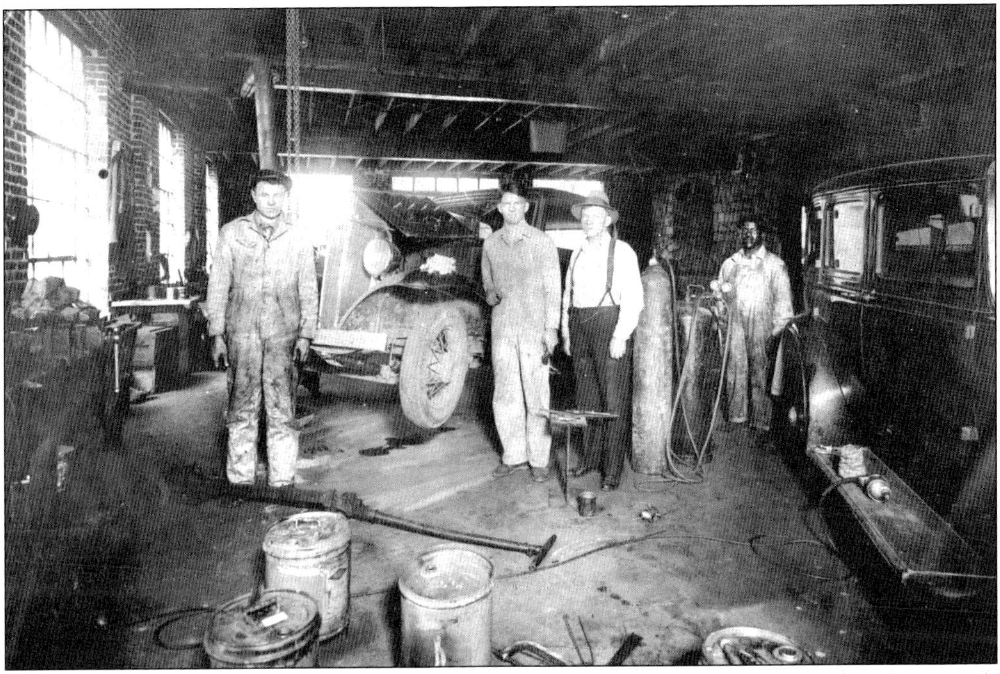

Morgan Motor Company was established in 1926 at Five Points. The men in this photograph work on cars inside the building. Pictured are, from left to right, Mack Craig Morgan II, Ernest Knotts, Mack Craig Morgan, and an unidentified man. (Courtesy of the Morgan family.)

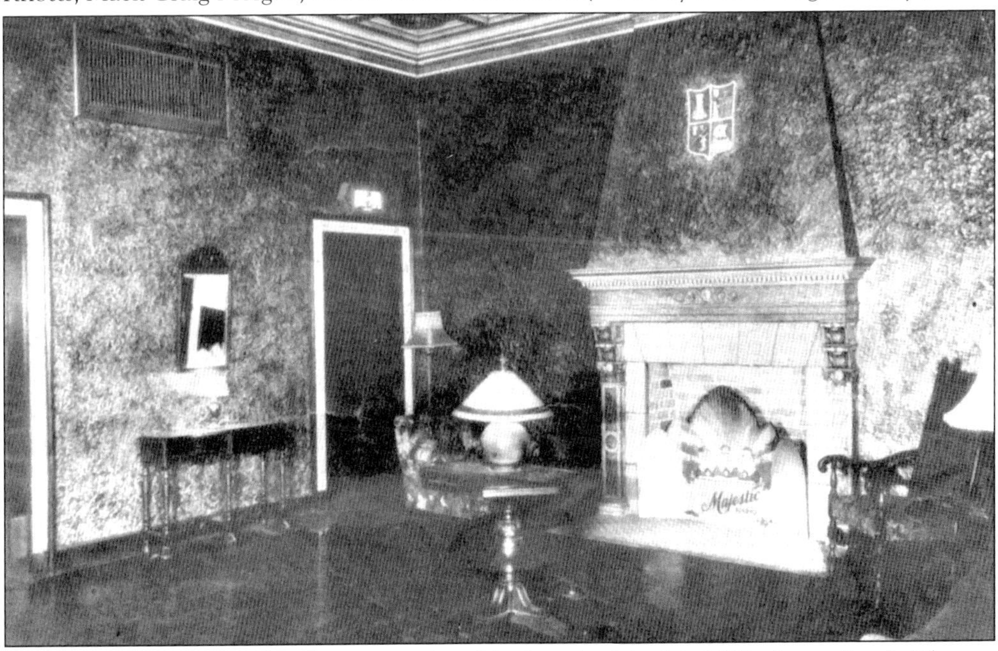

The interior of the Stanly Theater was lavishly furnished in this 1932 photo. Stanly Theater opened in December 1929. The balcony and projection room collapsed during a fire in 1937. The floors were mahogany, and the fireplaces were white marble. The theater, which could seat 700, was operated by Stanly Amusement Co. and managed by G.A. Hughes. (Courtesy of *The Stanly News and Press.*)

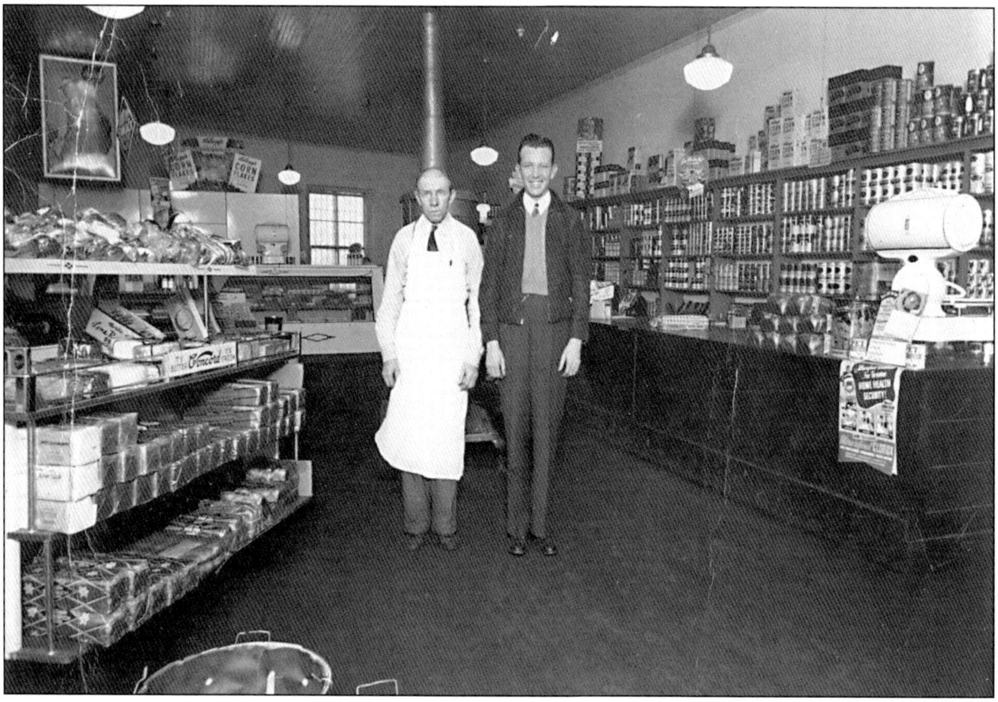

Two men standing in Townsend's store on 1095 Oakwood Street are flanked by rows of groceries. Note the large scale on the counter. (Courtesy of the Stanly County Museum.)

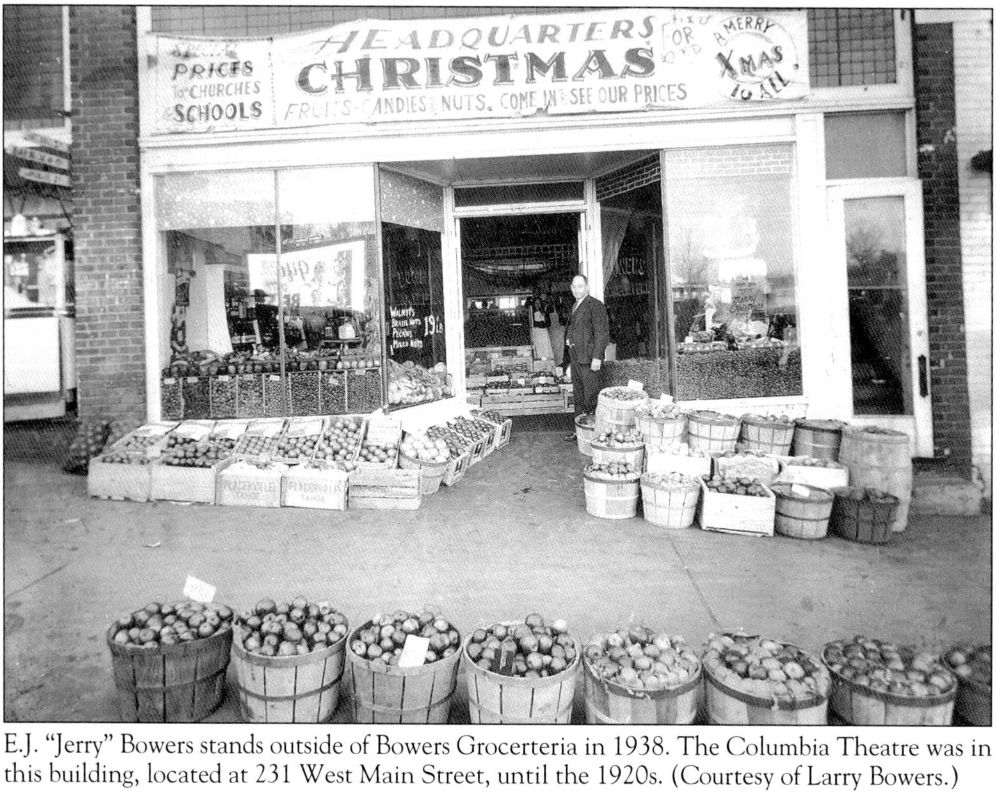

E.J. "Jerry" Bowers stands outside of Bowers Grocerteria in 1938. The Columbia Theatre was in this building, located at 231 West Main Street, until the 1920s. (Courtesy of Larry Bowers.)

Six

MILITARY

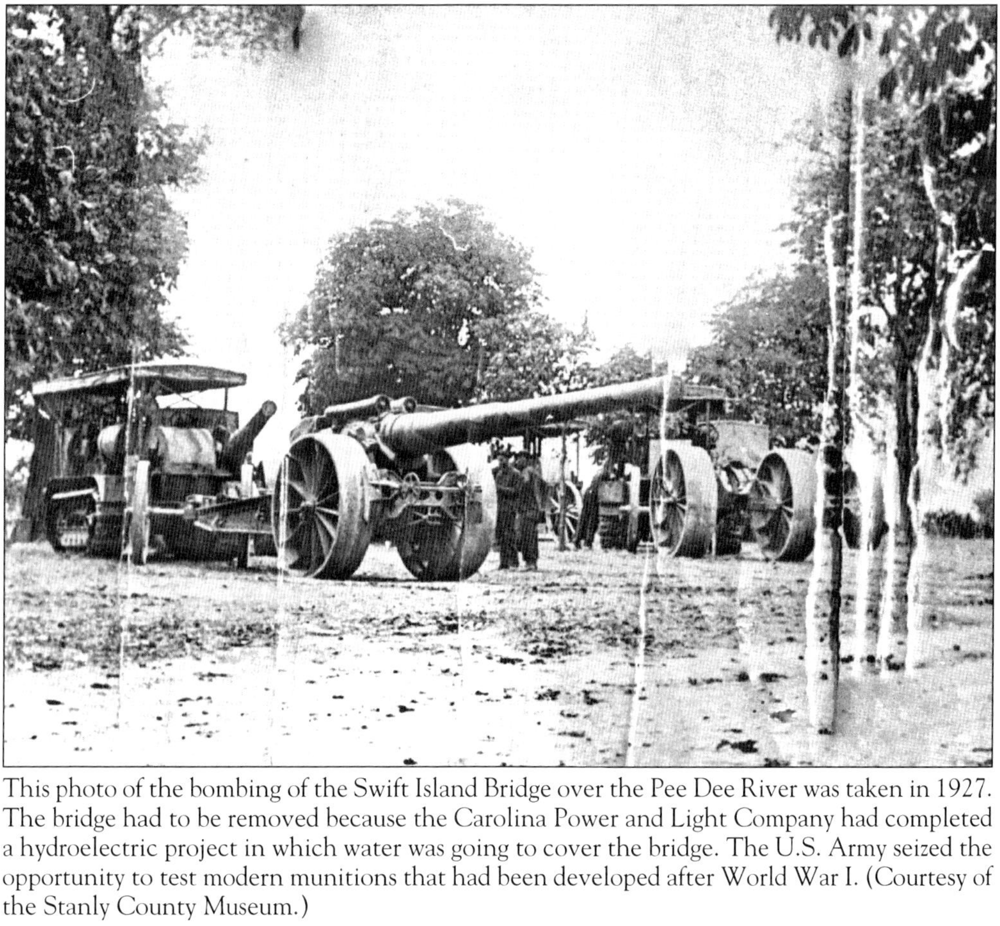

This photo of the bombing of the Swift Island Bridge over the Pee Dee River was taken in 1927. The bridge had to be removed because the Carolina Power and Light Company had completed a hydroelectric project in which water was going to cover the bridge. The U.S. Army seized the opportunity to test modern munitions that had been developed after World War I. (Courtesy of the Stanly County Museum.)

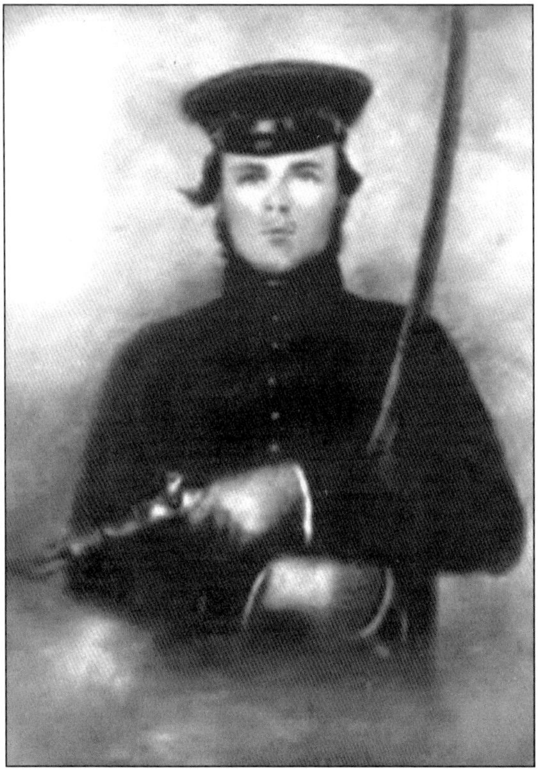

Pvt. Robert Allen Carter was a 24-year-old farmer when he came to Albemarle on May 5, 1861, to hear Dr. Richard Anderson give a speech. Stanly County had voted 763 to 85 in March of 1861 against secession. Carter was the first man to volunteer for service in the war. (Courtesy of Stanly County Museum.)

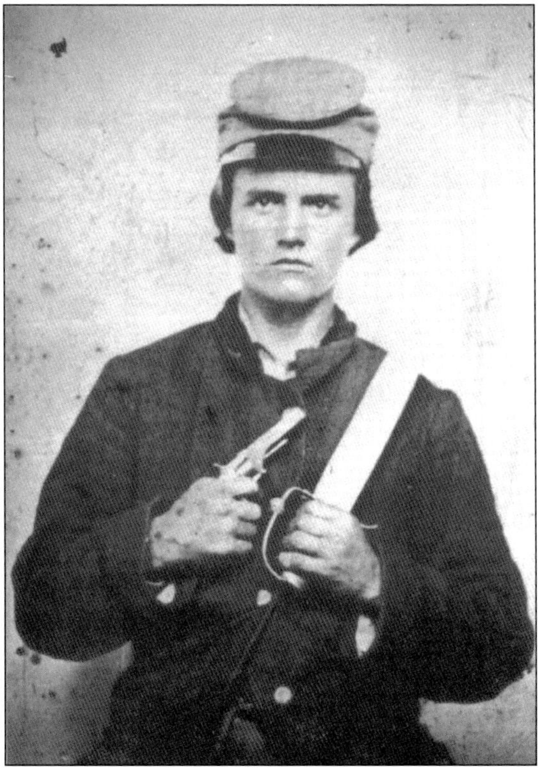

Pvt. Allen Carpenter, a 19-year-old man, enlisted with his brother Churchwell on July 29, 1861, in Albemarle. Allen and Churchwell were among the many North Carolina troops who participated in the famous Trimble-Pettigrew-Pickett's Charge at the Battle of Gettysburg on July 3, 1863. (Courtesy of the Stanly County Museum.)

Eli Monroe Huneycutt was a 23-year-old farmer when he enlisted on March 25, 1862, with Company H, 42nd Regiment North Carolina Troops. On July 30, 1864, Huneycutt fought in one of the most unusual battles of the Civil War: the Battle of the Crater. (Courtesy of the Stanly County Museum.)

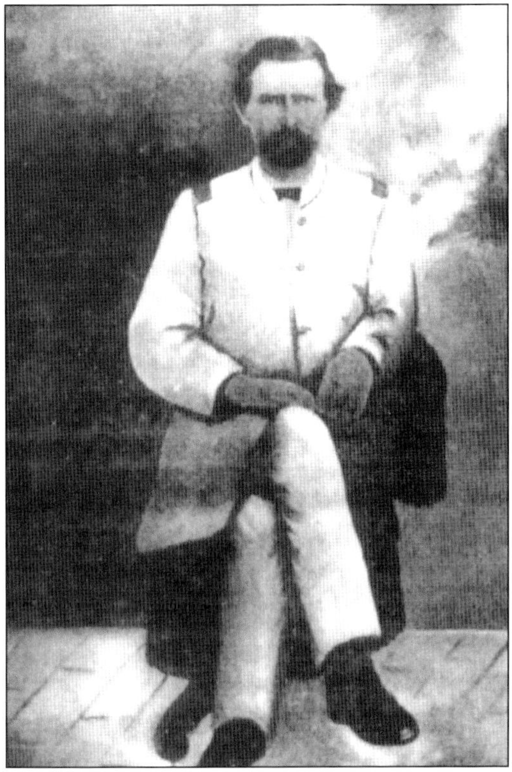

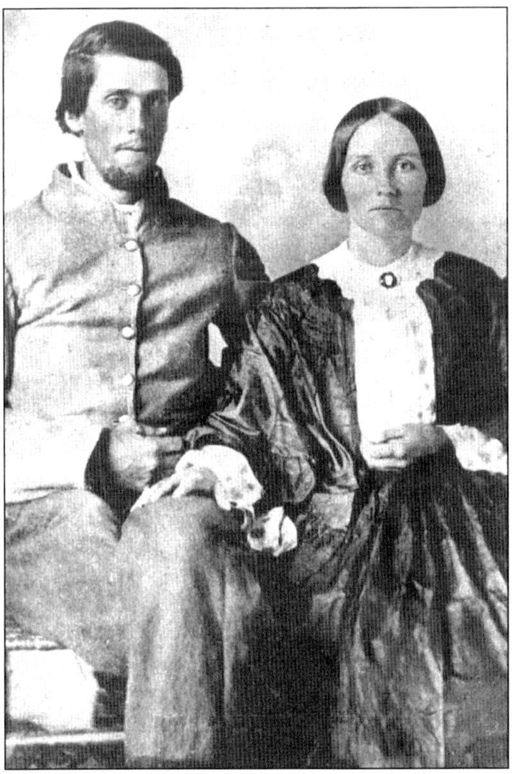

Pvt. Jacob Shoffer, a farmer, was 28 years old when he enlisted with Company C, 42nd Regiment North Carolina Troops (Gibbs Prison Guard) on May 15, 1862. He was discharged from service on October 2, 1862, after being diagnosed with "phthisis pulmonalis," which is more commonly known as tuberculosis. In March of 1864, he enlisted again. (Courtesy of the Stanly County Museum.)

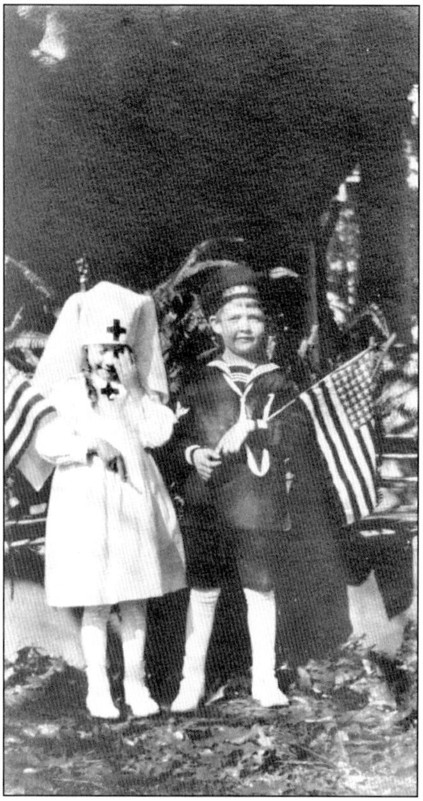

William Ridenhart and Elmina Hearne participate in the Red Cross Parade on Armistice Day on November 11, 1918, during World War I. (Courtesy of the Stanly County Museum.)

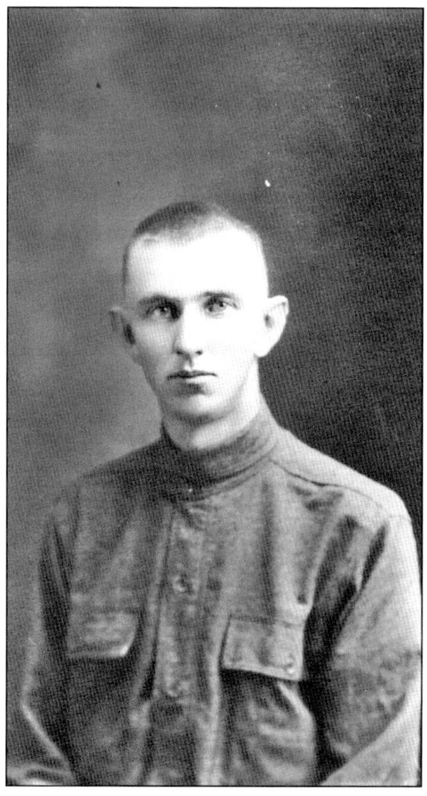

John Moose poses in his World War I uniform. (Courtesy of the Stanly County Museum.)

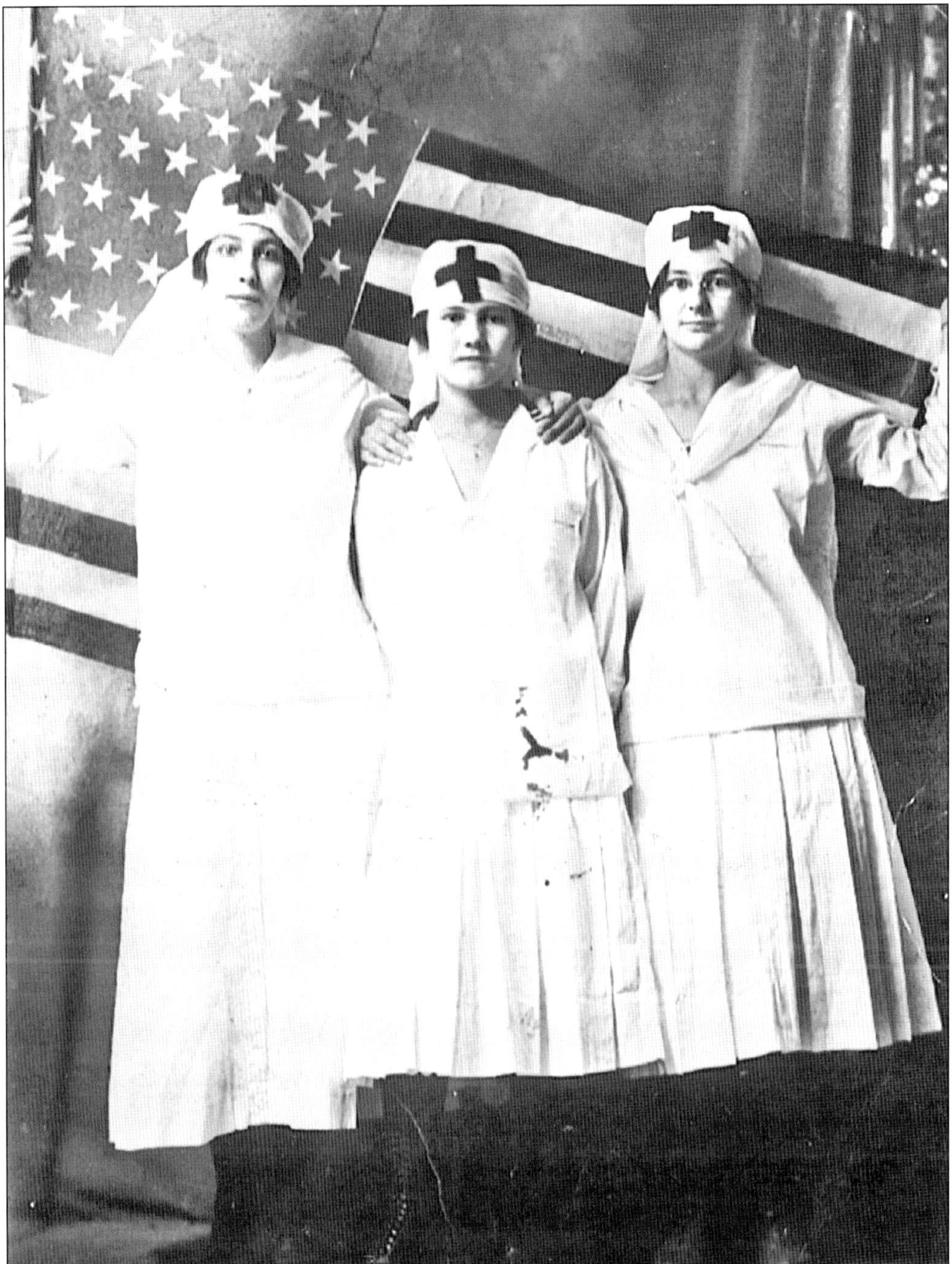

Stanly County nurses aided the troops who served in World War I. Nurses Esther Kimball, Bertha Glover, and Daisy Arie pose in front of a United States flag for this 1917 photograph. (Courtesy of the Stanly County Museum.)

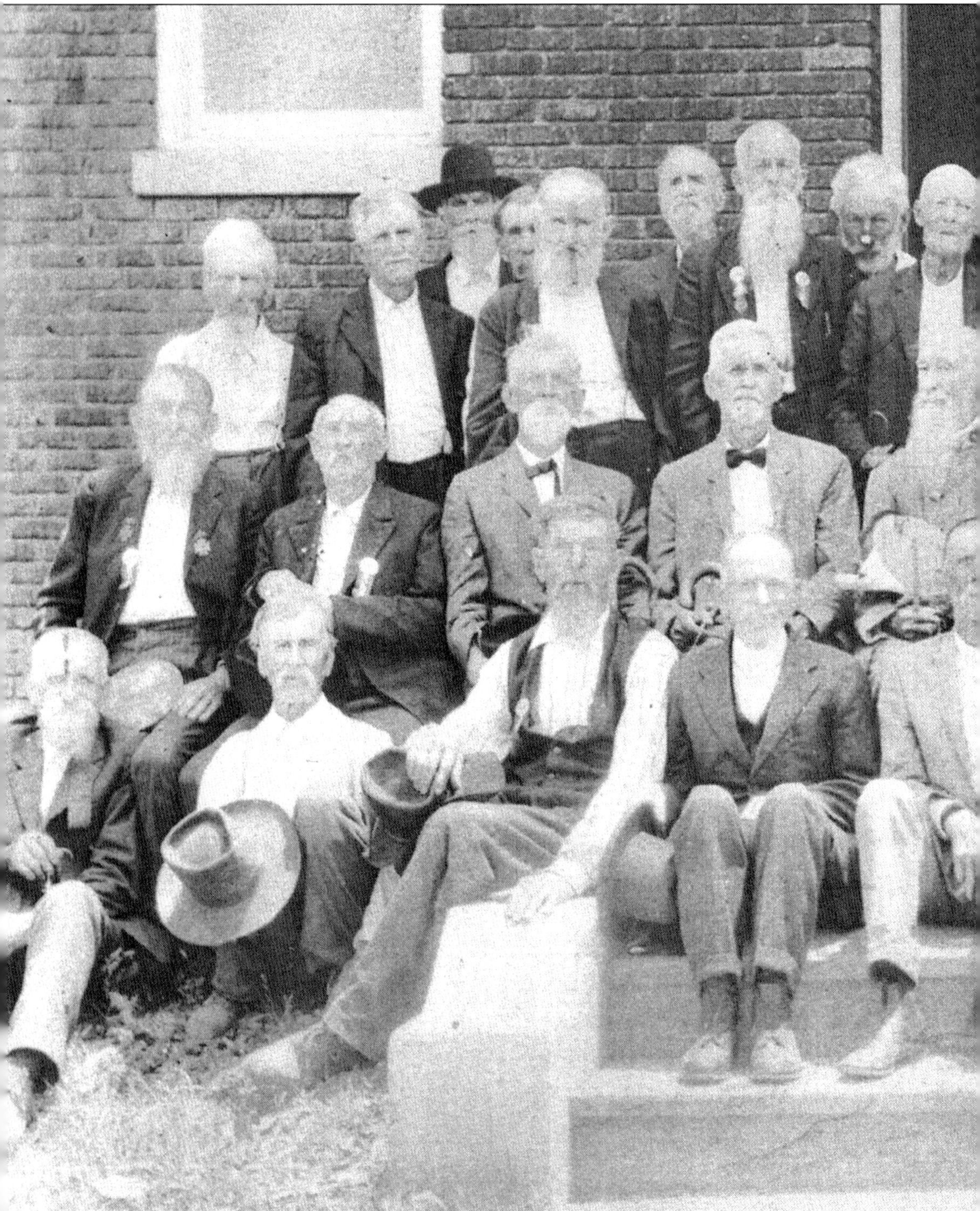

Stanly County voted 763 to 85 in March of 1861 against secession. When North Carolina seceded, however, Stanly County still sent six companies to fight. The surviving Stanly County Civil War veterans pose in this image, *c.* 1924. Veteran Nelson Alexander Clayton (front row,

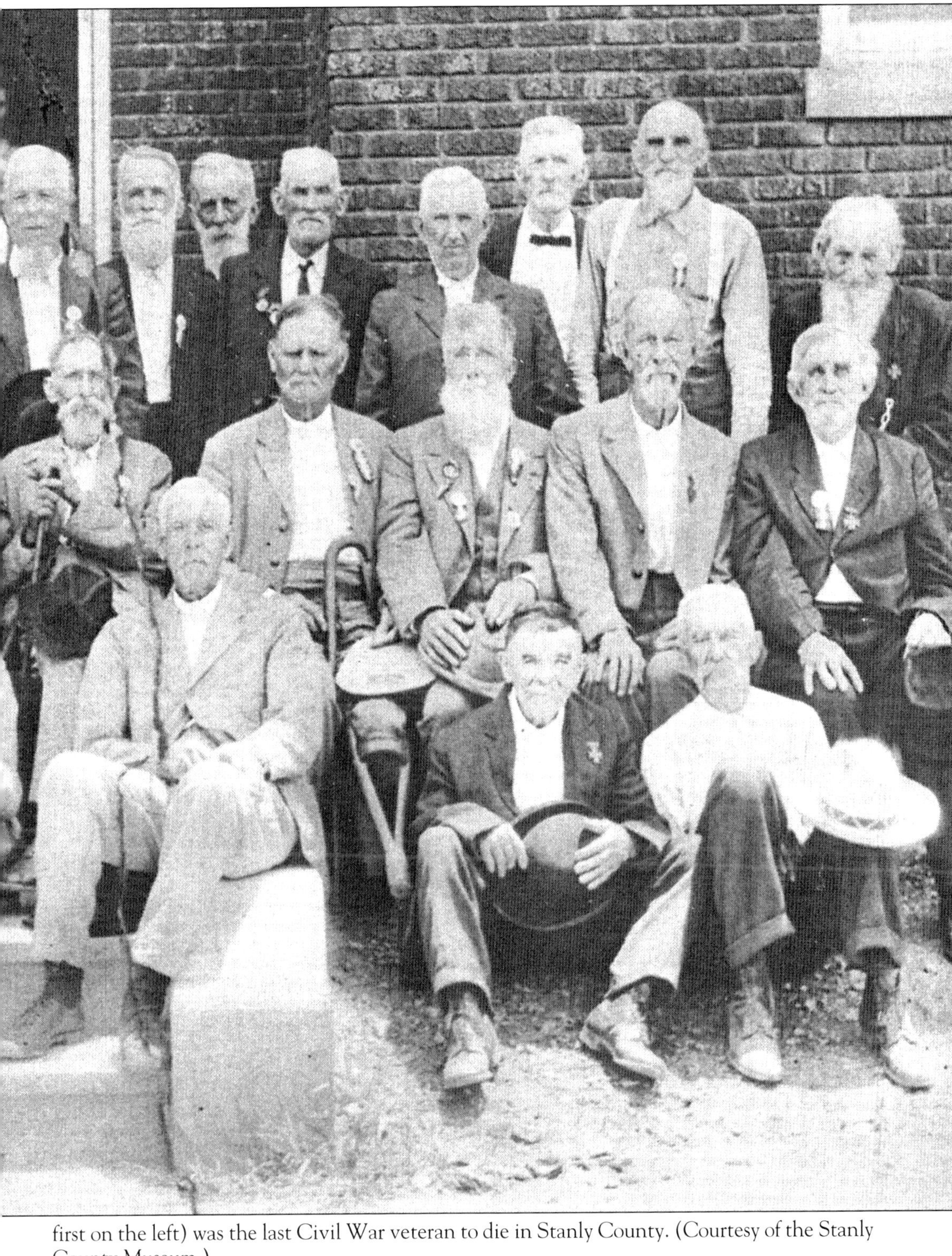

first on the left) was the last Civil War veteran to die in Stanly County. (Courtesy of the Stanly County Museum.)

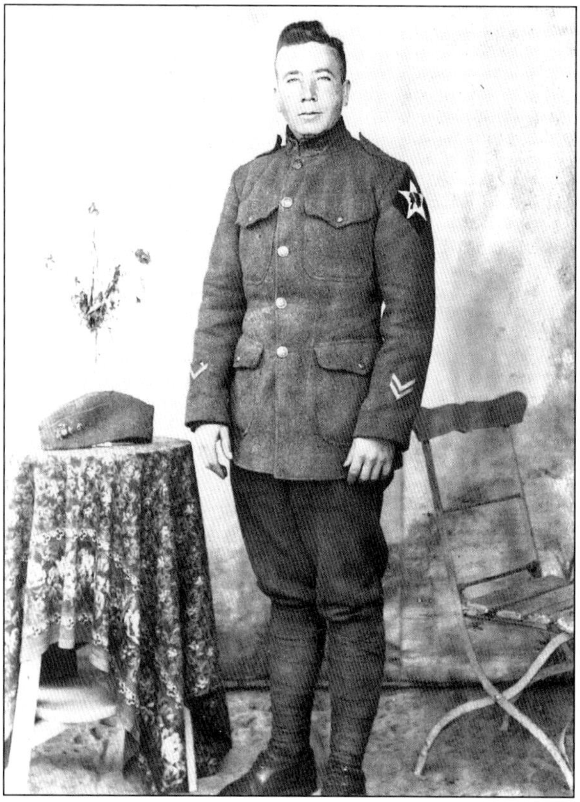

Samuel Raymond Boyce poses for a portrait in his World War I uniform. His hat rests on a table beside him. World War I ended on November 11, 1918. (Courtesy of the Stanly County Museum.)

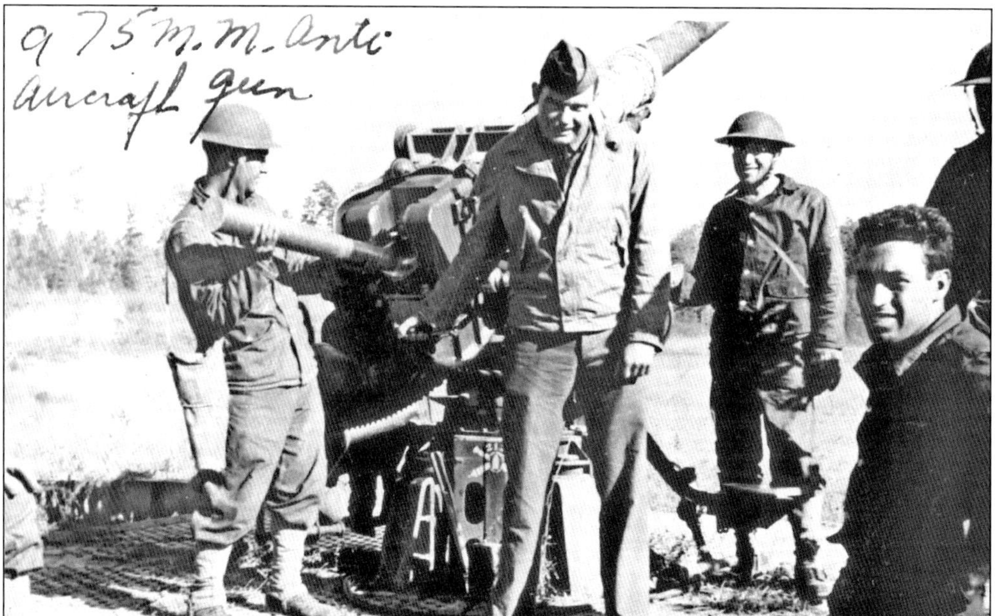

A soldier loads a 75mm anti-aircraft gun during World War II army maneuvers in the fall of 1941. (Courtesy of the Stanly County Museum.)

Marshall Burns Boyce, a marine in World War II, continued his father's legacy of serving in the U.S. Armed Forces. His father, Samuel Raymond Boyce, served in World War I. (Courtesy of the Stanly County Museum.)

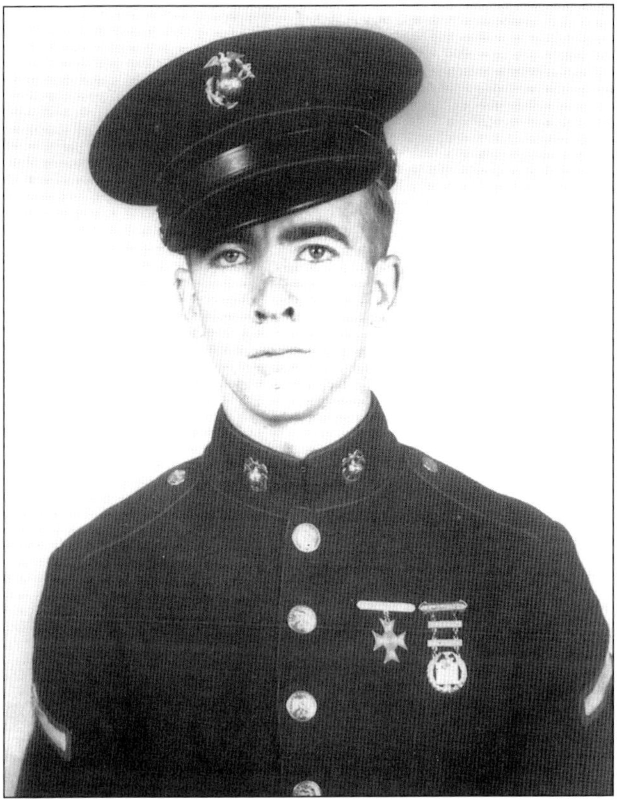

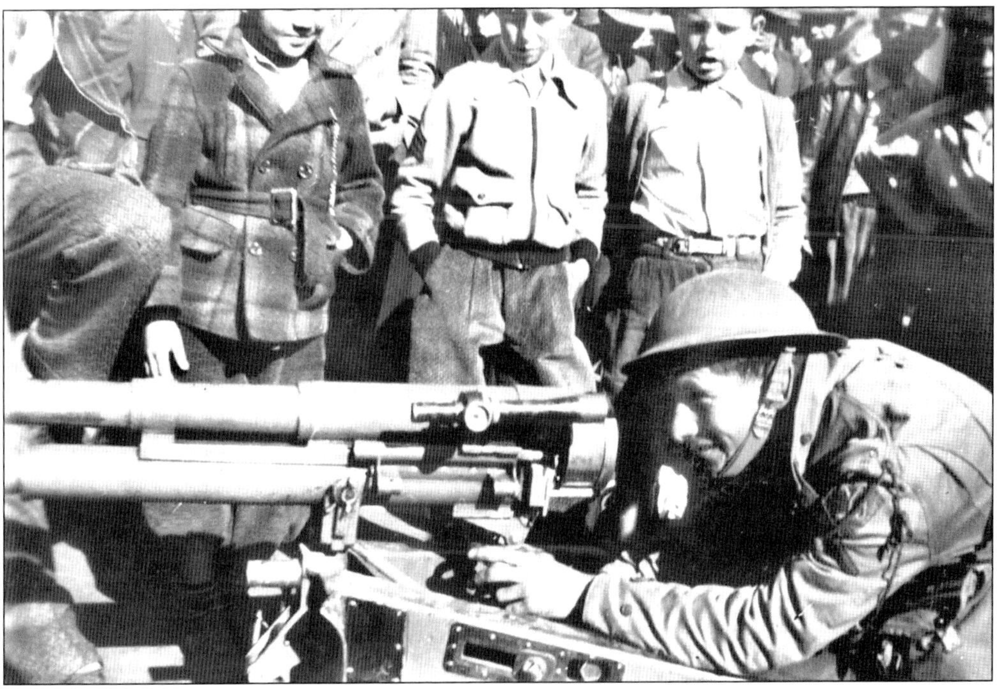

Local children Johnny Youngblood and Doug Phillips observe a soldier operating a gun during World War II maneuvers in 1941. (Courtesy of the Stanly County Museum.)

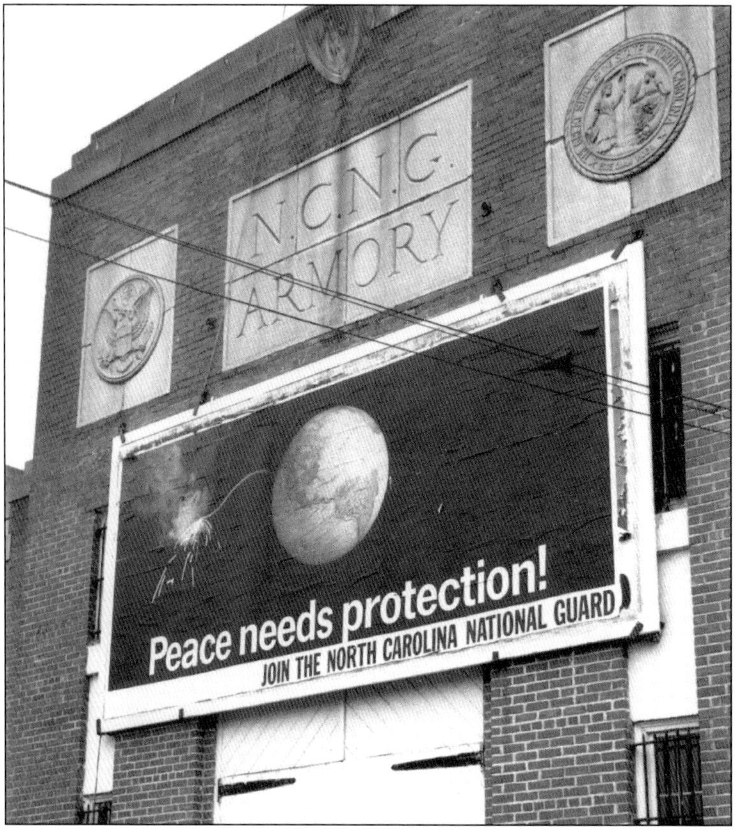

The North Carolina National Guard Armory operated on North Third Street in 1937. They had meetings and stored tanks and jeeps. The armory also housed a shooting range at one time. The building is now a senior center. (Courtesy of the Stanly County Museum.)

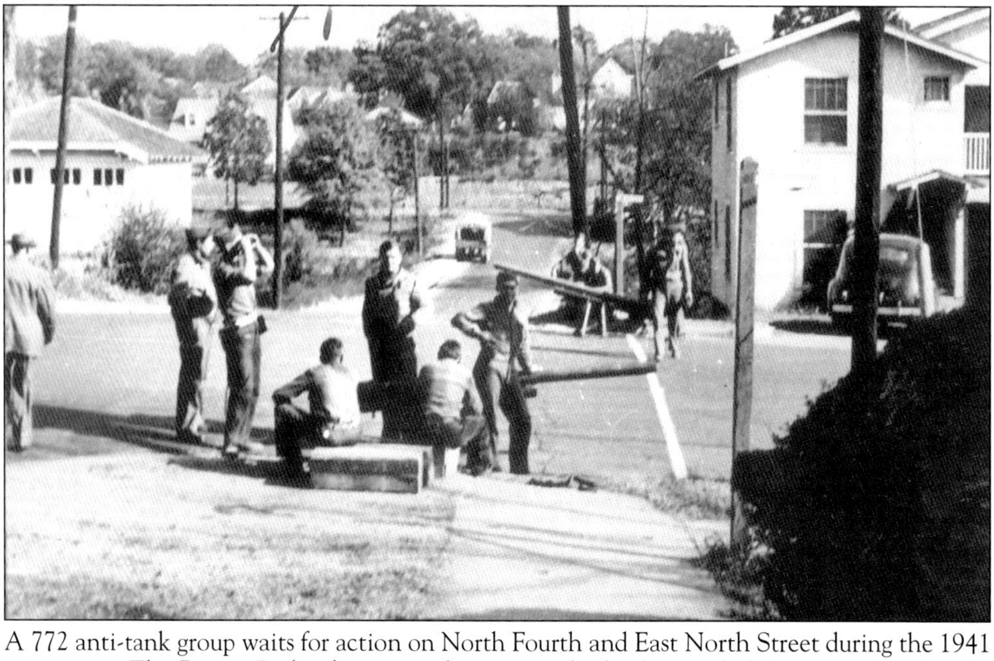

A 772 anti-tank group waits for action on North Fourth and East North Street during the 1941 maneuvers. The Brown-Parker house can be seen in the background. (Courtesy of the Stanly County Museum.)

Soldiers passing through Albemarle enjoy refreshments from local resident Mary Ellen Patterson. Also pictured are, from left to right, Privates Pritchard, Eldred, Ptacek, and Sergeant Cox. An apartment on Fourth and North Street can also be seen in the background. (Courtesy of the Stanly County Museum.)

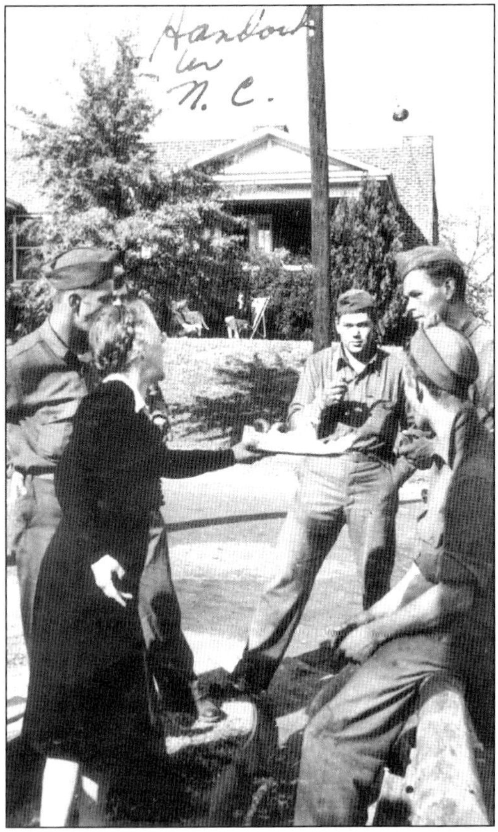

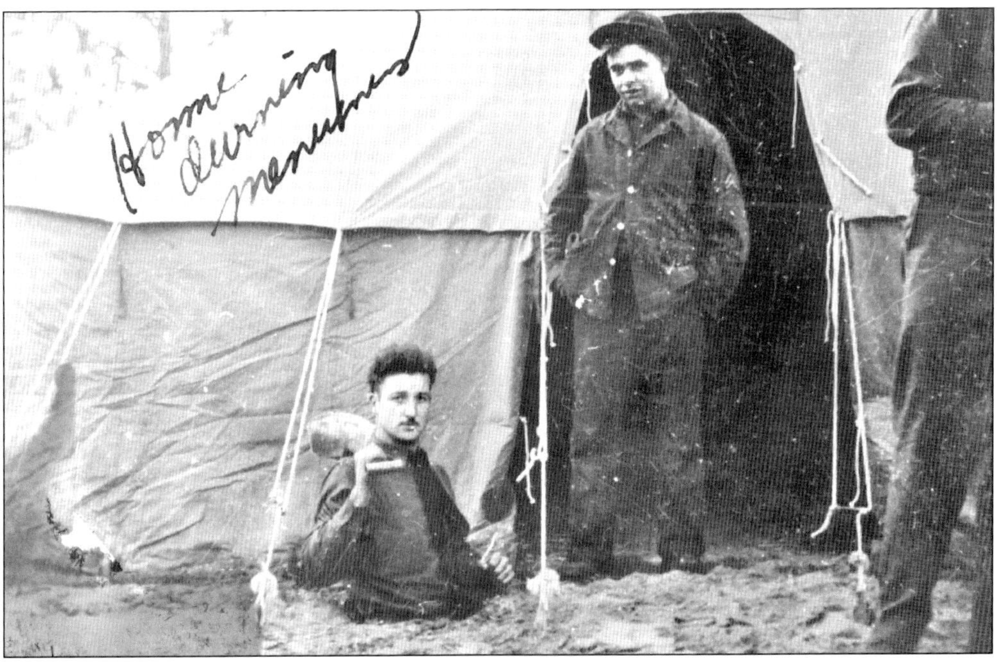

Corporal Michalak observes Sergeant Wilcox digging a hole during the 1941 maneuvers. (Courtesy of the Stanly County Museum.)

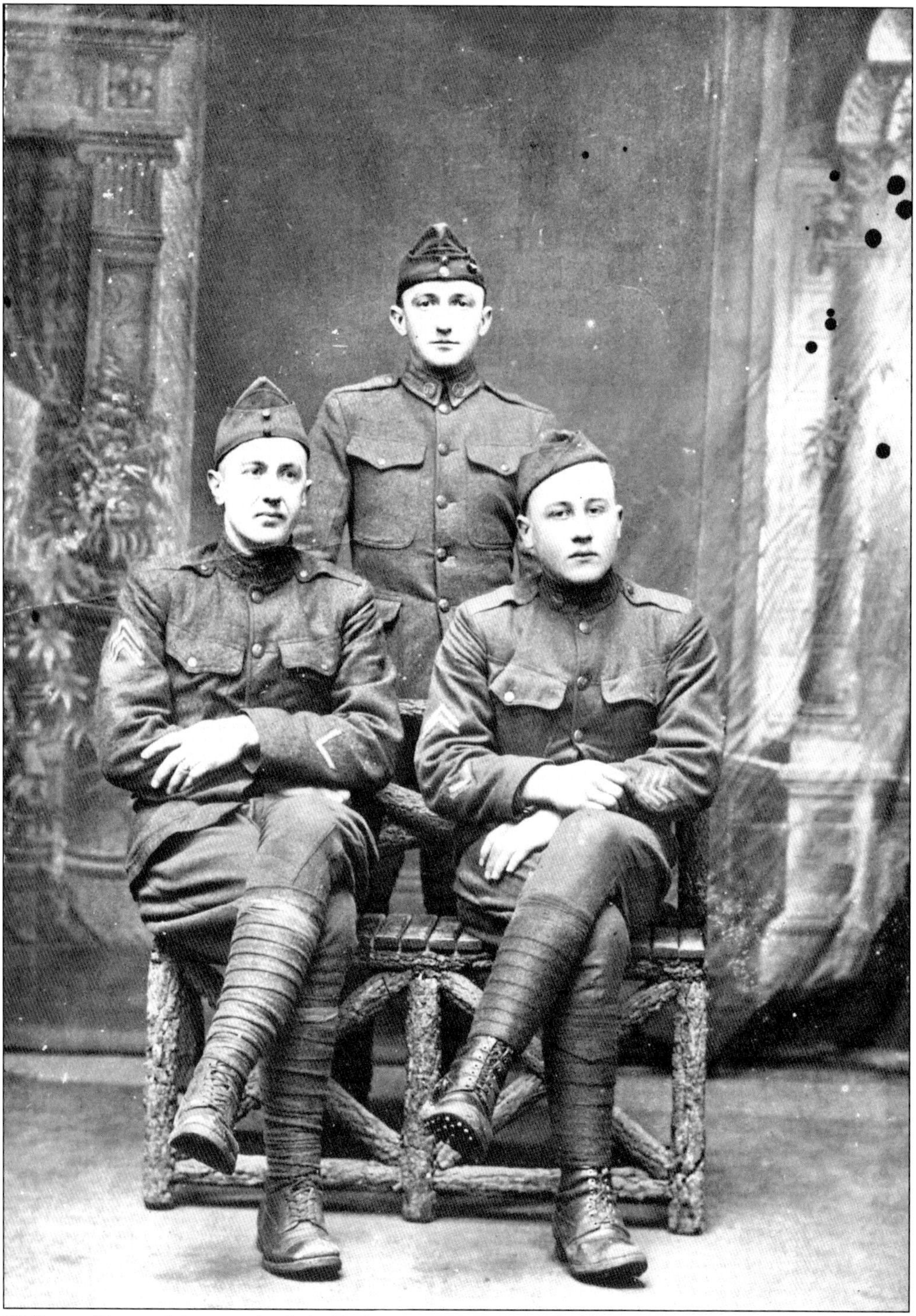

William Henry Morrow (right), Robert Lee Morrow (left), and their cousin ? Whitfield (standing) served together in France during World War II. (Courtesy of Jane Rogers.)

William W. "Bill" Love sits on a bench with his grandmother, Nancy Morton Love, in front of his grandfather's grocery store in 1946. His grandfather, William Wesley Love, operated the grocery store on North Fourth Street. Bill Love served in the Army Air Corps. (Courtesy of William W. "Bill" Love.)

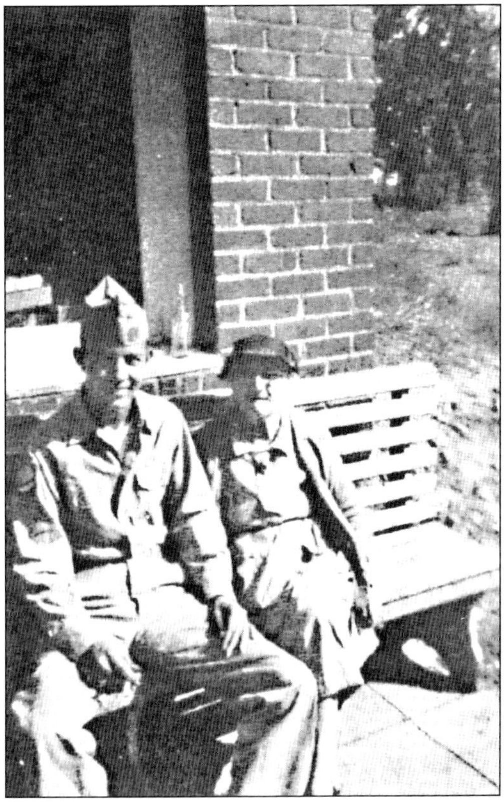

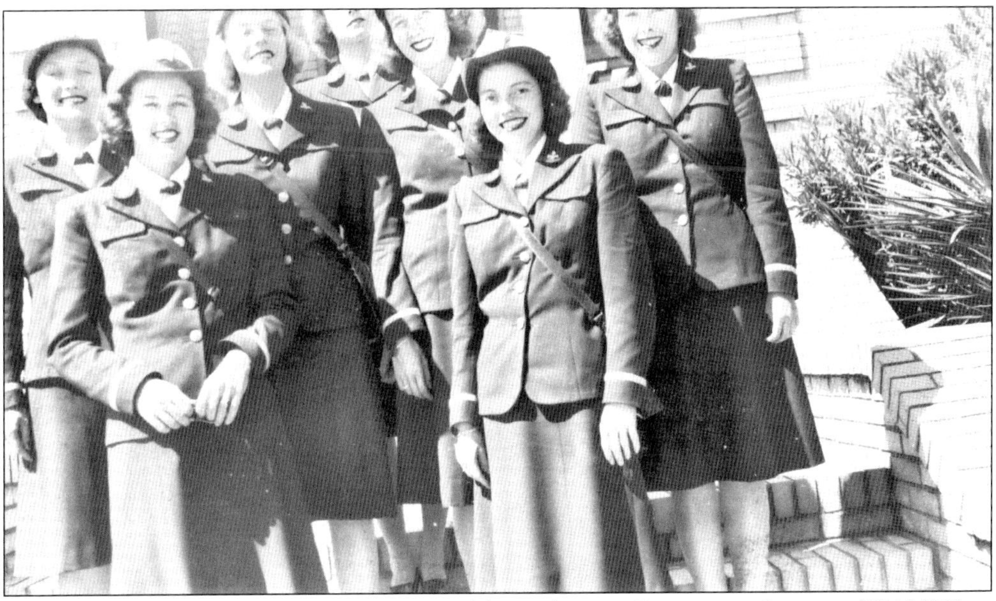

In 1943, members of the Women Accepted for Volunteer Emergency Services (WAVES), a World War II women's naval group, pose with Patricia Ross (right front). (Courtesy of the Stanly County Museum.)

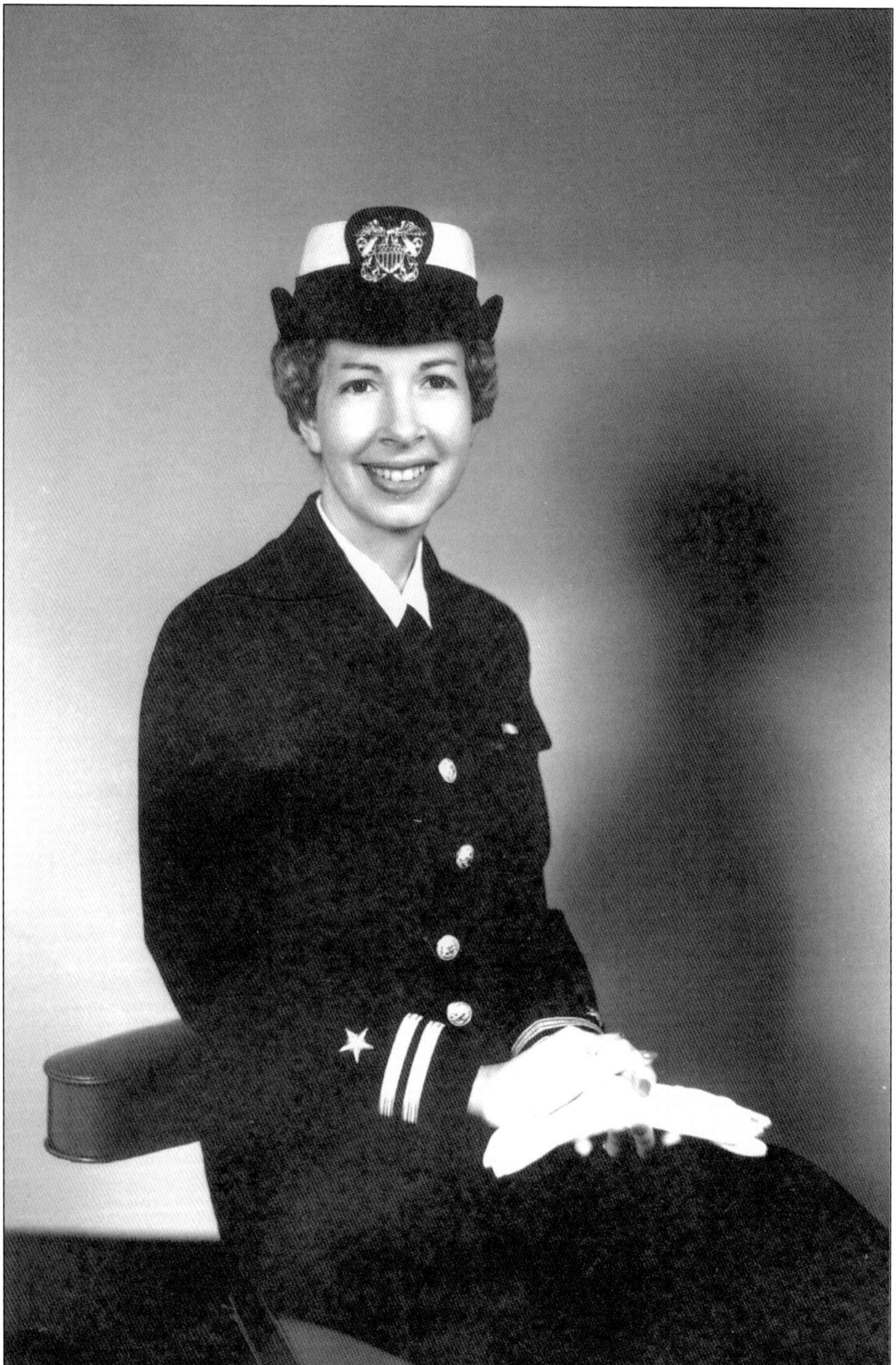

Nancy H. Baker served in the U.S. Navy in May of 1977. After retiring as a captain from the navy, she served as a personnel manager for the City of Albemarle. (Courtesy of the Stanly County Museum.)

Seven

Fashion

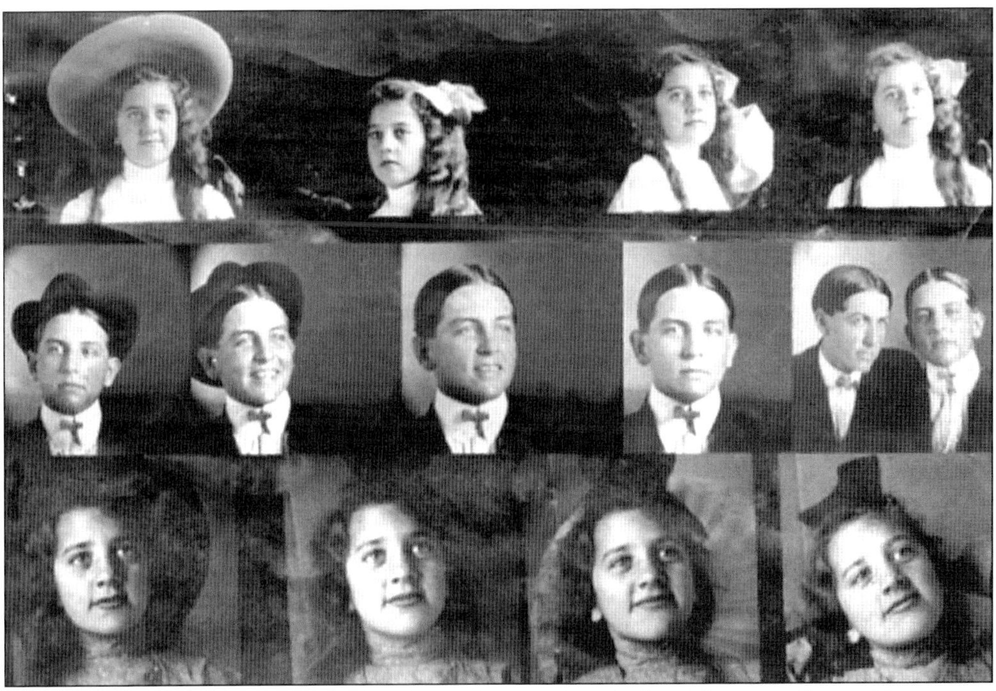

Shown here are portraits of John Spinks and an unidentified girl from a collage. (Courtesy of the Stanly County Museum.)

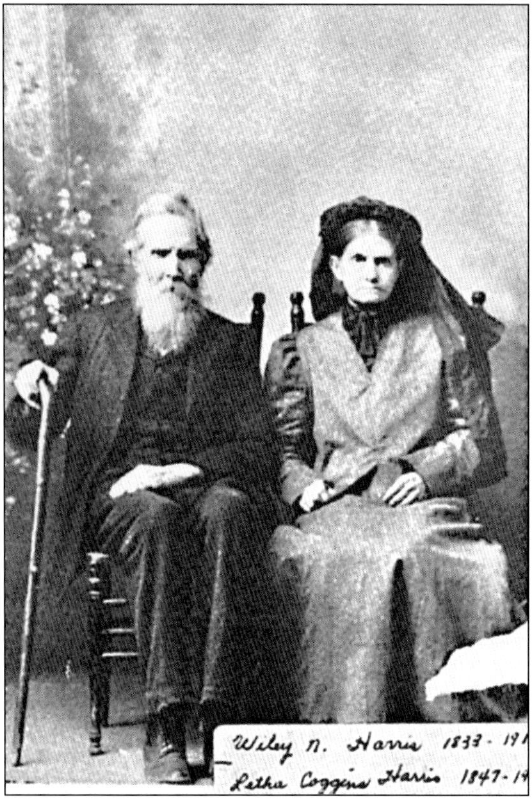

Wiley N. Harris (1833–1912) and Letha Coggins Harris (1847–1913) sit together for their portrait. (Courtesy of the Stanly County Museum.)

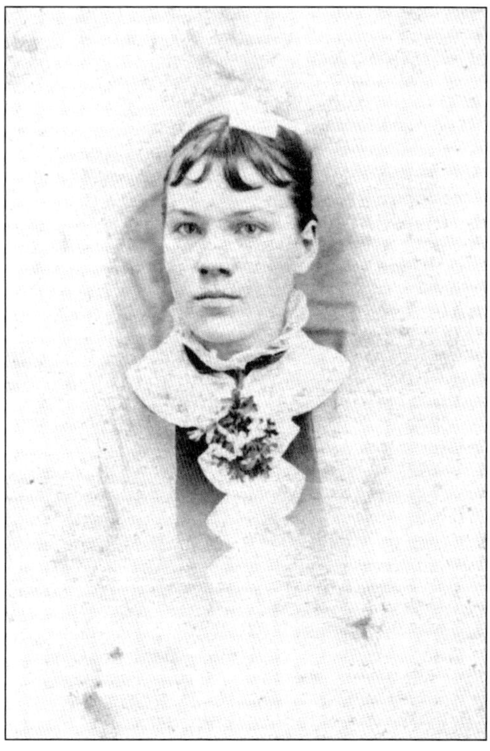

"Ever Ella be the same/Changing nothing but your name/if you meet a nice young man/Try to catch him if you can." This poem was found on the back of the photograph pictured here. (Courtesy of the Patterson family.)

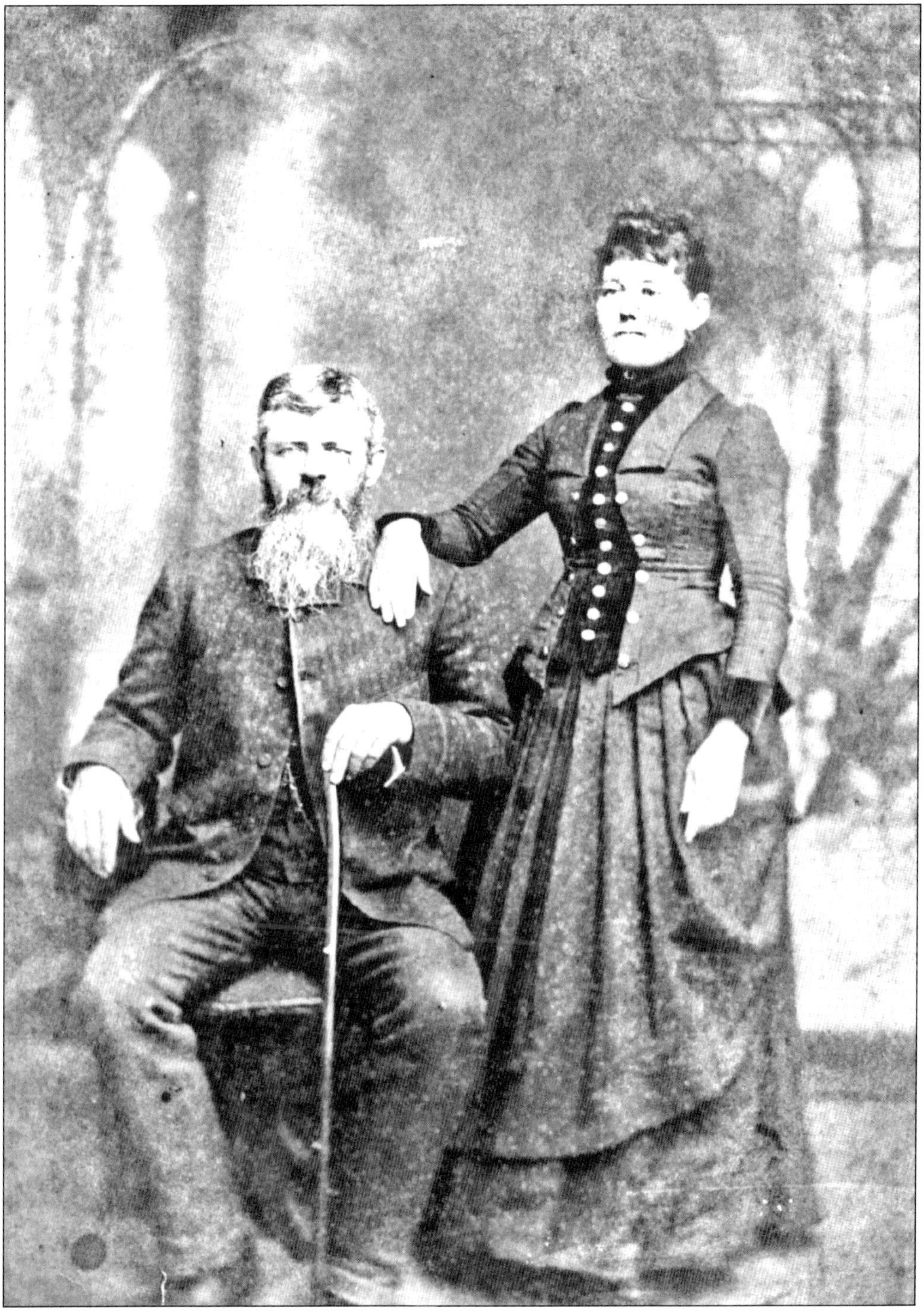

W.S. Cooper photographs Mr. and Mrs. John Atkins in the late 1800s. Mr. Atkins is seated with his cane while Mrs. Atkins stands at his side, resting a hand on his shoulder. The J.S. Atkins House was on the corner of South Second Street and West North Street. (Courtesy of the Stanly County Museum.)

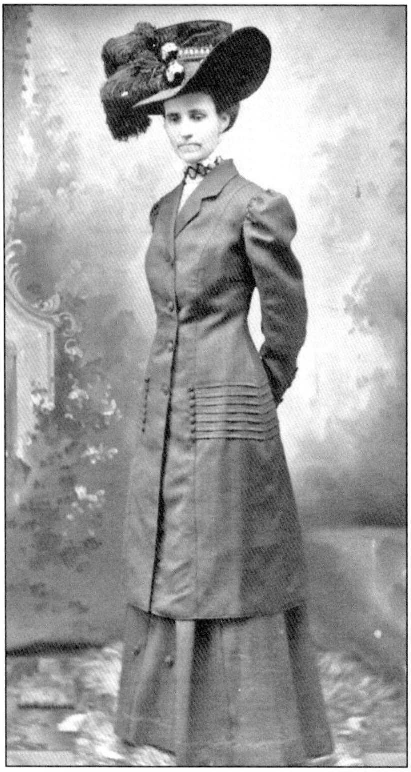

A lady poses for the J.J. Cook photography studio c. late 1800s. Note the elegant hat trimmed in feathers. (Courtesy of the Stanly County Museum.)

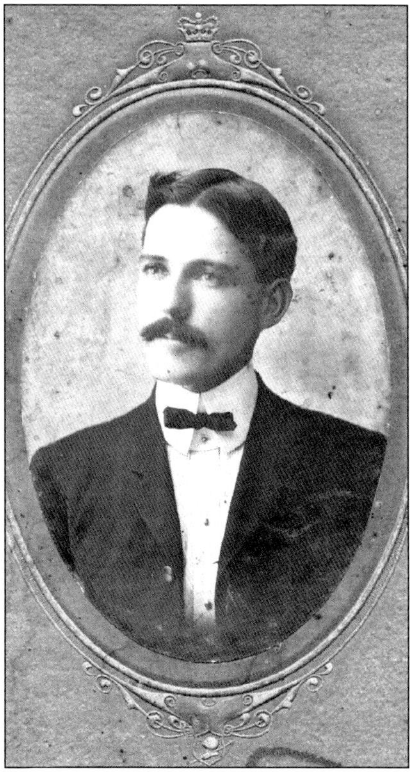

Charles Bolick is fashionably dressed in a suit and bowtie with studs running down the front of his shirt in the early 1900s. (Courtesy of the Stanly County Museum.)

Mrs. John F. Kirk poses with an unidentified woman. Ida Ross Kirk married John F. Kirk, and she died on January 28, 1925. (Courtesy of the Patterson family.)

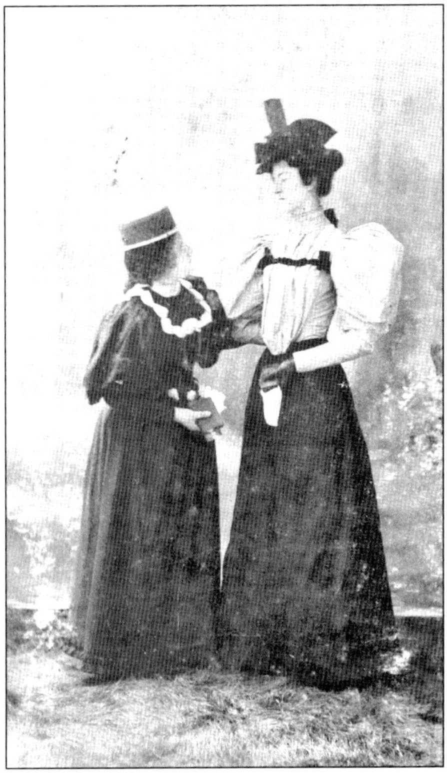

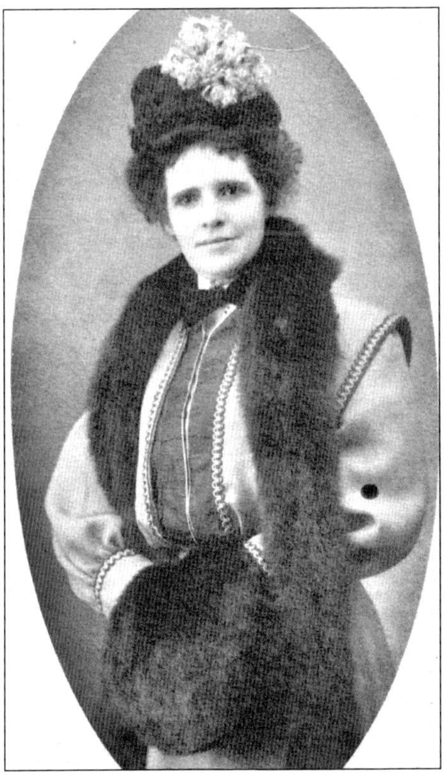

Mrs. Eugene Ewing poses in a fur muff, scarf, and hat in the early 1900s. (Courtesy of the Stanly County Museum.)

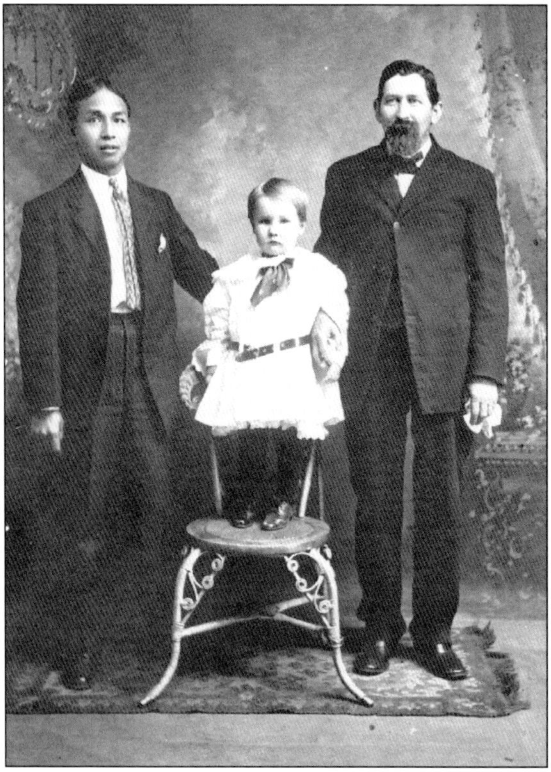

Lum ? (left) operated the laundry for owner Noah J. Pennington (right) and his son Worth (center). This photo dates from the early 1900s. (Courtesy of the Stanly County Museum.)

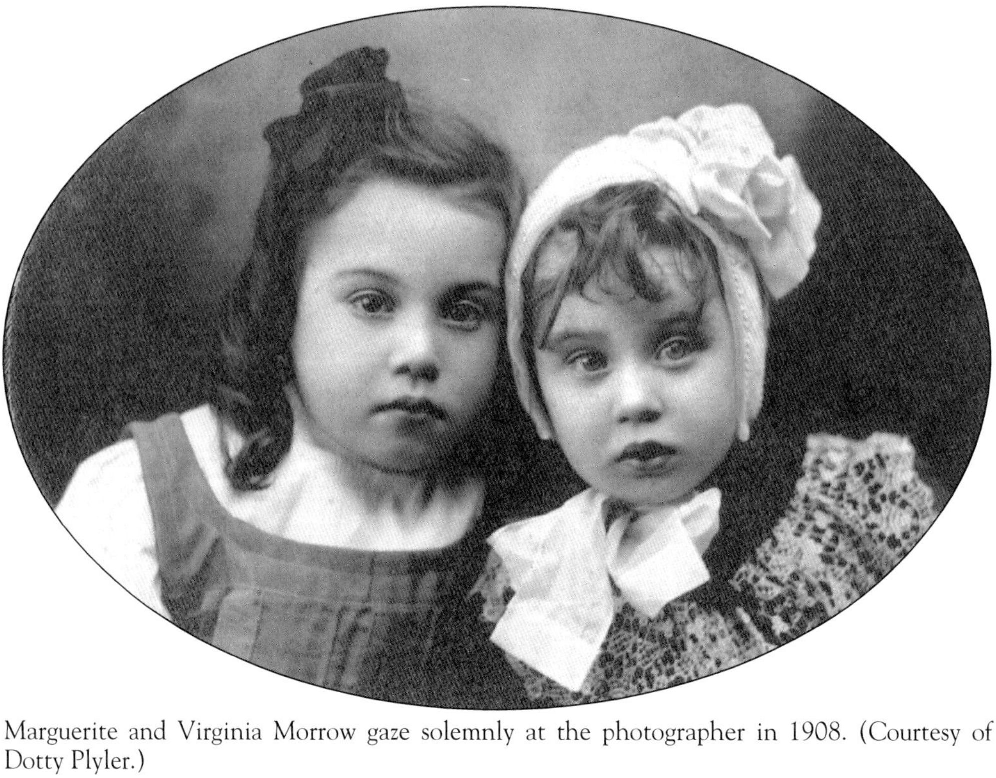

Marguerite and Virginia Morrow gaze solemnly at the photographer in 1908. (Courtesy of Dotty Plyler.)

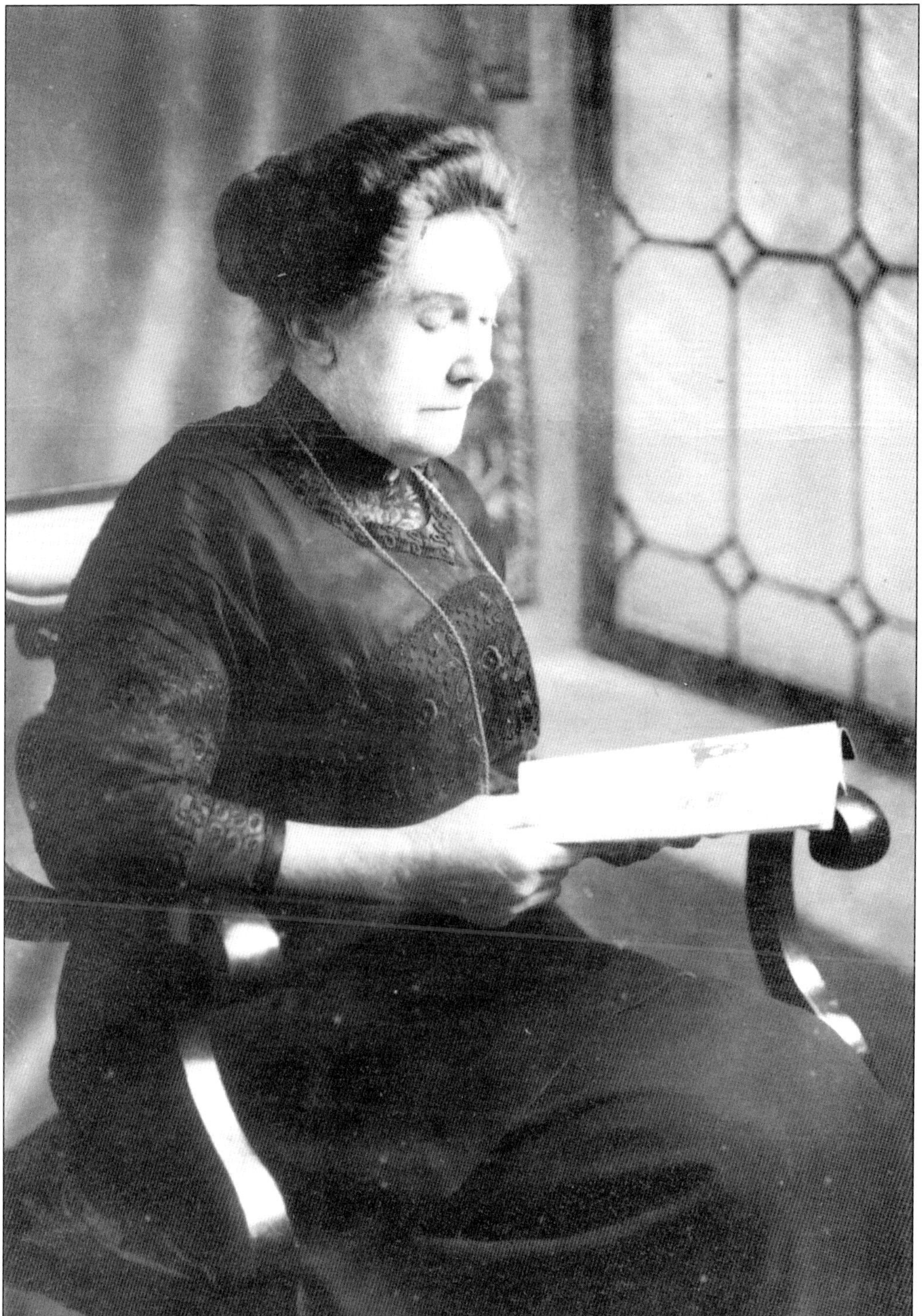

Frances Ufford was sent to North Carolina as a home missionary in 1875. She founded Albemarle Normal and Industrial Institute, a school for girls in Albemarle. The school closed in 1929. (Courtesy of the Stanly County Museum.)

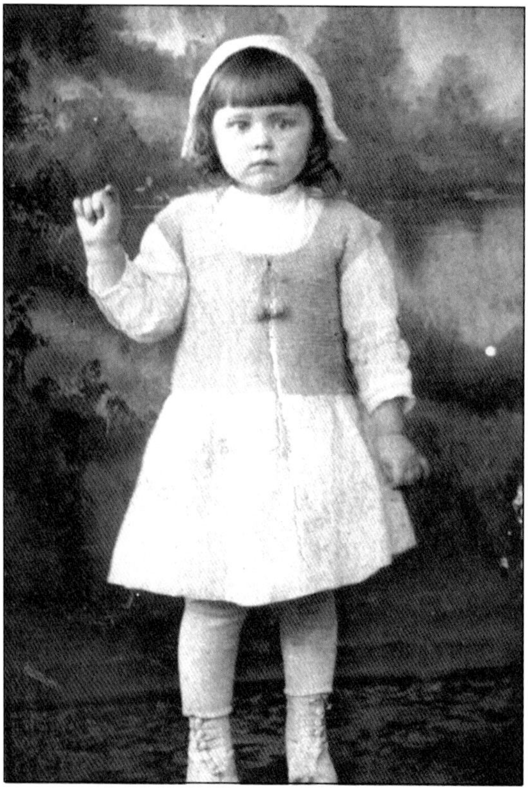

Mary Alice Starr was the daughter of Alice Mabry Starr. (Courtesy of the Stanly County Museum.)

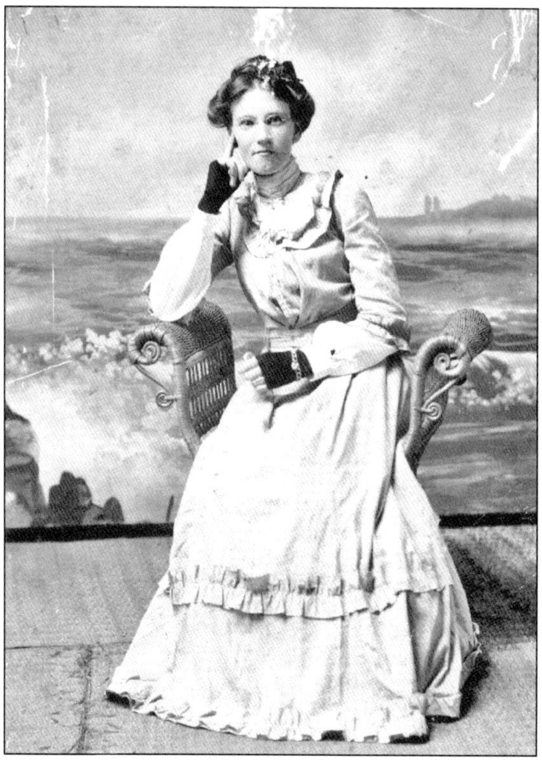

Laura Mullinix, a student at Frances Ufford's school, is photographed in a thoughtful pose, c. 1900–1902. Note the black fingerless gloves. Mullinix was a student with Pattie Marks. (Courtesy of the Stanly County Museum.)

Mary Louise Kleuppelberg Townsend, the daughter of S.H. Hearne, poses in a double-breasted jacket and an elaborate hat with an intricately braided brim. (Courtesy of the Stanly County Museum.)

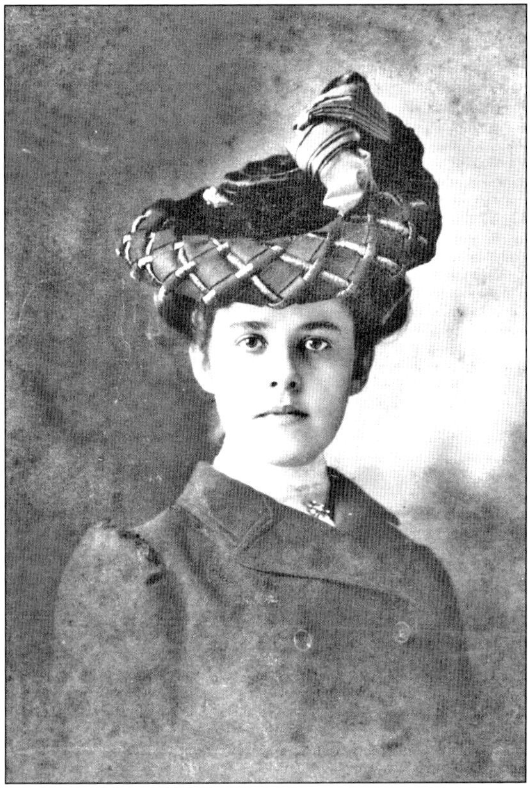

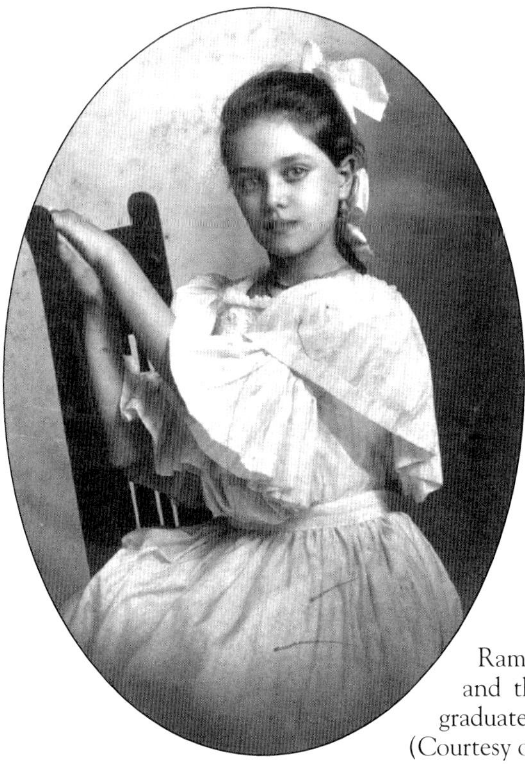

Ramelle Smith was the daughter of R.L. Smith and the sister of Lee Smith, the first female to graduate with a law degree from Duke University. (Courtesy of Dr. and Mrs. Whitman Smith.)

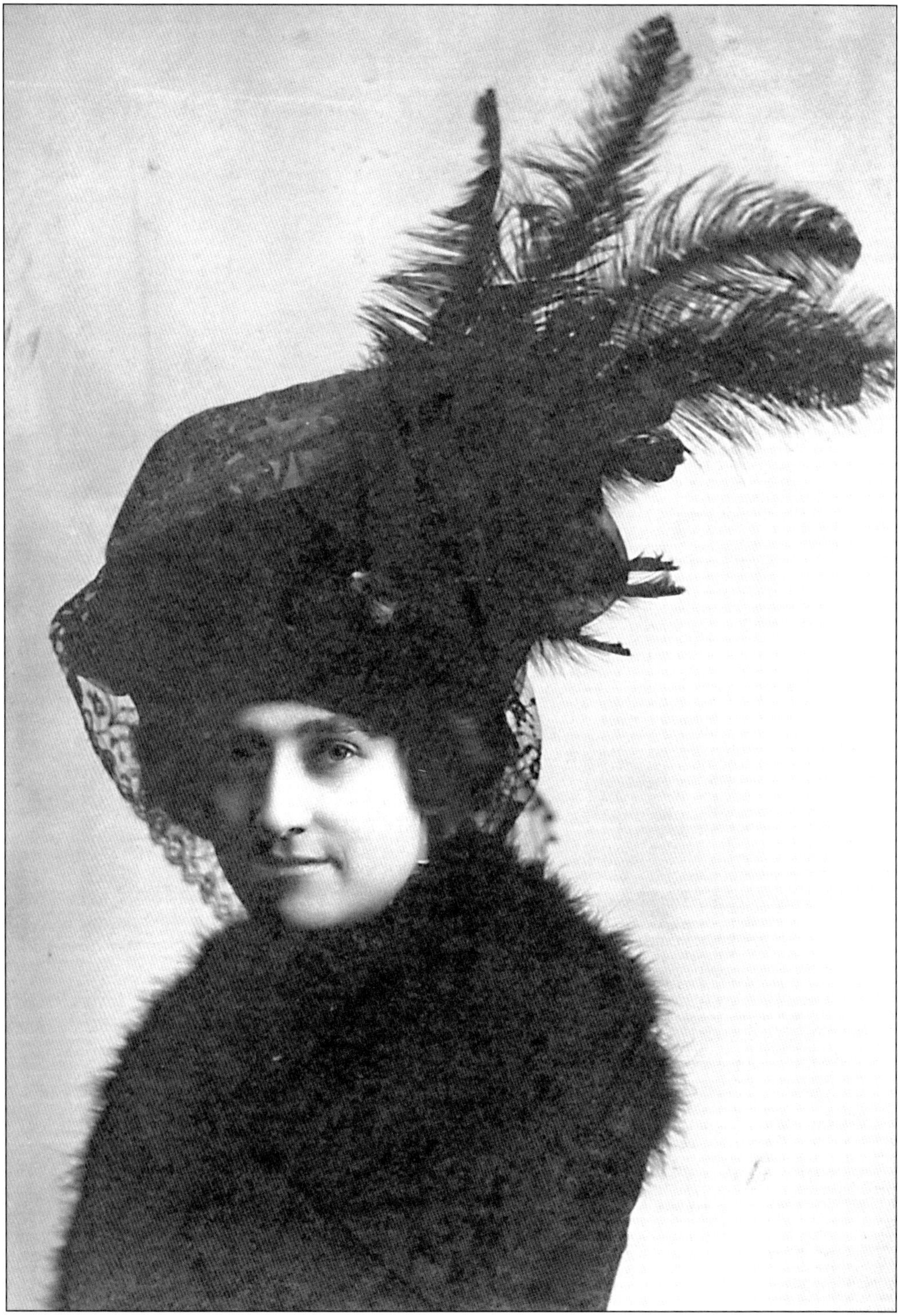

Mrs. J.C. Hall, born Edith Mae Fitzgerald, poses in her stylish hat in the early 1900s. Dr. J.C. Hall owned Hall's Pharmacy. The couple was married on October 16, 1901. (Courtesy of Dent Turner.)

B.L. Parkinson poses for Scotts Studio in 1916. He was married to Dera Dry Parkinson, a distinguished educator. (Courtesy of the Stanly County Museum.)

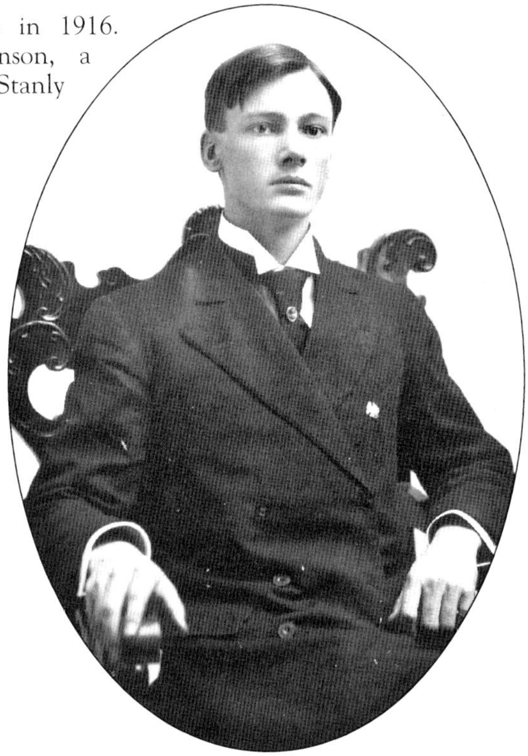

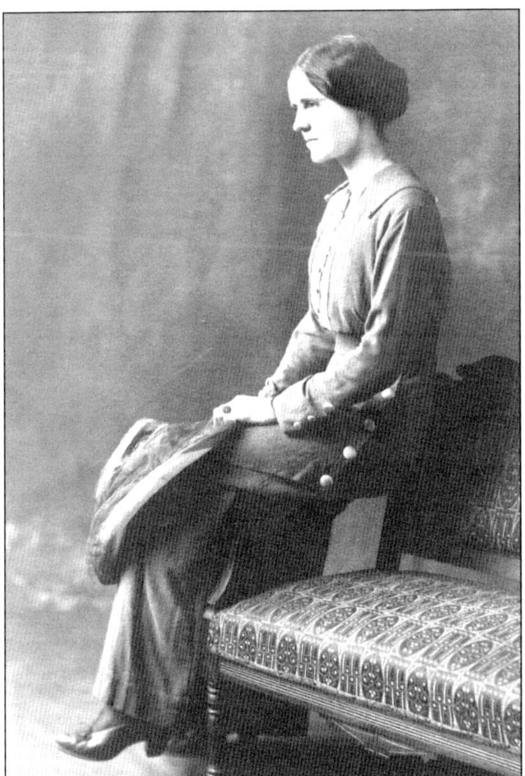

Dera Dry Parkinson rests on the arm of a chair in 1915, holding her large, gauze-trimmed hat while staring pensively into the distance. An educator, she married B.L. Parkinson of Albemarle. (Courtesy of the Stanly County Museum.)

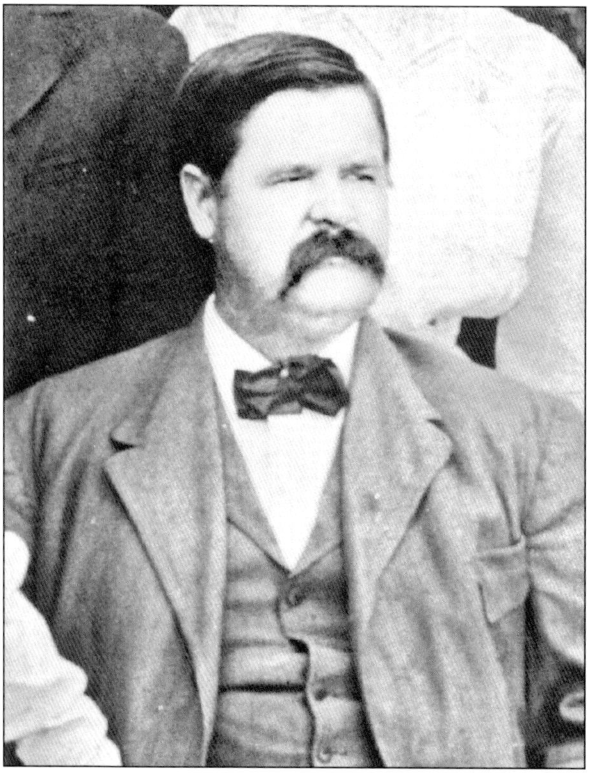

Dr. D.P. Whitley moved to Albemarle in 1918. Although the flu epidemic killed thousands, his records show that he only lost 7 of the 3,000 sufferers he treated. (Courtesy of the Stanly County Museum.)

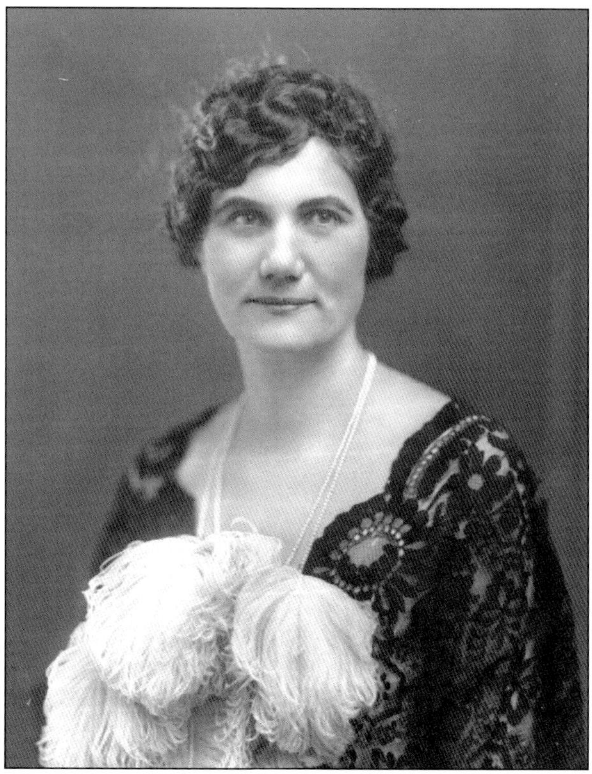

Letha Parker Starnes is elegantly dressed in lace and pearls around 1910–1920. She is also holding an ostrich feather fan. She was born April 2, 1884. (Courtesy of Gene Starnes.)

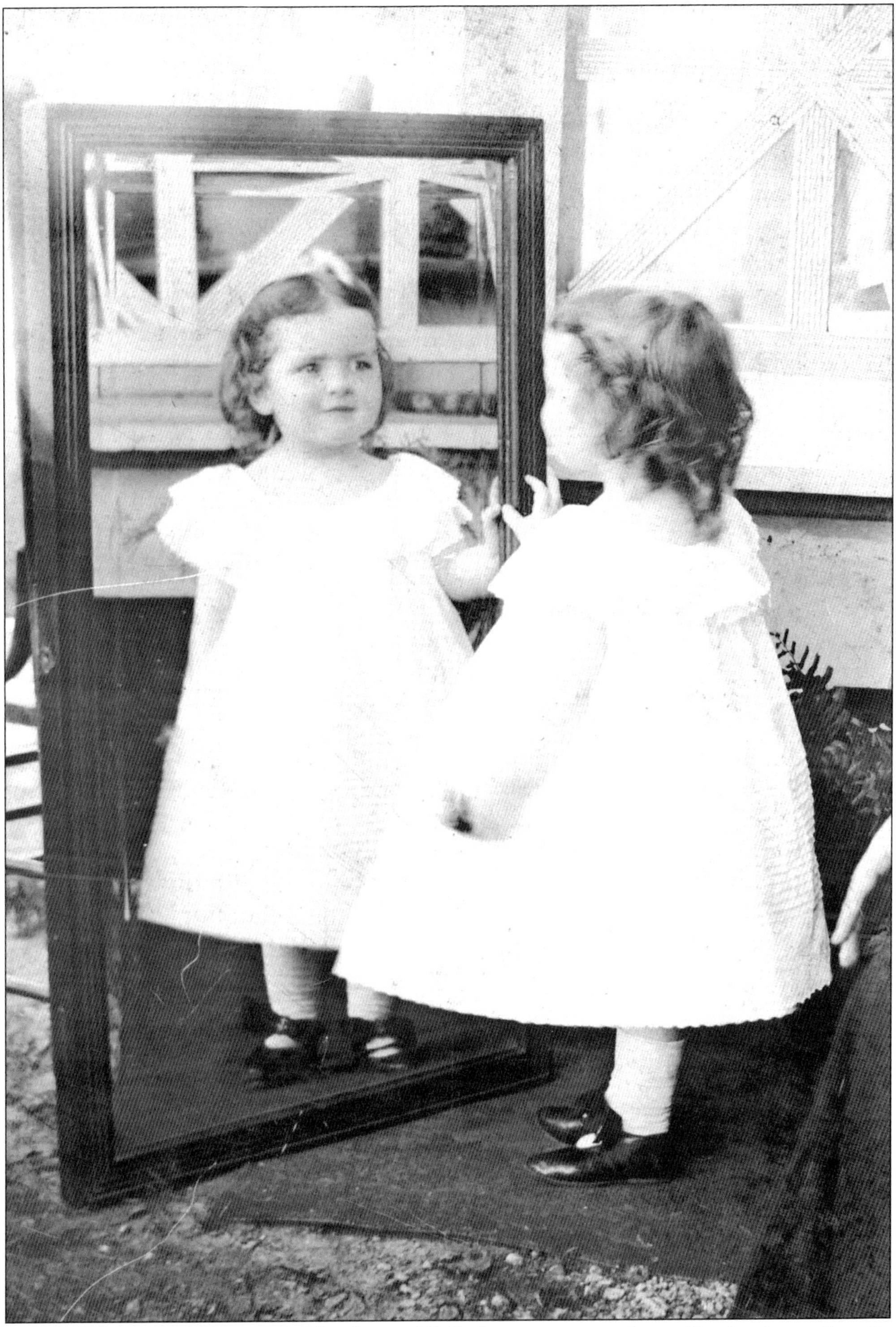

Elizabeth Austin Patterson, the daughter of R.E. Austin, peers at her reflection in a mirror in 1915. She later married Frank Bernard Patterson. (Courtesy of the Patterson family.)

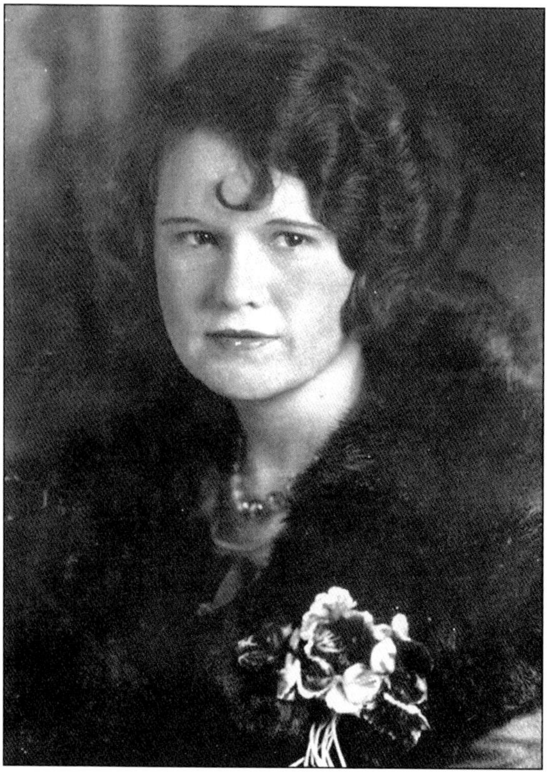

In the 1920s, Ethel ? posed for Finks Studio, which was located above Hall's Pharmacy. She posed with pearls and a large fur collar framing her face. (Courtesy of the Stanly County Museum.)

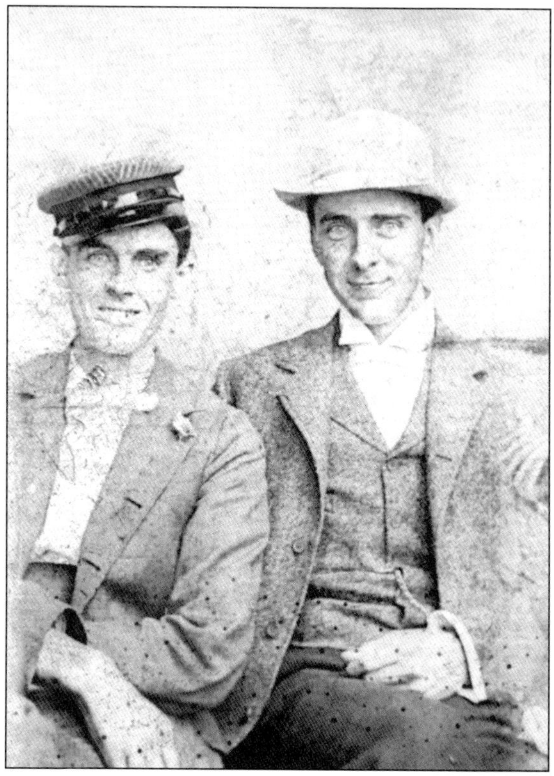

The following poem was found on the back of this photograph in the Pattersons' possession: "Preserve as your would you own hearts dearest treasures, nothing showed ever induce you to part with it ever, John and Rufus." One of the men pictured here is Rufus E. Austin, who was born October 19, 1866, and died January 11, 1917. (Courtesy of the Patterson family.)

Eight

RELIGION

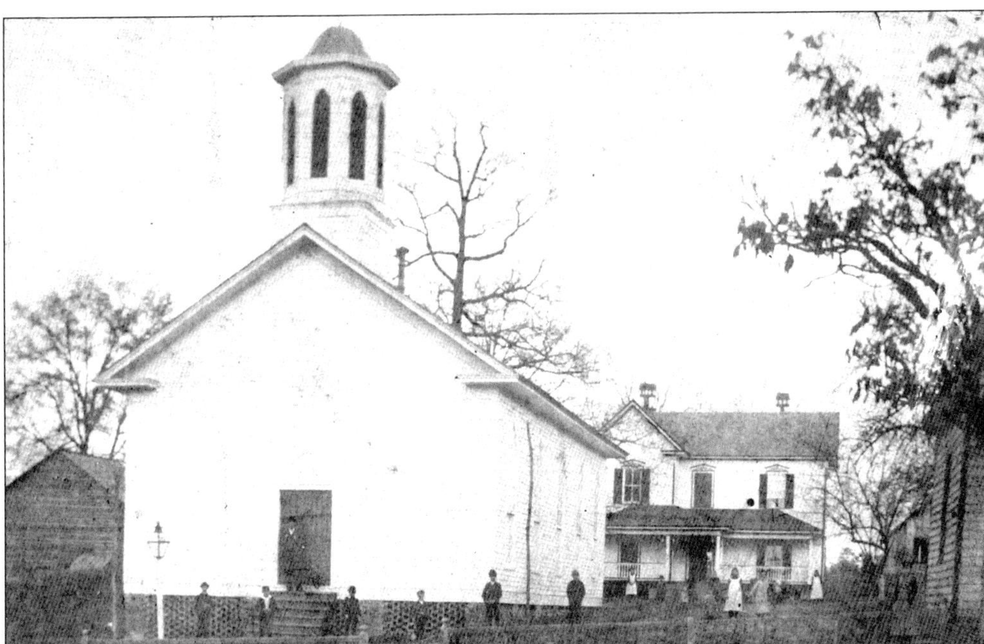

In this photograph, people are shown gathering outside of an Albemarle church and parsonage in 1893. (Courtesy of the Stanly County Museum.)

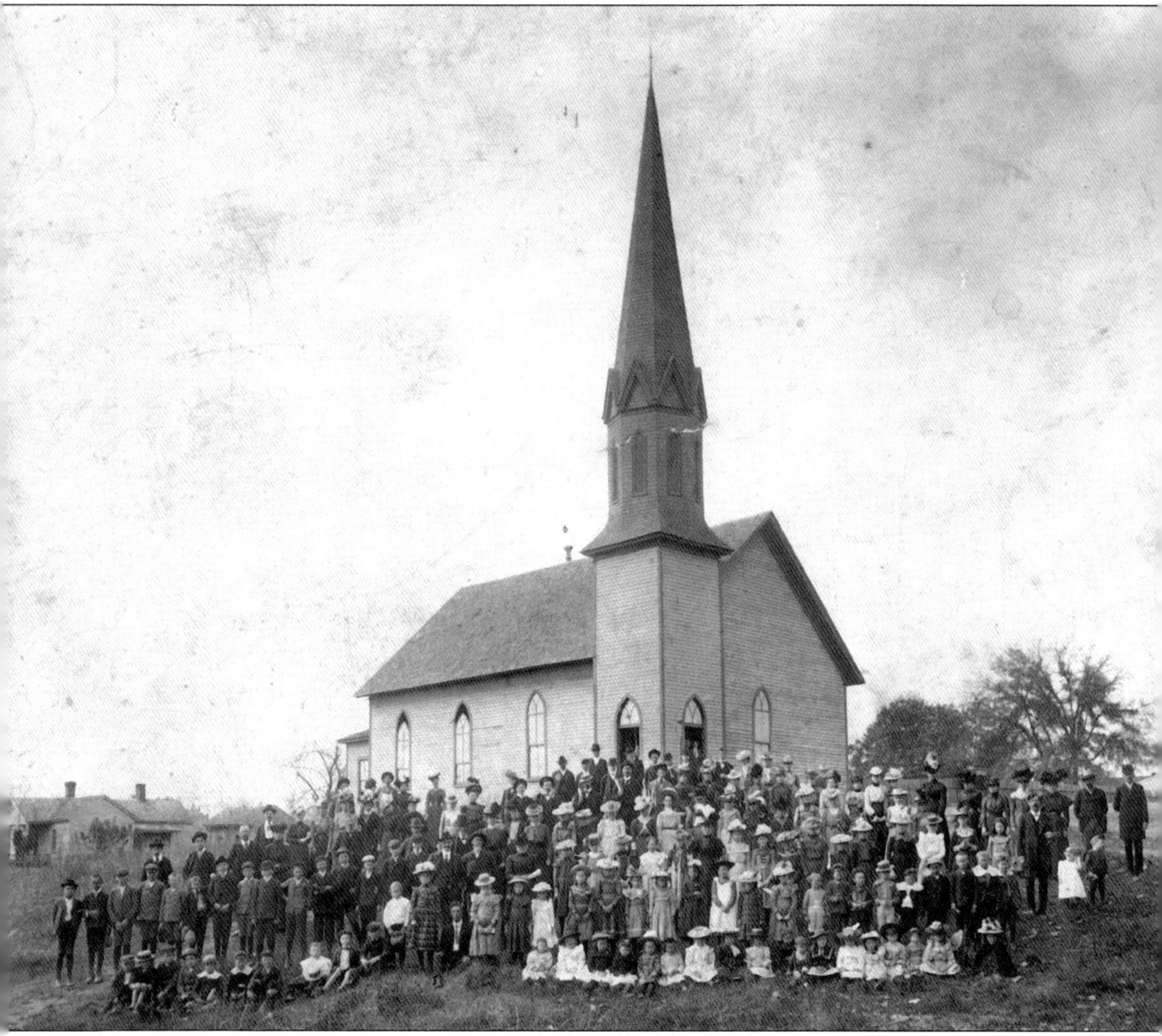

The congregation of First Baptist Church, located at North and Third Streets, gathers together in the early 1890s. Members met with Rev. J.M. Bennett in the courthouse before the church was built. (Courtesy of the Stanly County Museum.)

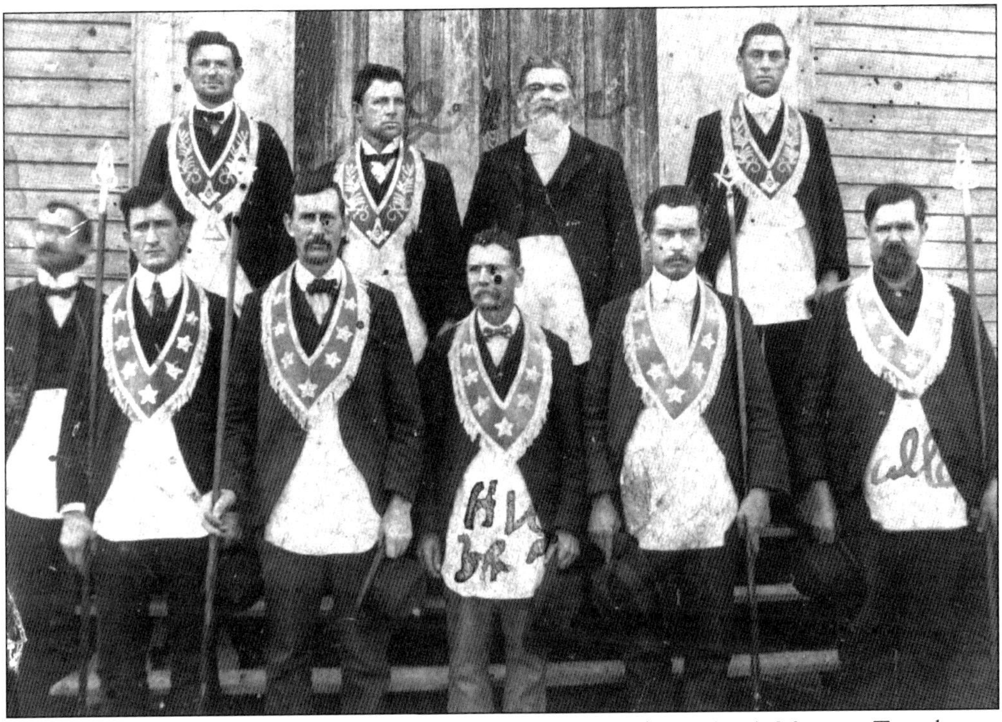

An early Masonic group in Stanly County poses in the early 1900s. A Masonic Temple was located at the southeast corner of Main and First Streets. It burned in the early 1900s. (Courtesy of the Stanly County Museum.)

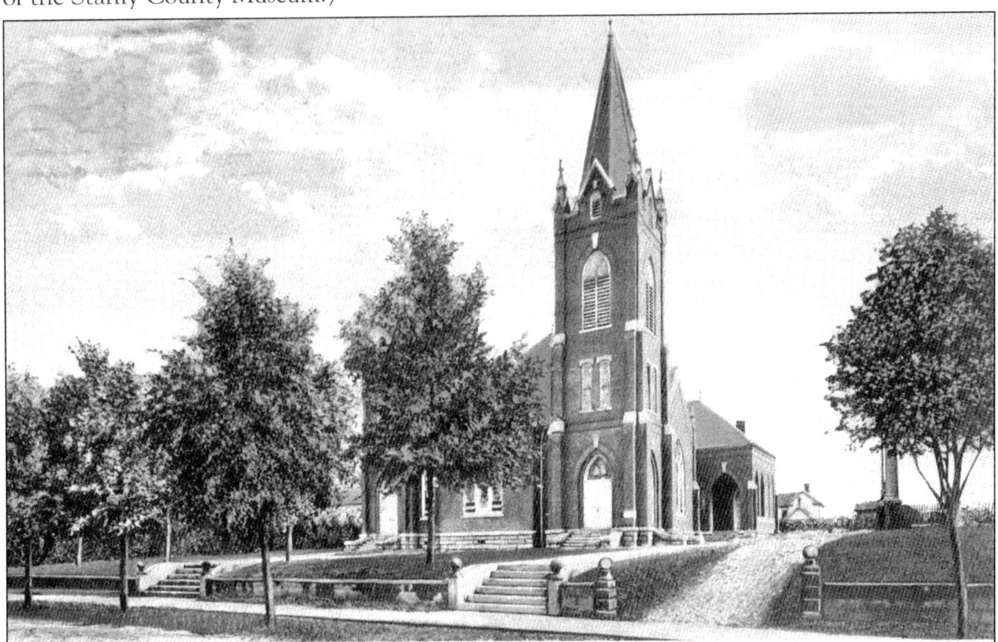

Daniel Freeman donated the lot on North Second Street to the Central United Methodist Church. The church was organized in 1831. This is the third church building, built in 1900. (Courtesy of the Stanly County Museum.)

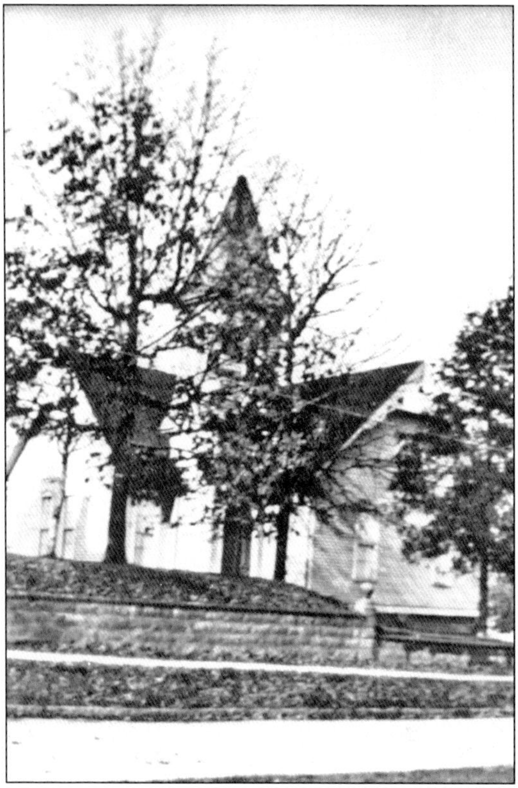

The original First Presbyterian Church was located on the southeast corner of North First and West North Street. First Presbyterian was organized in 1898. The church was built in 1900 and torn down in the 1920s. (Courtesy of the Stanly County Museum.)

The current First Presbyterian Church was built in a restrained Beaux Arts style in 1924 at 126 West North Street. (Courtesy of the Stanly County Museum.)

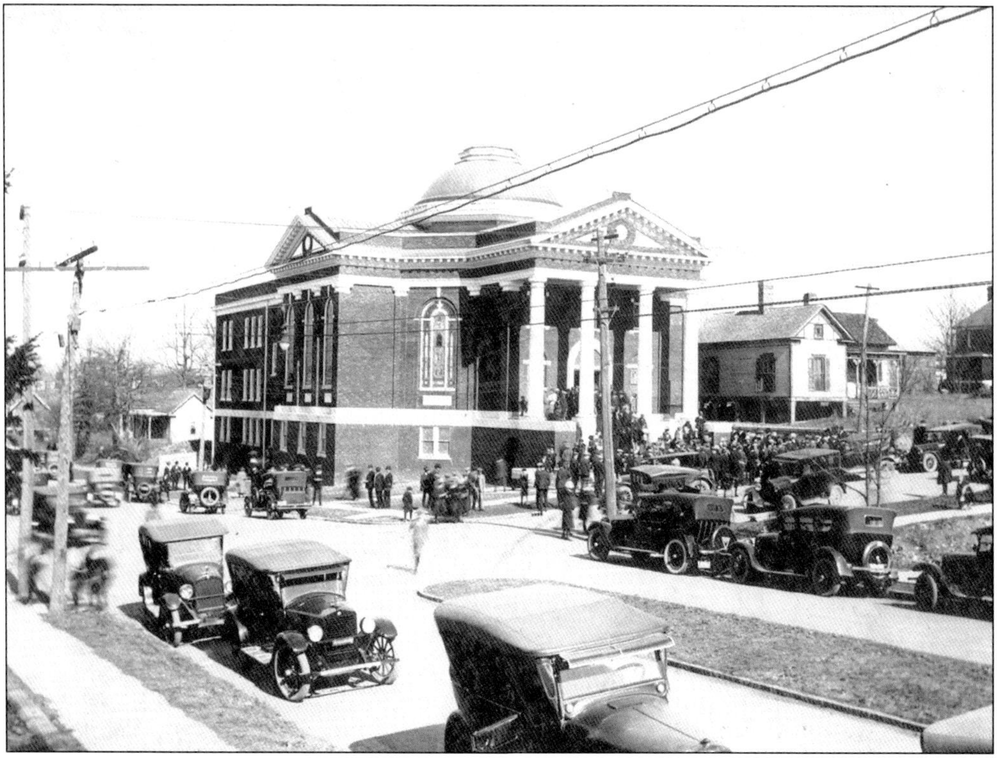

The First Baptist Church was built in the 1890s on the southwest corner of North Third Street and East North Street. The Reverend R.H. Herring, who was pastor from 1901 to 1904, is pictured in the inset. (Courtesy of the Stanly County Museum.)

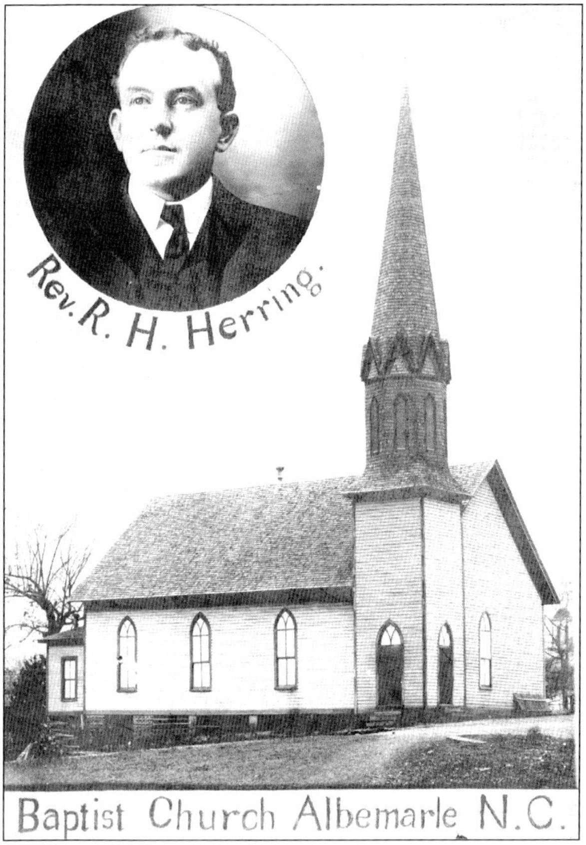

Judson McLendon, an African-American stone mason and minister, designed and built St. Delight Holiness Church in 1927 on the north side of Glendale Avenue. The church is mainly constructed of white flint rock and fieldstone. A cross was designed in rock over the entrance. (Courtesy of the Stanly County Museum.)

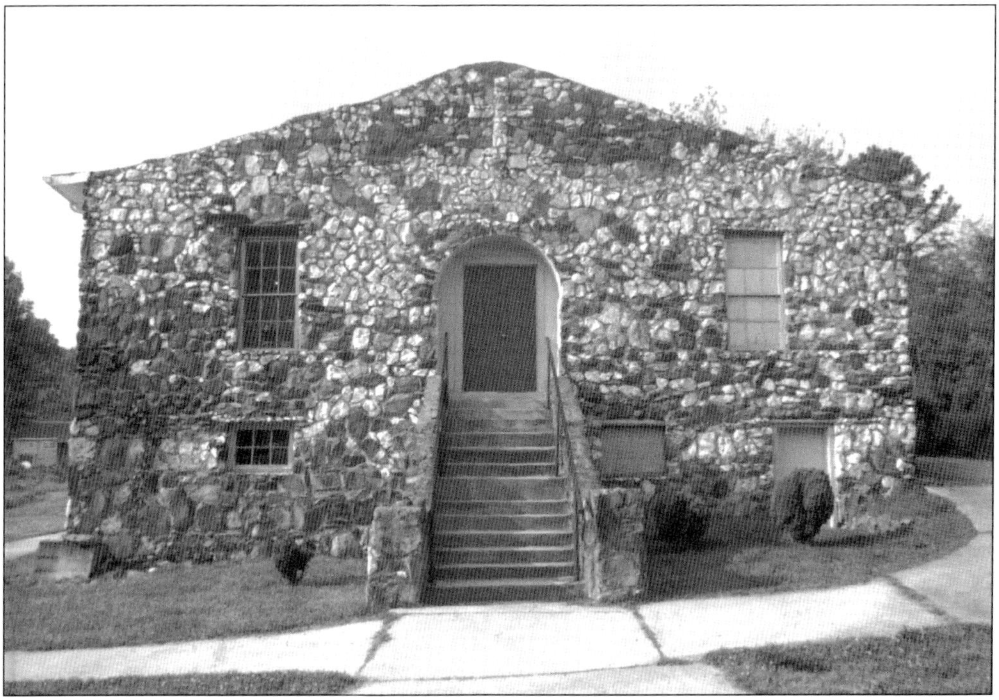

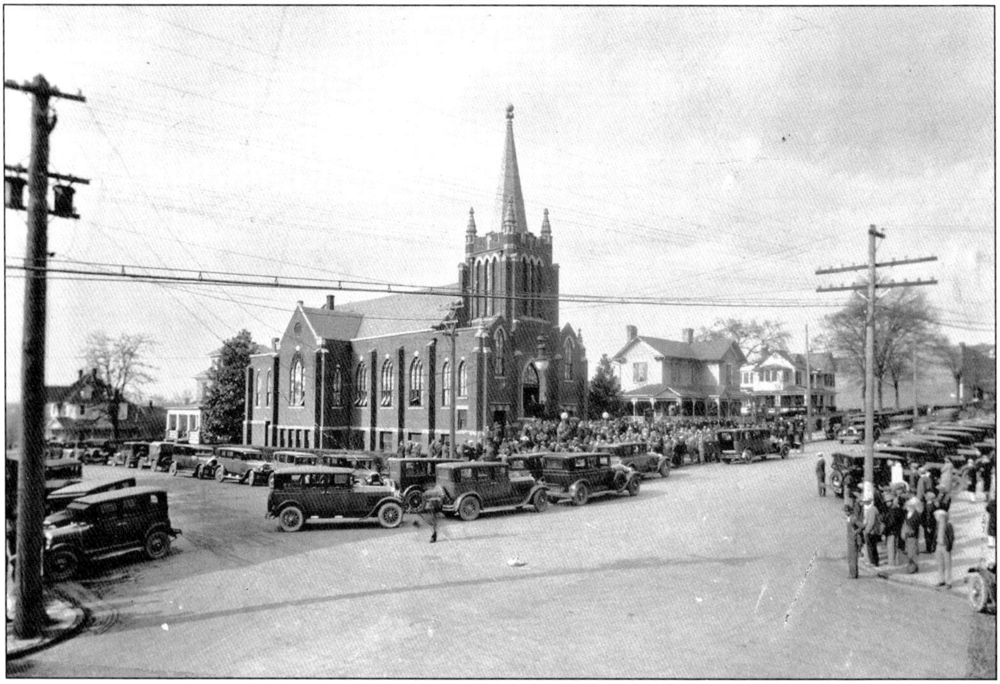

A crowd gathers at the First Lutheran Church for John S. Efird's funeral in 1927. The church was built in 1909. Efird donated land to the church, and the Christian Education Building was built there in 1931. (Courtesy of the Stanly County Museum.)

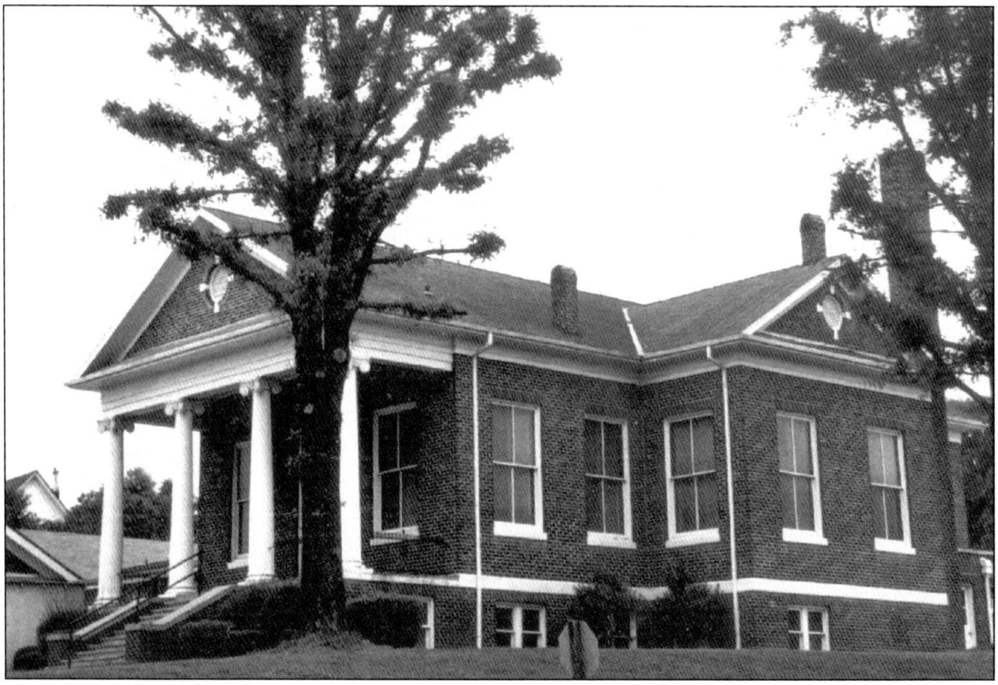

The Congregational Christian Church was organized in 1912. The first church was built in 1913. The second church, shown in this image, was built in 1928. (Courtesy of the Stanly County Museum.)

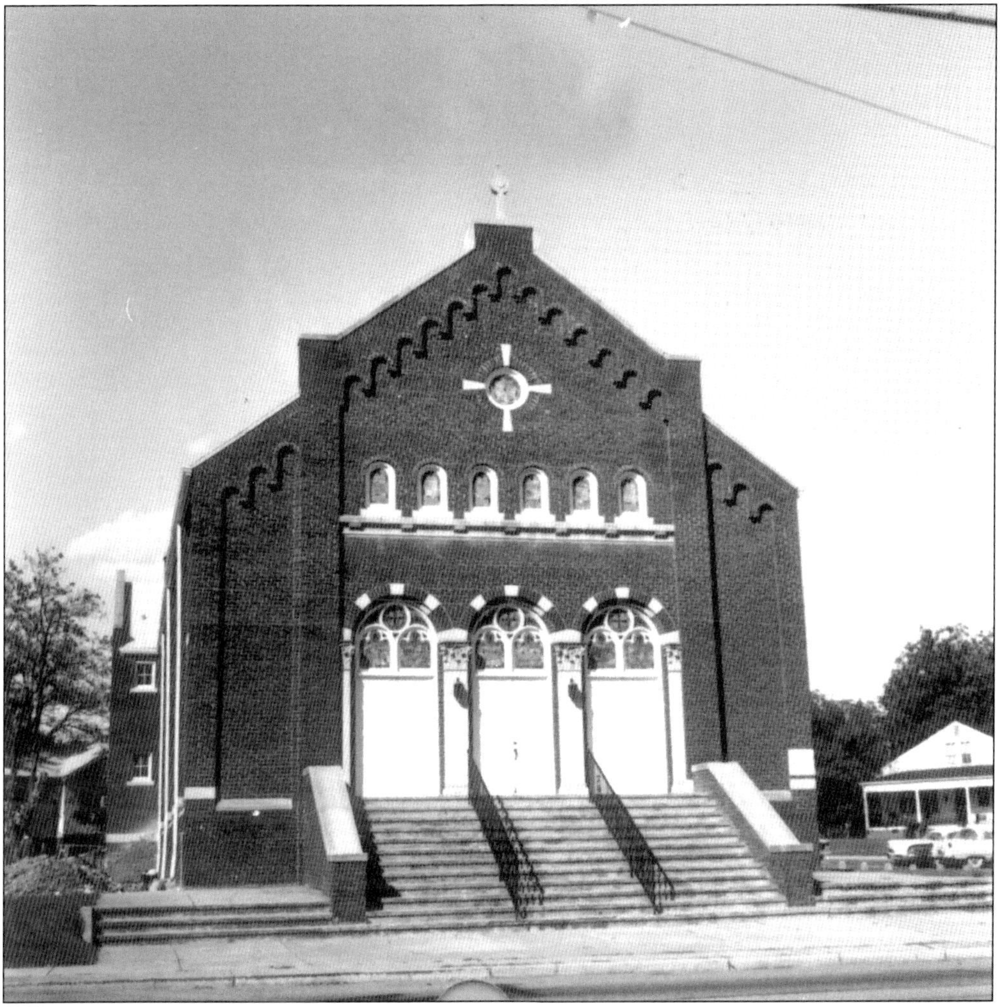

The Main Street United Methodist Church was organized in 1909. The current church was built in 1928 after the original building burned down. The church was originally called First Methodist Presbyterian Church. (Courtesy of the Stanly County Museum.)

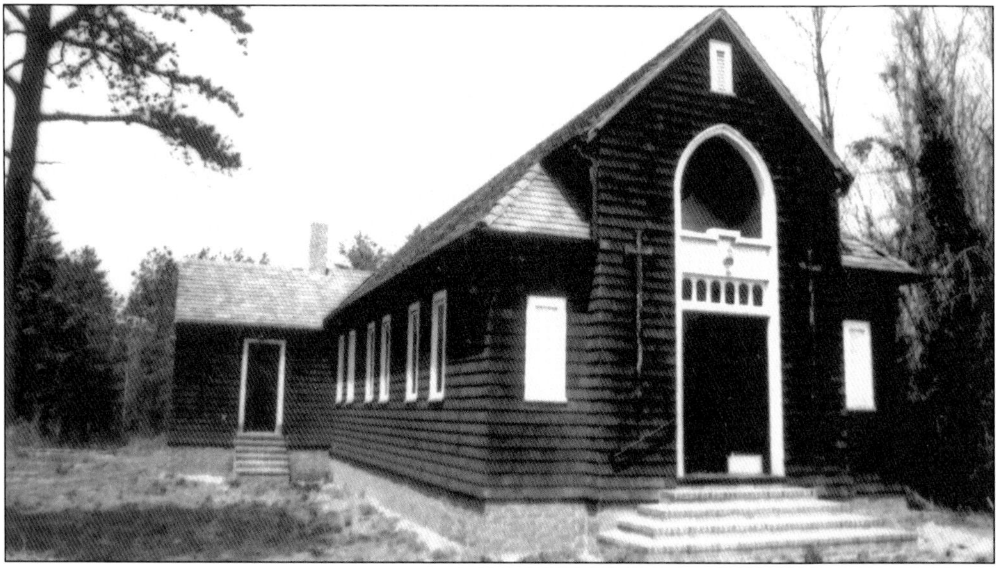

The first Catholic church in Albemarle, Annunciation Catholic Church, was built in 1934. Originally named Our Lady of the Annunciation, it was located on the corner of North Second Street and Montgomery Avenue. It later moved to Rock Creek Park. (Courtesy of the Stanly County Museum.)

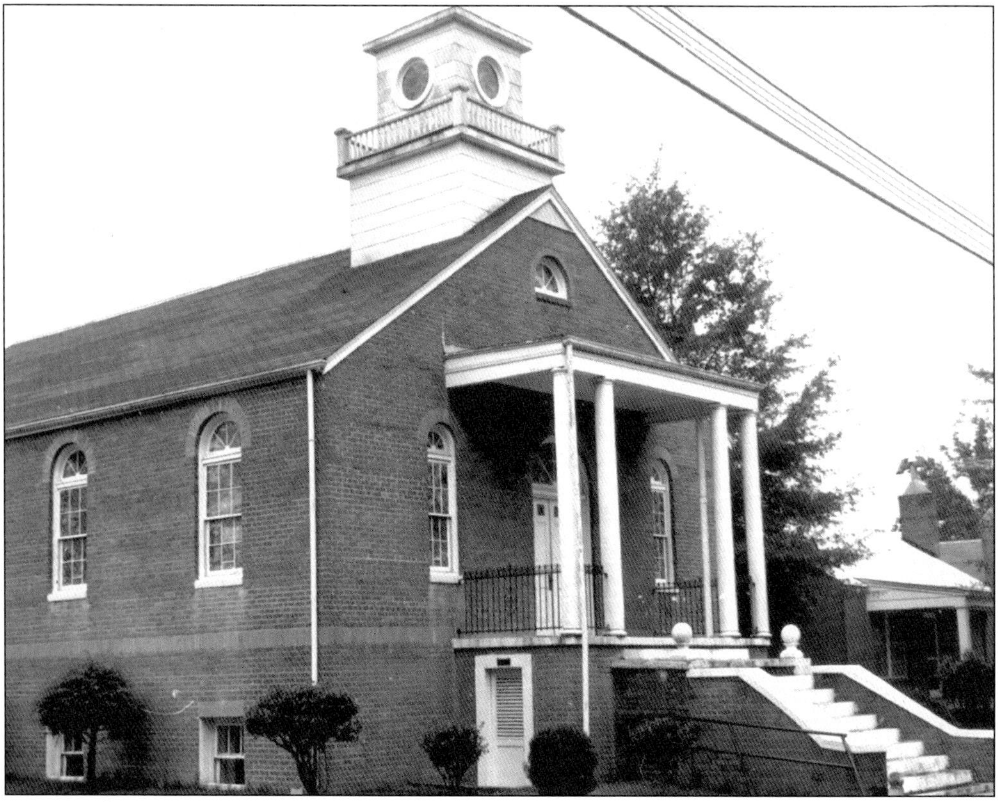

Immanuel Baptist Church is located on Old Charlotte Road. It was first organized in 1945. (Courtesy of the Stanly County Museum.)

Nine

ARCHITECTURE

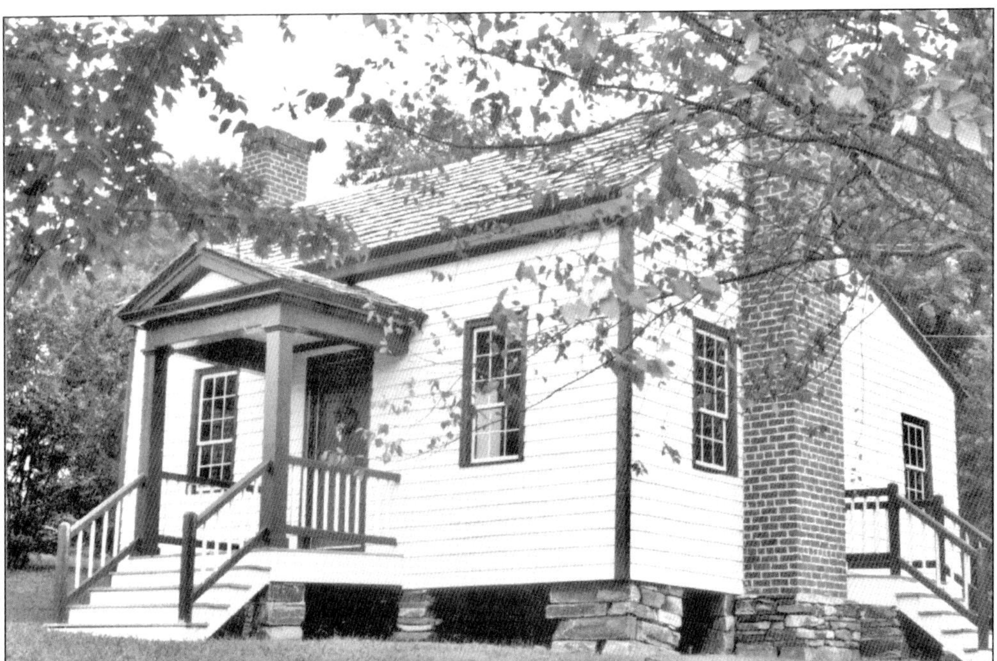

The Freeman-Marks House was built in 1835 by Daniel Freeman. It is now the oldest house standing in Albemarle. Samuel J. Pemberton lived in this house while he co-authored the *North Carolina Criminal Code and Digest*. (Courtesy of the Stanly County Museum.)

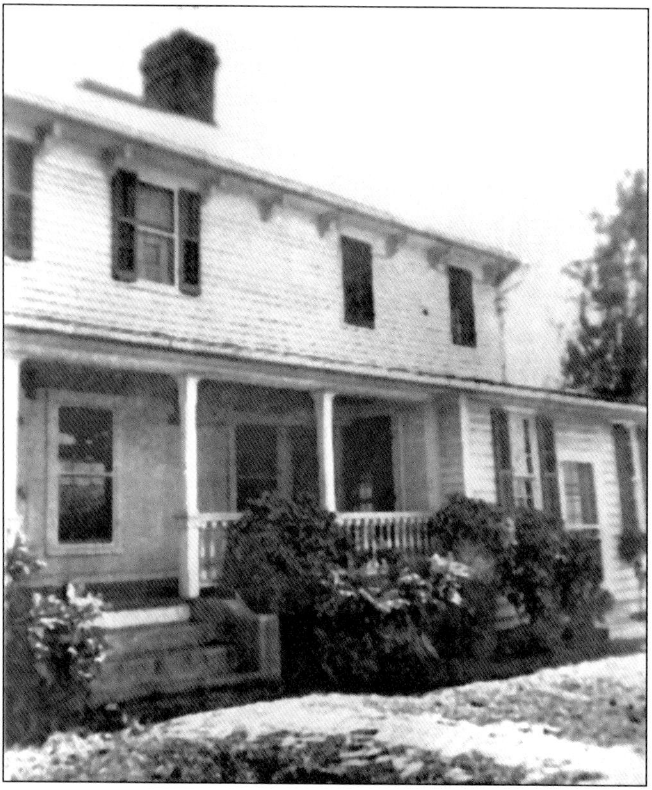

Eben Hearne built the Hearne Inn in 1828 on South First Street. (Courtesy of the Stanly County Museum.)

The I.W. Snuggs House was built in 1852. Named after its most famous occupant, I.W. "Buck" Snuggs, the ninth sheriff of Stanly County, it is the third oldest house standing in Albemarle. Stanly County's prominent artist Roger Thomas created this print. (Courtesy of Roger Thomas.)

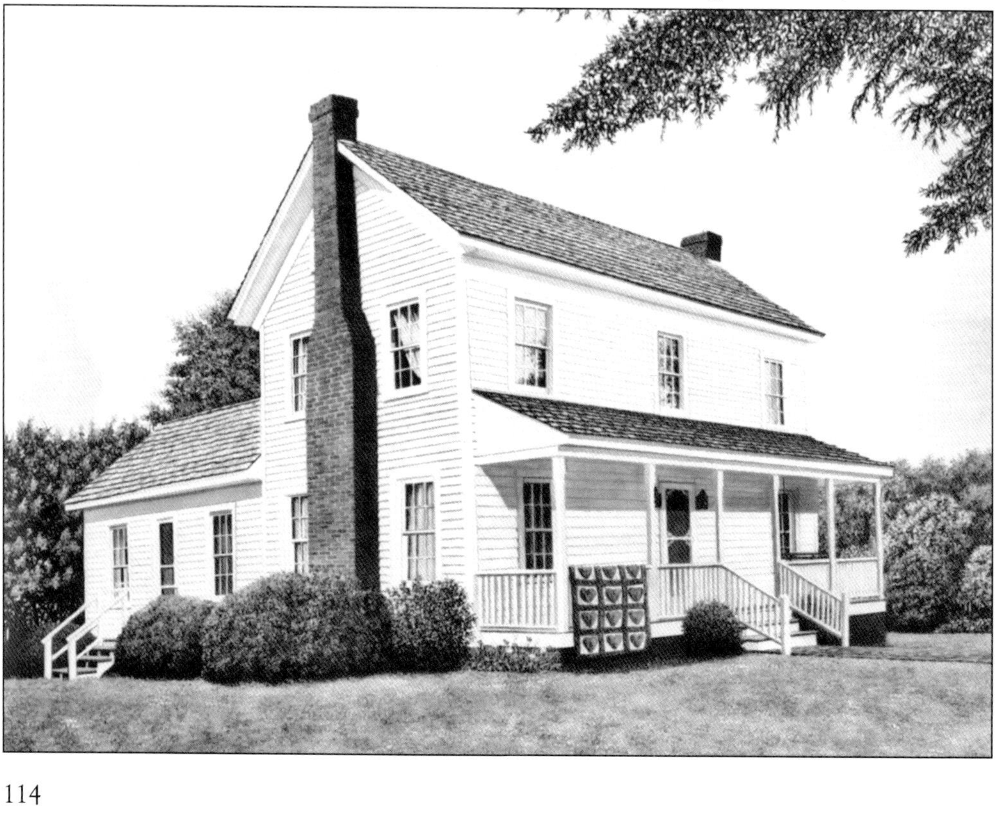

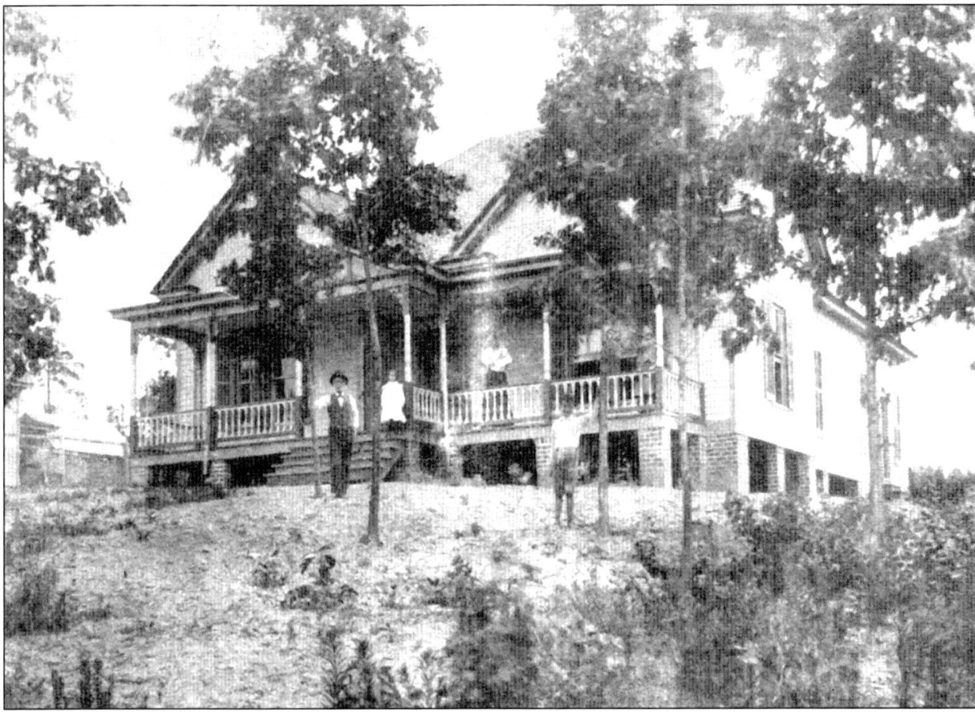

The Dry family poses in front of their home in 1898. Pictured are, from left to right, G.M Dry, Grace (on the porch steps), Laura (in the middle of the porch holding Helene, who is less then a month old), Chester, and Dera (on the far right on the porch). The Dry house is located at 522 East Main Street. The house was altered in 1909 to a two-story Victorian, but it burned in 2003. (Courtesy of the Stanly County Museum.)

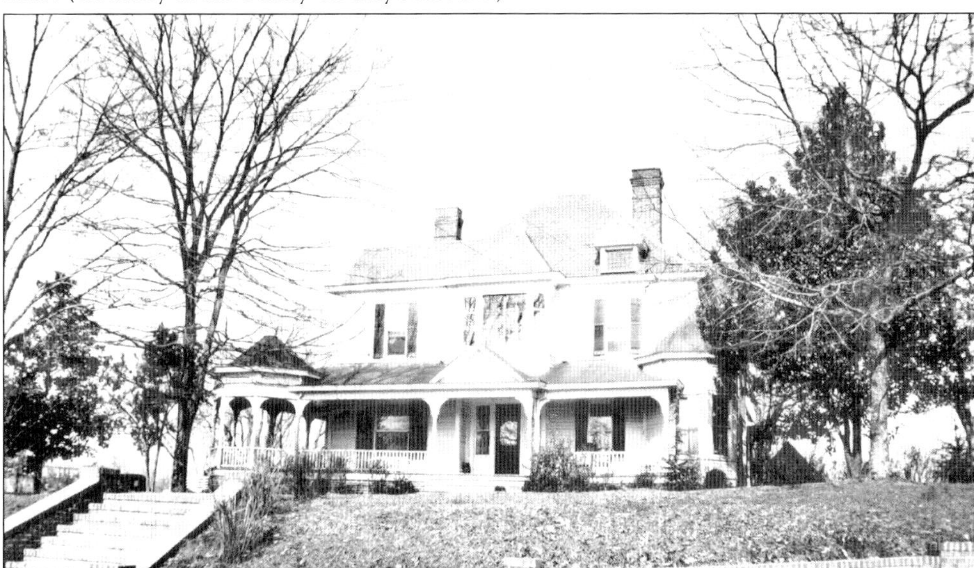

The Brown-Parker House was built in 1891 at 427 Pee Dee Avenue by L.A. Moody for James Milton Brown (1851–1923), an attorney, and Martha Cornelia Anderson (1866–1935). (Courtesy of the Stanly County Museum.)

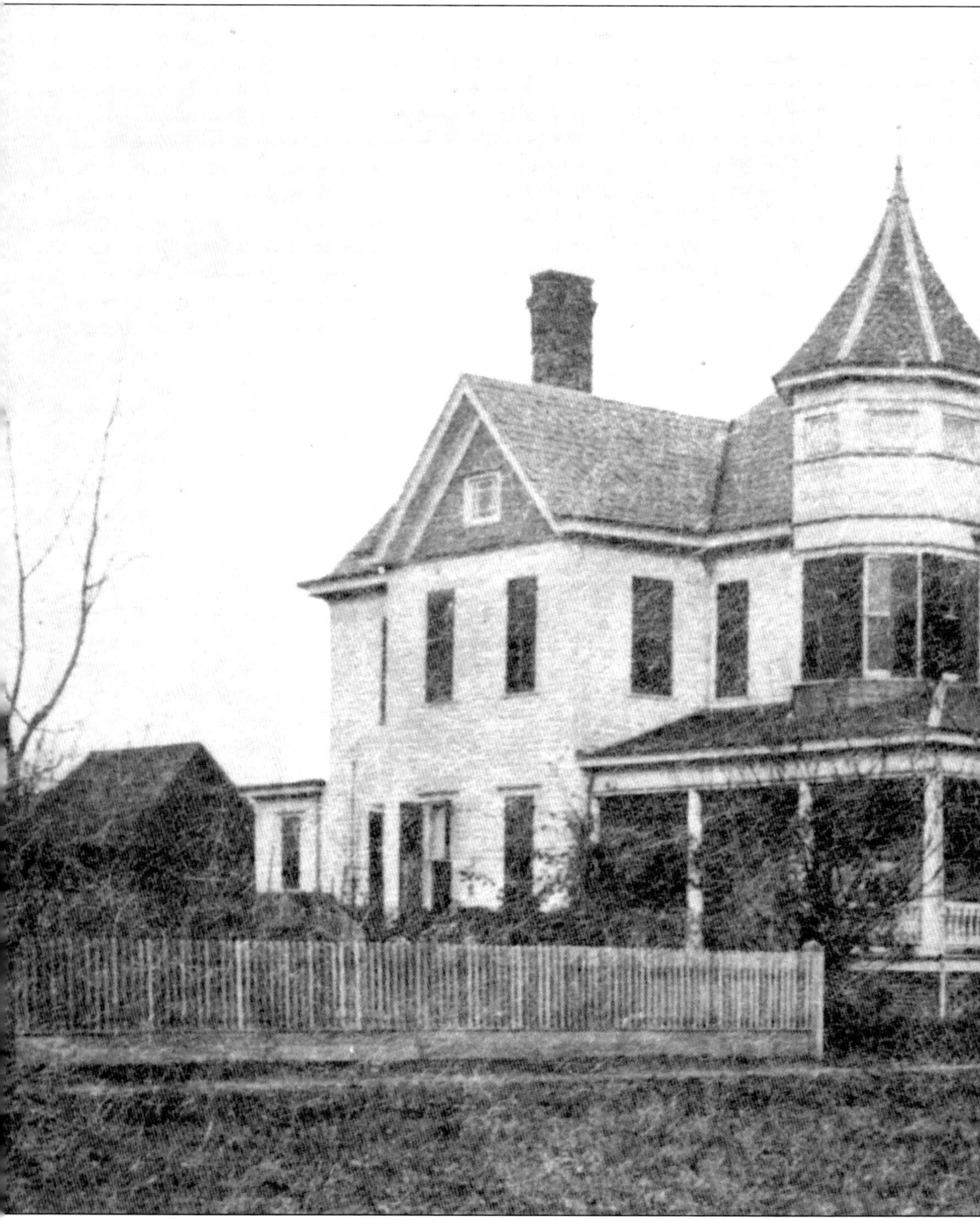

The Asbury-Parker house, located on East North Street, was demolished in 1977. It has now

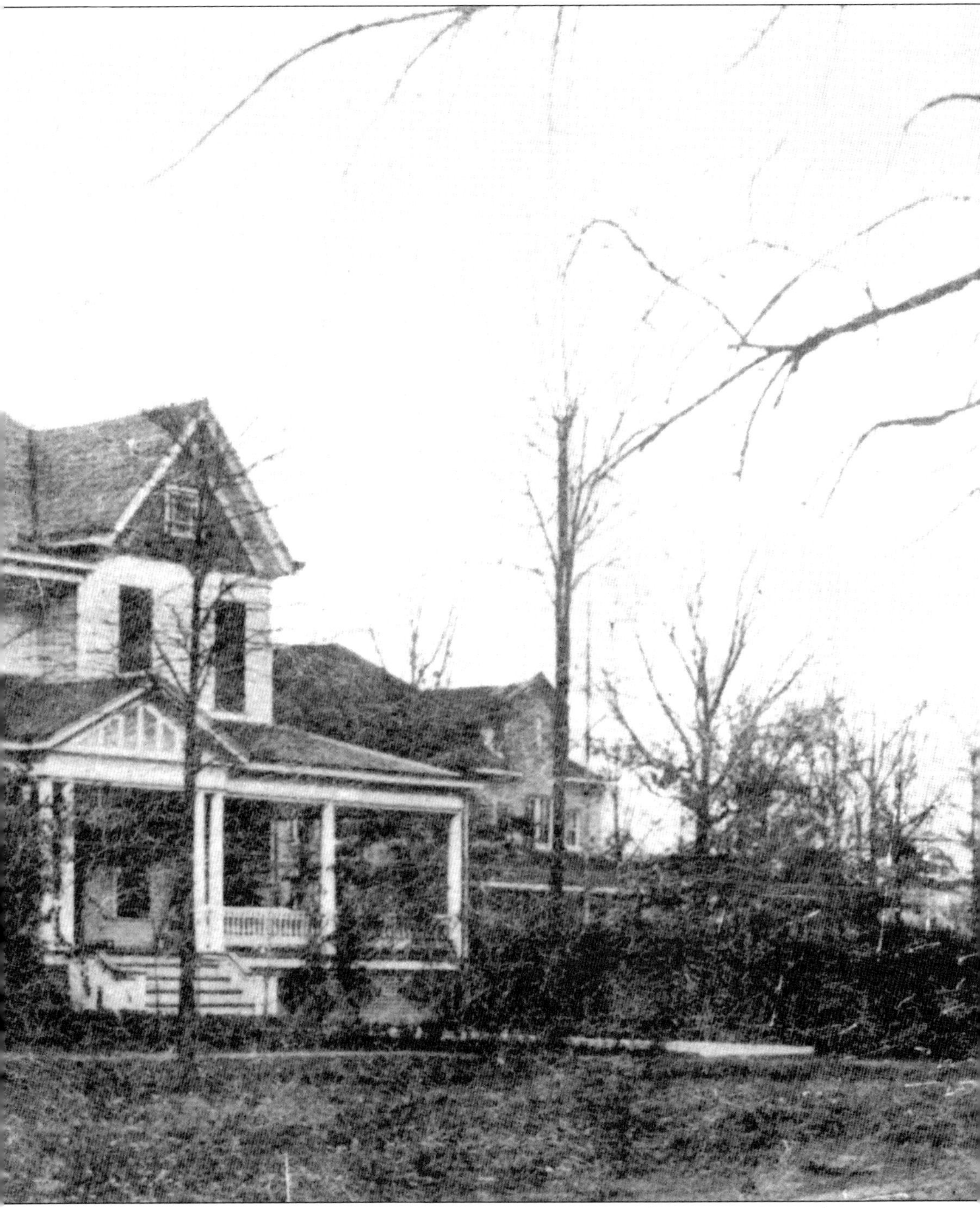

become the First Baptist Church parking lot. (Courtesy of the Stanly County Museum.)

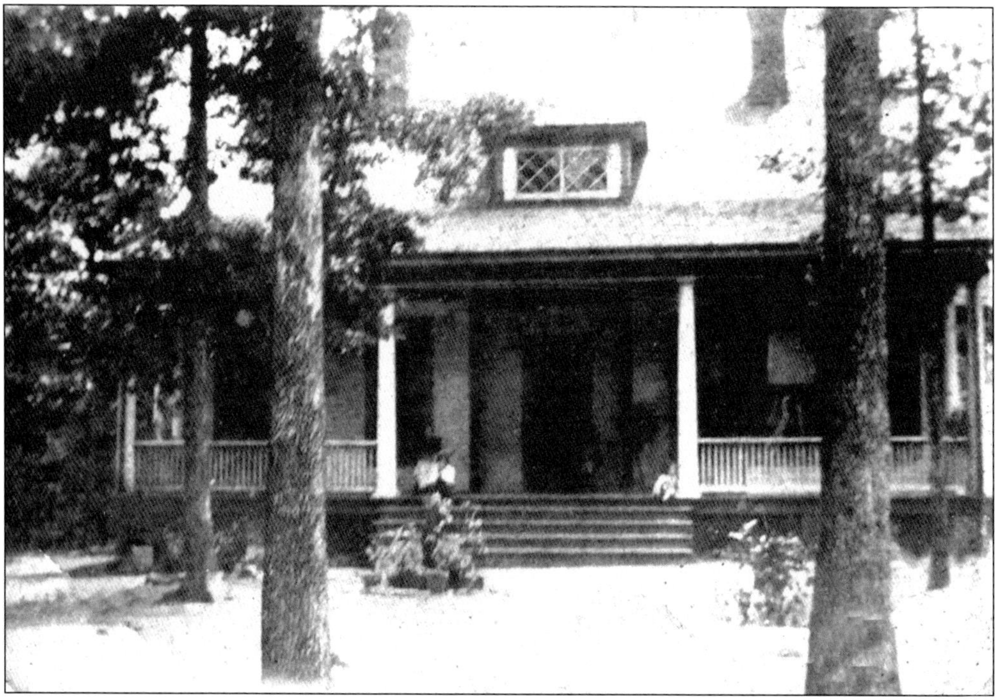

The Morrow House, also known as Oakmarle, was built in 1899. Mr. and Mrs. James McKnight Morrow donated 1,800 acres of land to the State of North Carolina in the 1930s, thereby forming Morrow Mountain. (Courtesy of Dotty Plyler.)

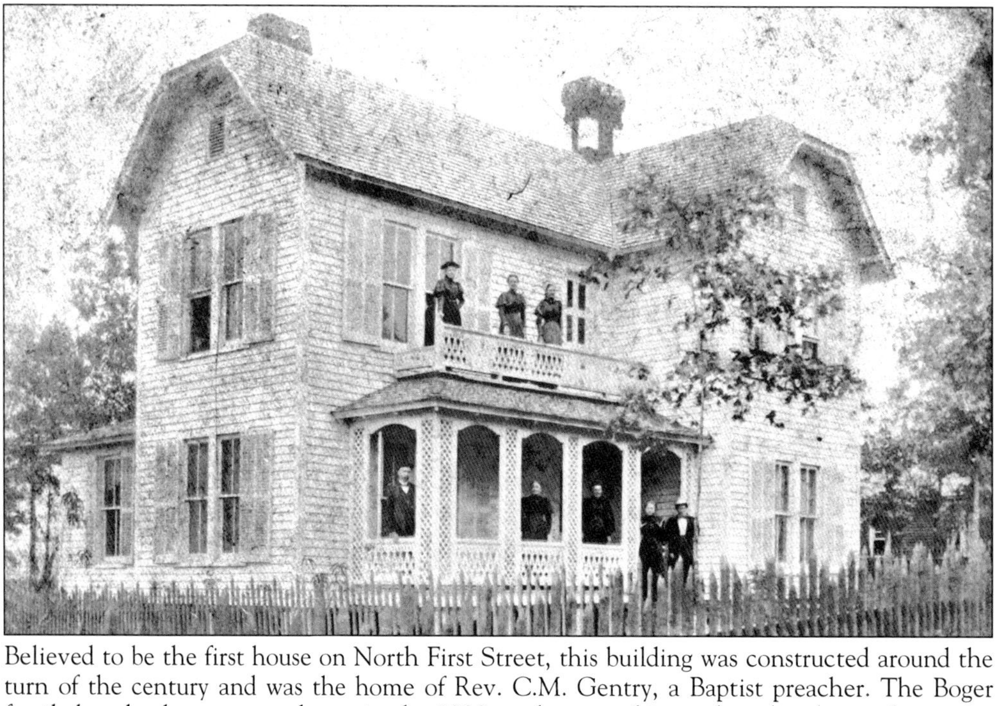

Believed to be the first house on North First Street, this building was constructed around the turn of the century and was the home of Rev. C.M. Gentry, a Baptist preacher. The Boger family bought the two-story house in the 1920s and operated it as a boarding house during the 1930s. (Courtesy of the Stanly County Museum.)

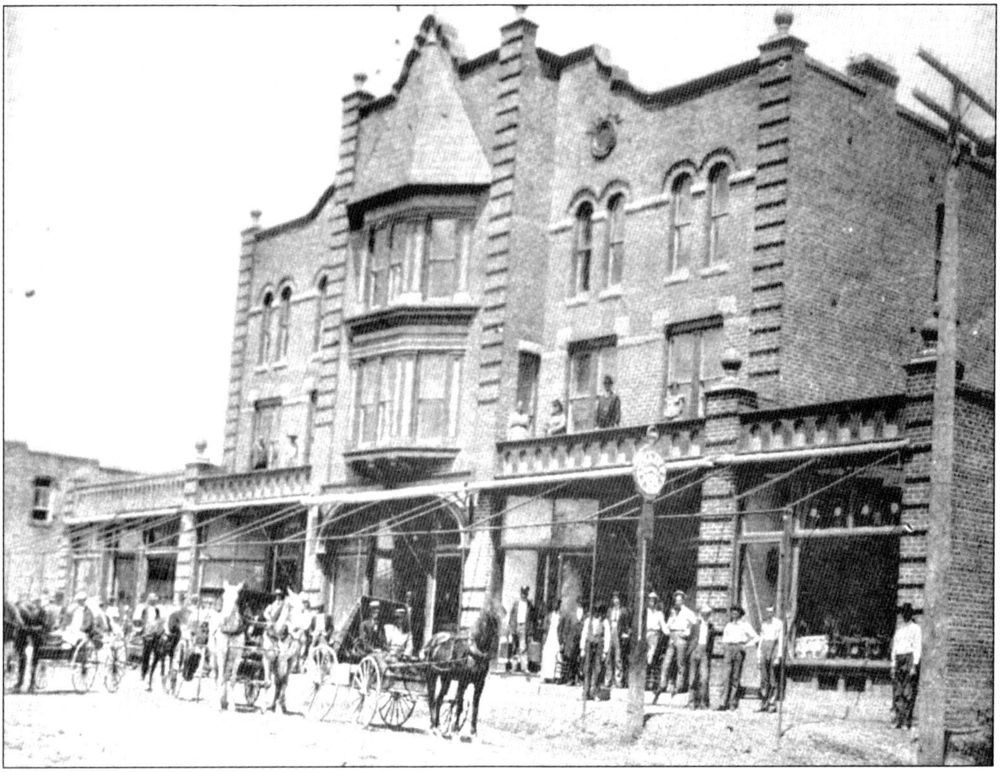

W.T. Huckabee Sr. owned the Central Hotel until 1947. Mr. Huckabee is pictured here on the balcony to the left. Dr. Sebe Kluttz is standing below the dormer windows, and Mr. F.E. Starnes is in front of the original Starnes Jewelry store before it relocated. (Courtesy of the Stanly County Museum.)

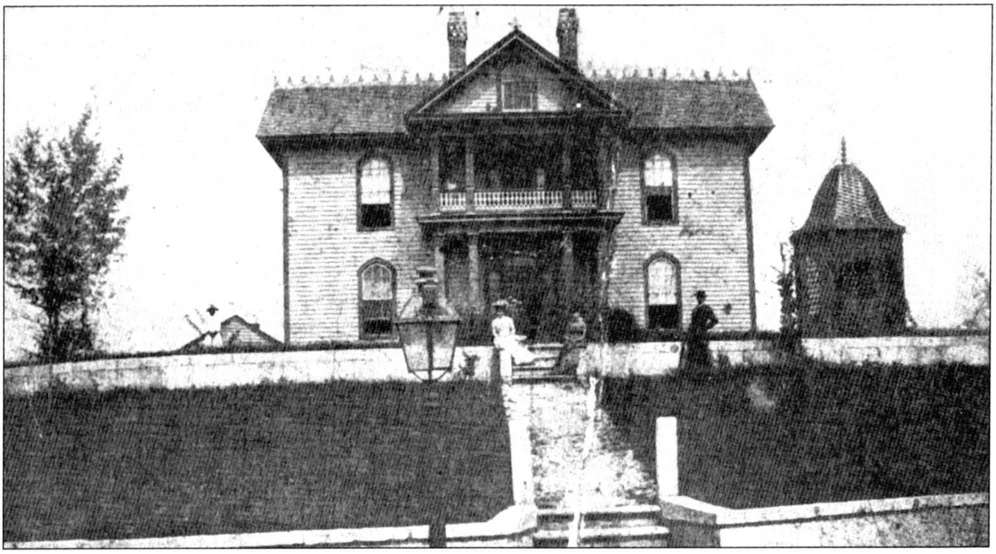

John S. Efird's original house was in the Victorian style. (Courtesy of the Stanly County Public Library.)

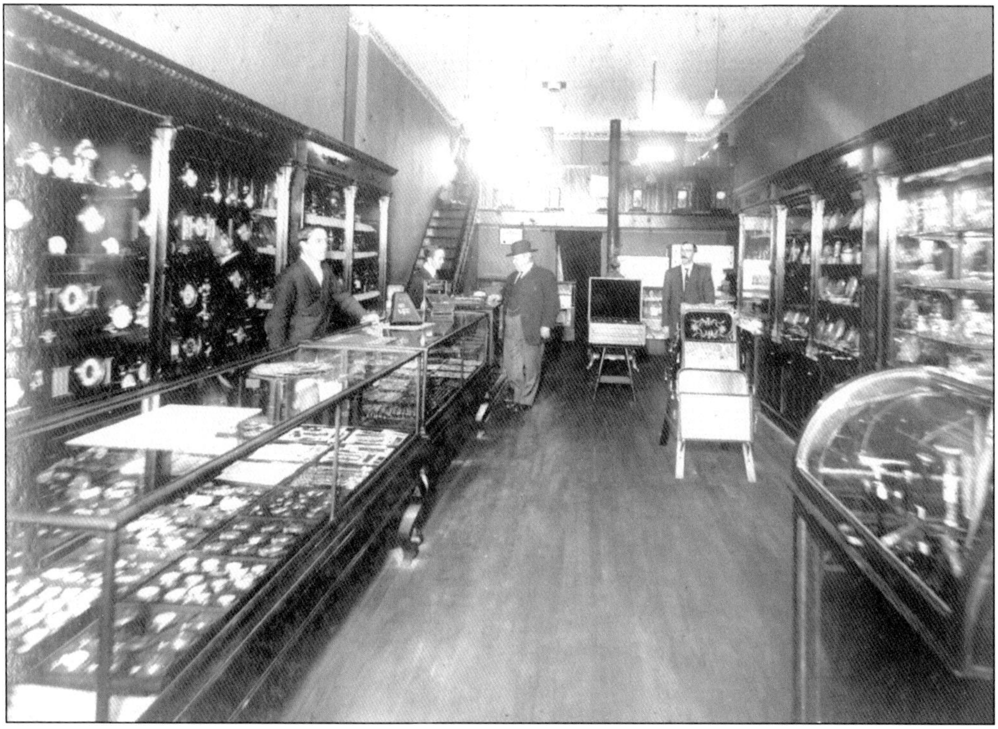

Starnes Jewelry was built in 1907 on West Main Street by F.E. Starnes. It is currently owned and managed by F.E. Starnes's grandson, Francis Eugene "Gene" Starnes III. Notice the beautiful display cases in the Queen Anne style. (Courtesy of the Stanly County Museum.)

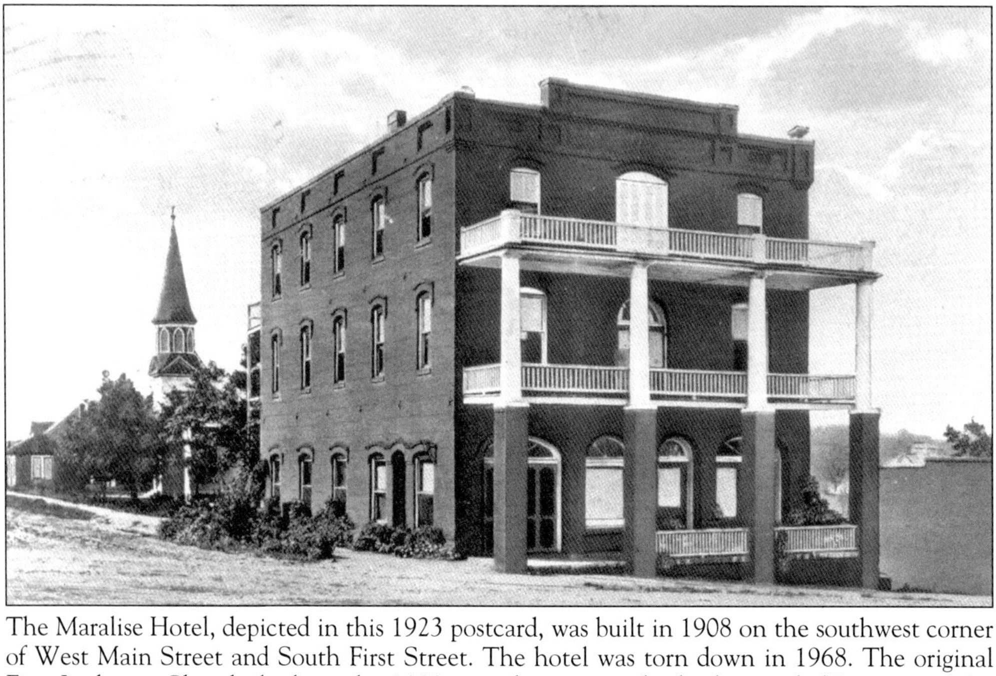

The Maralise Hotel, depicted in this 1923 postcard, was built in 1908 on the southwest corner of West Main Street and South First Street. The hotel was torn down in 1968. The original First Lutheran Church, built in the 1880s, can be seen in the background. (Courtesy of the Stanly County Museum.)

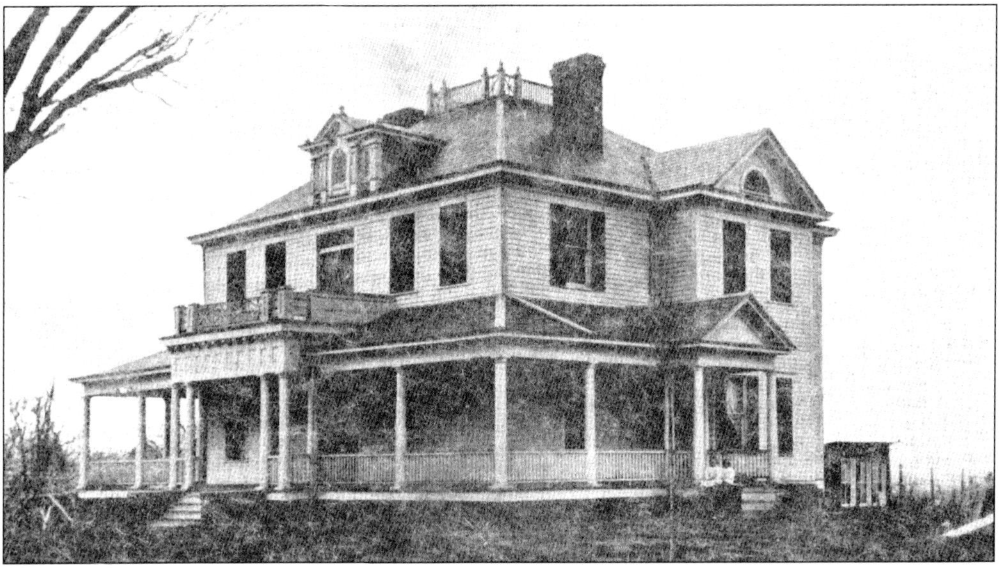

The Thomas C. Hearne house was built in 1909 at 434 West South Street. This house was built in the Colonial Revival style and was the third house on that property. (Courtesy of the Stanly County Museum.)

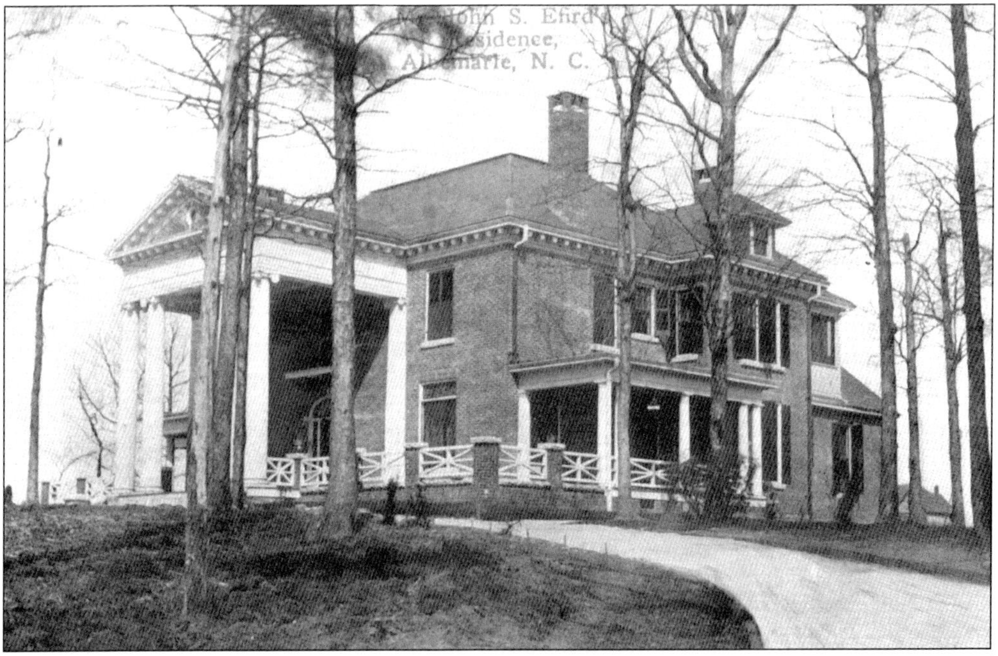

The John S. Efird house was built on West Main Street between 1910 and 1915. (Courtesy of the Stanly County Museum.)

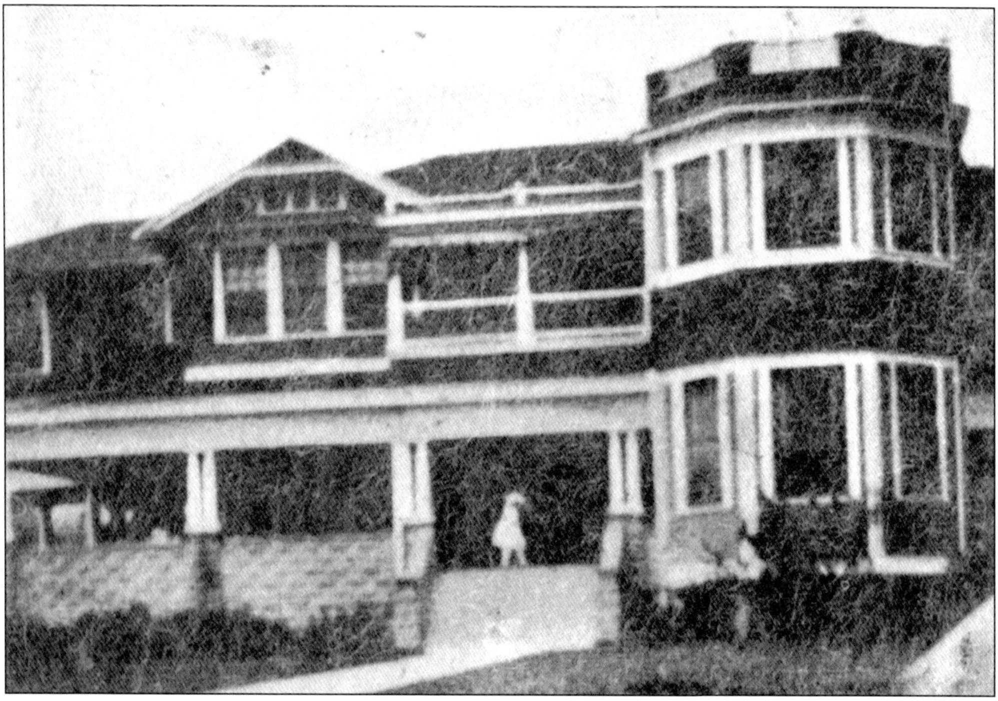

According to the 1902 Sanborn Map, B.D. Langdale's home was located at 43 South Second Street. The house was torn down and replaced by the Lutheran Fellowship Hall. (Courtesy of the Stanly County Public Library.)

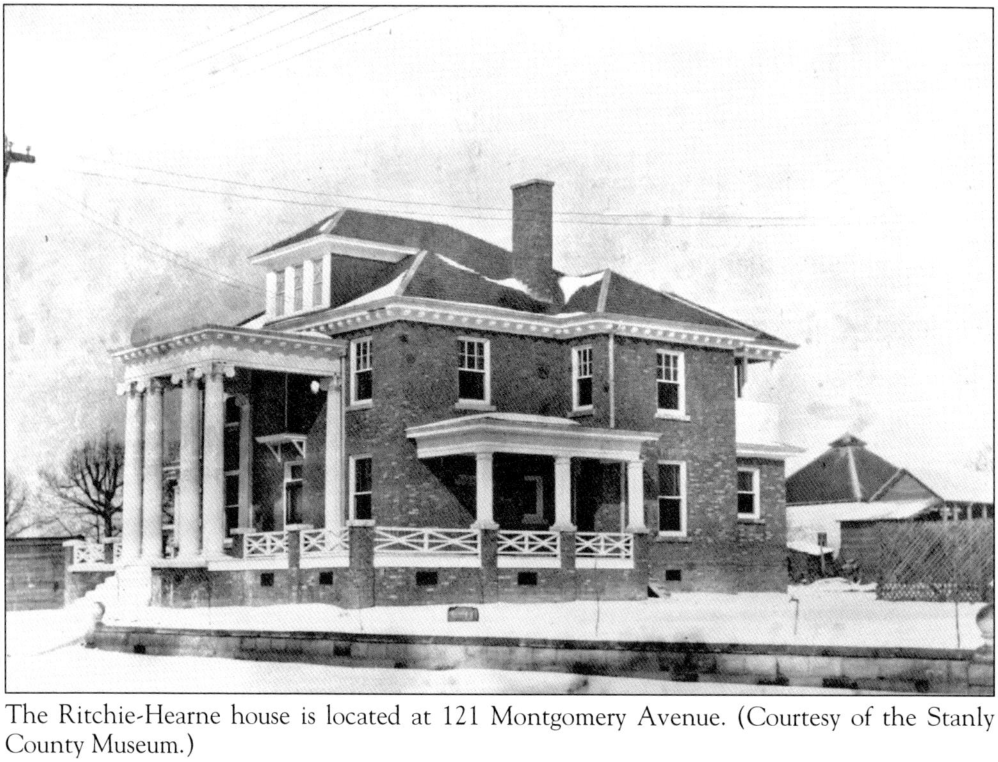

The Ritchie-Hearne house is located at 121 Montgomery Avenue. (Courtesy of the Stanly County Museum.)

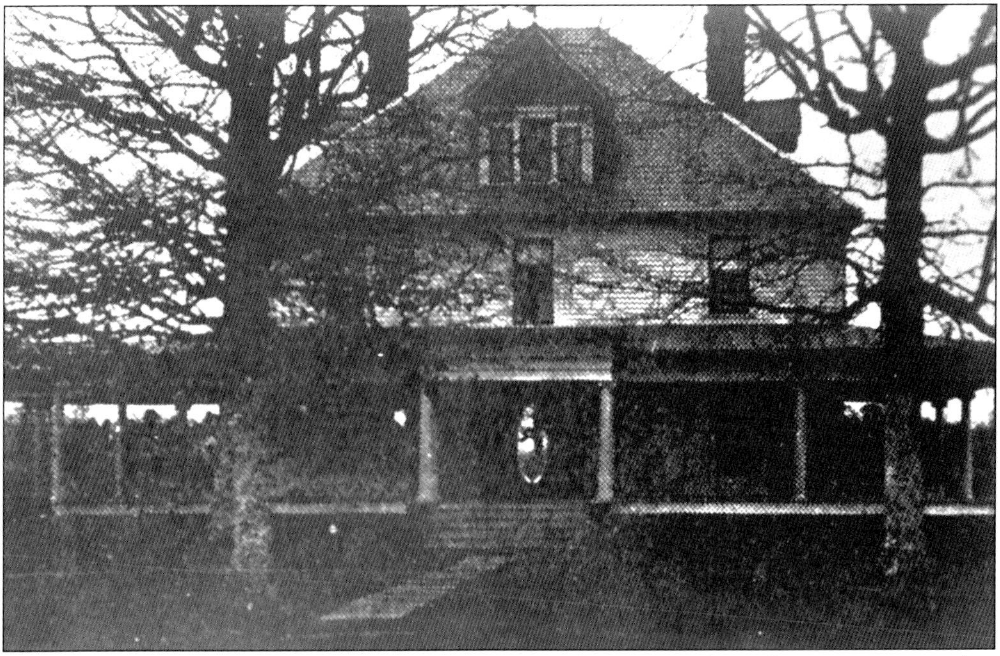

The Ben Foreman home, located at 416 North Second Street, is shown here as it appeared in 1912. (Courtesy of the Stanly County Museum.)

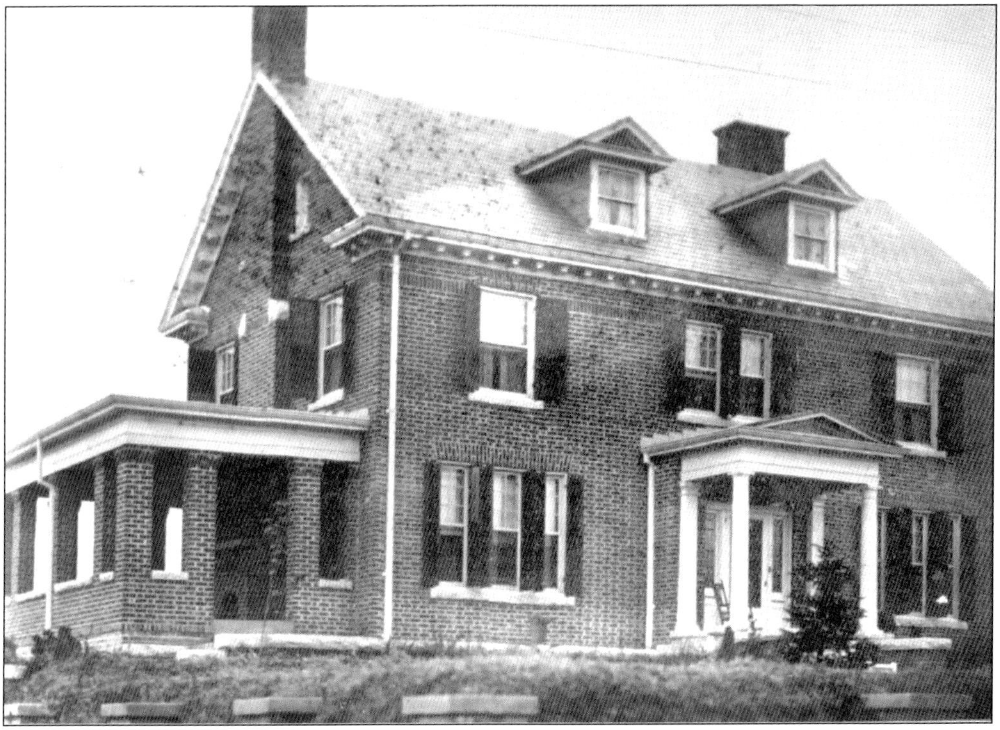

The Hall house was designed in the Colonial Revival style by Louis Asbury and built in 1912. J.C. Hall owned Hall's Pharmacy at 135 West Main Street and 120 North Second Street. (Courtesy of the Stanly County Museum.)

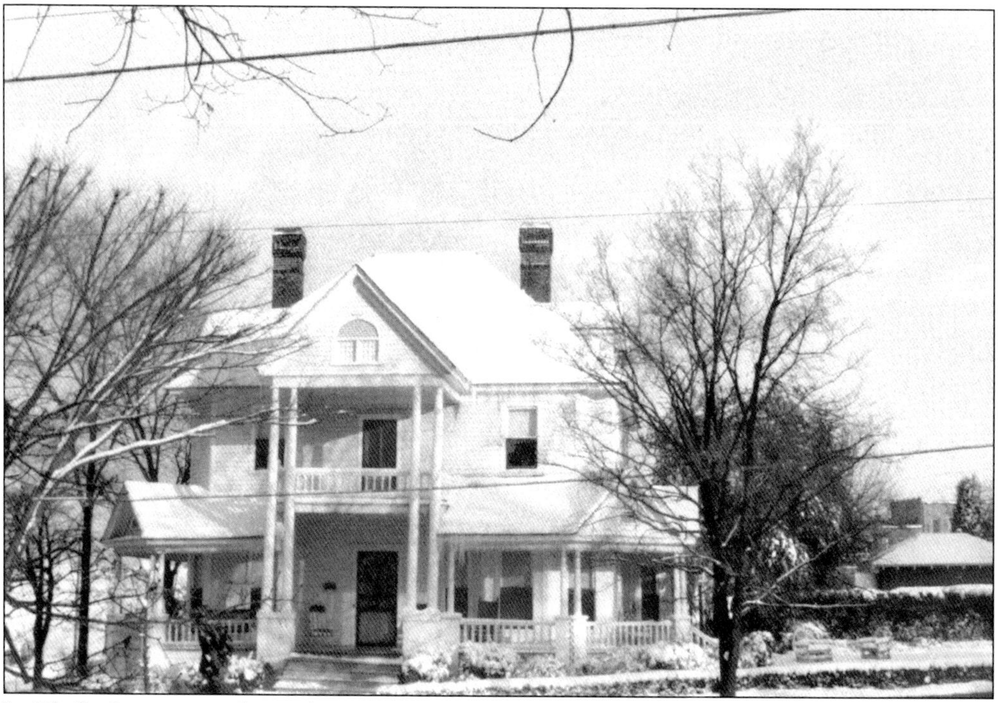

J. Efird's house was located on West South and First Street. (Courtesy of the Stanly County Museum.)

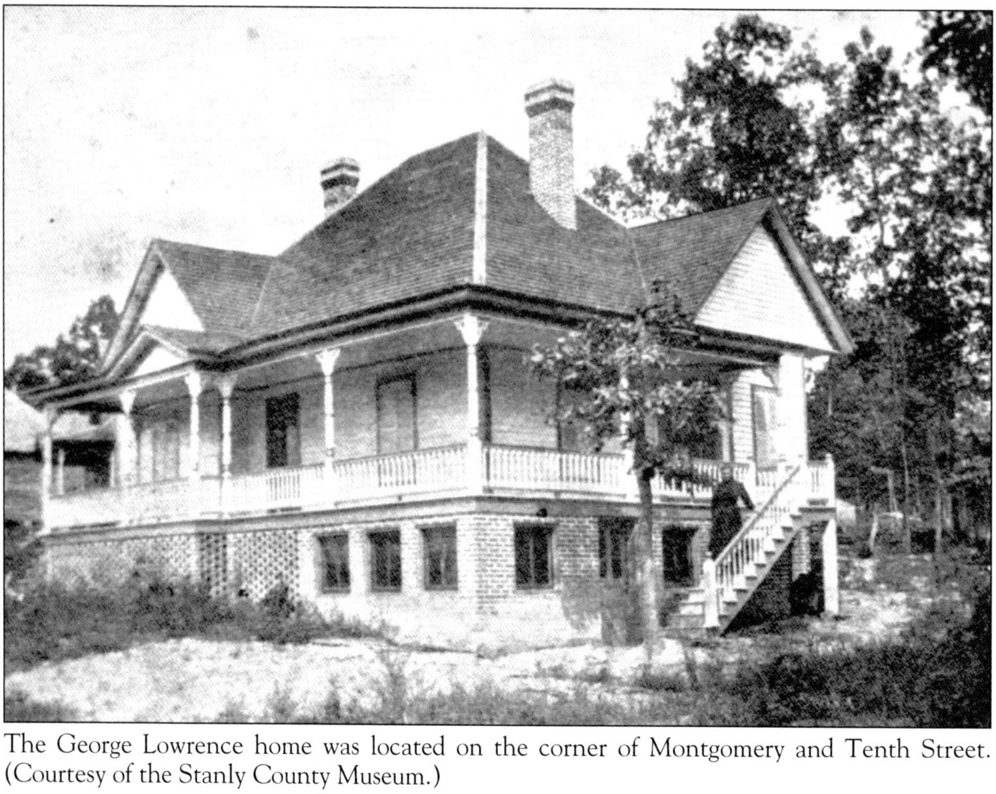

The George Lowrence home was located on the corner of Montgomery and Tenth Street. (Courtesy of the Stanly County Museum.)

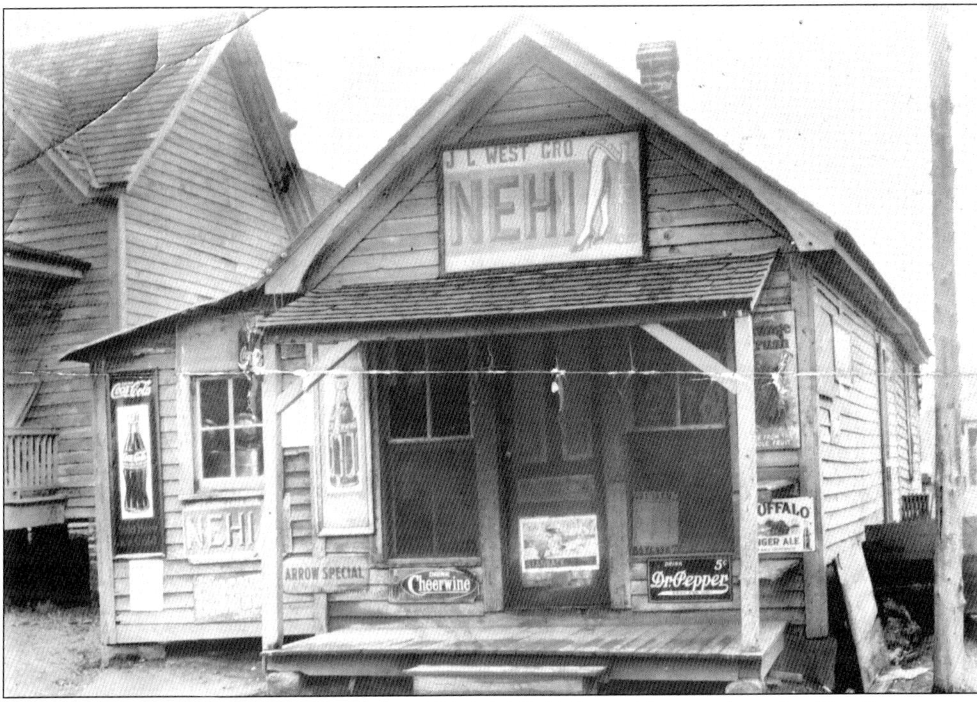

The J.L. West Grocery was located in Efird Mill Village. Notice that the Dr. Pepper sign advertises drinks for 5¢. (Courtesy of the Stanly County Museum.)

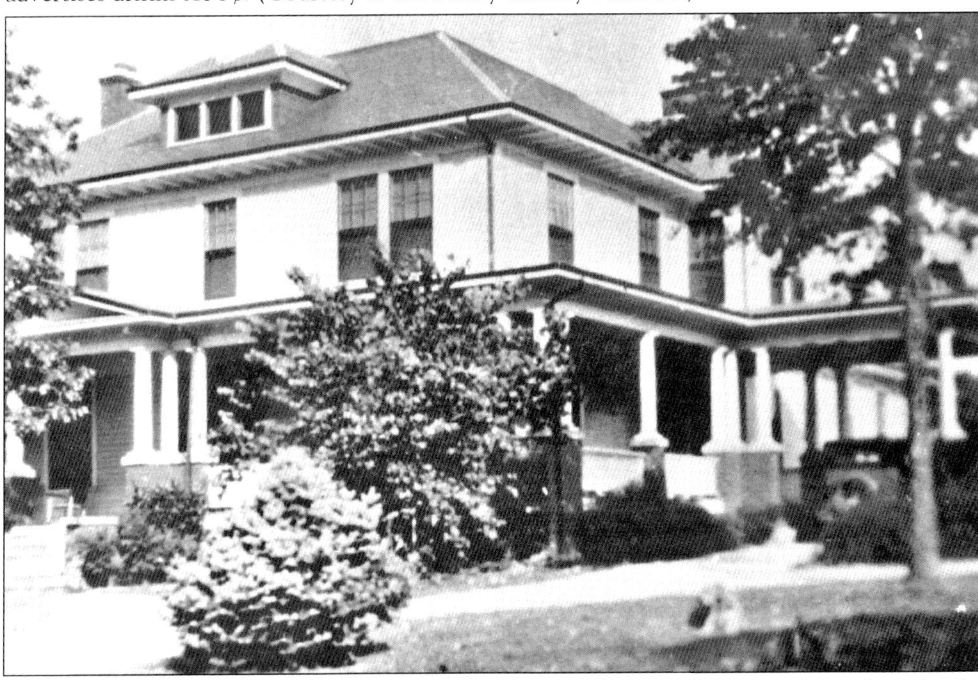

Depicted in this image is the Groves house on 506 North Second. It is now a parking lot for a Catholic church. James Alonzo "Governor" Groves was an executive at Wiscassett Mill. He also built a summer home, Grovestone, in the 1930s. Groves was married to Nelle Hearne. (Courtesy of the Stanly County Museum.)

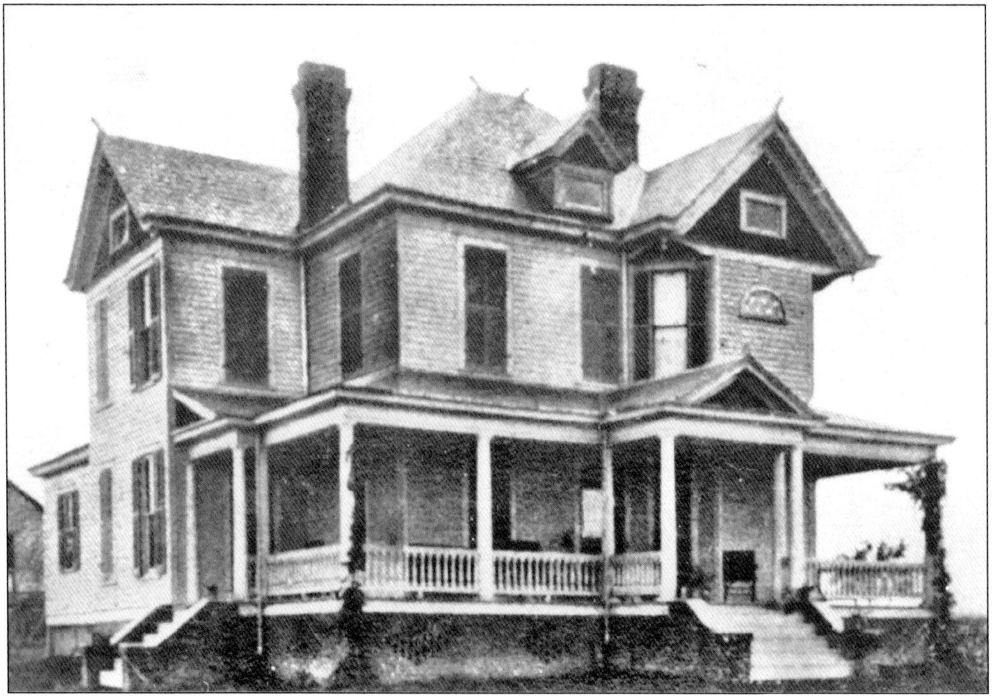

The Palmer House was once located on West Main Street and was a boarding house at one time. Charlie Palmer founded Palmer Stone Works in the early 1900s. (Courtesy of the Stanly County Museum.)

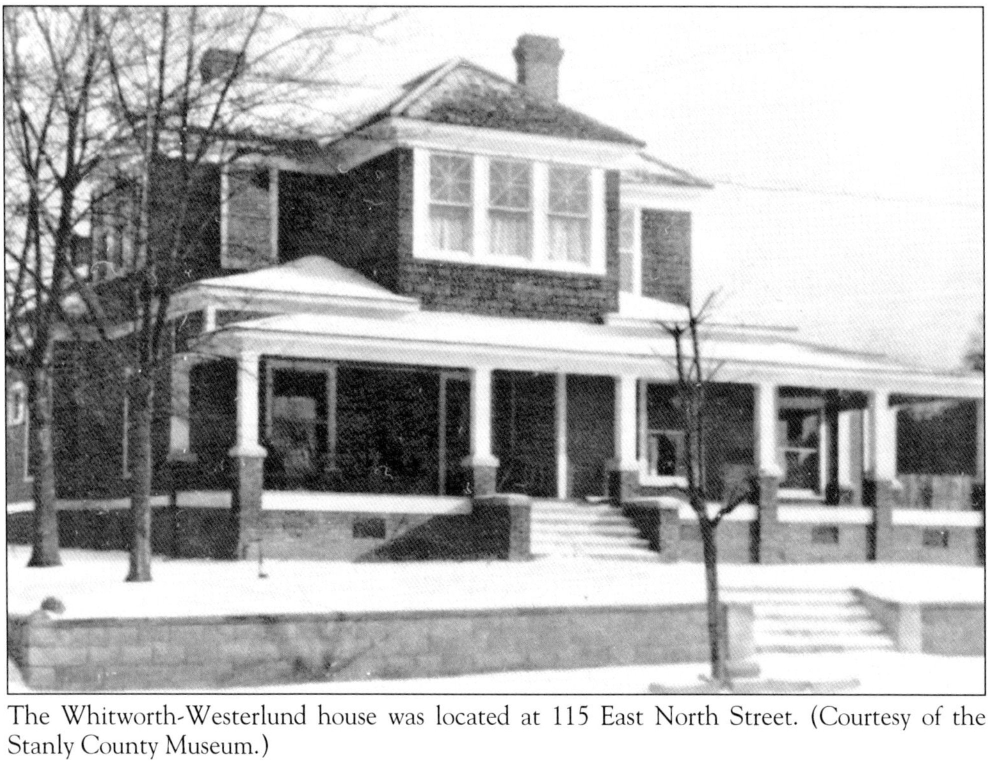

The Whitworth-Westerlund house was located at 115 East North Street. (Courtesy of the Stanly County Museum.)

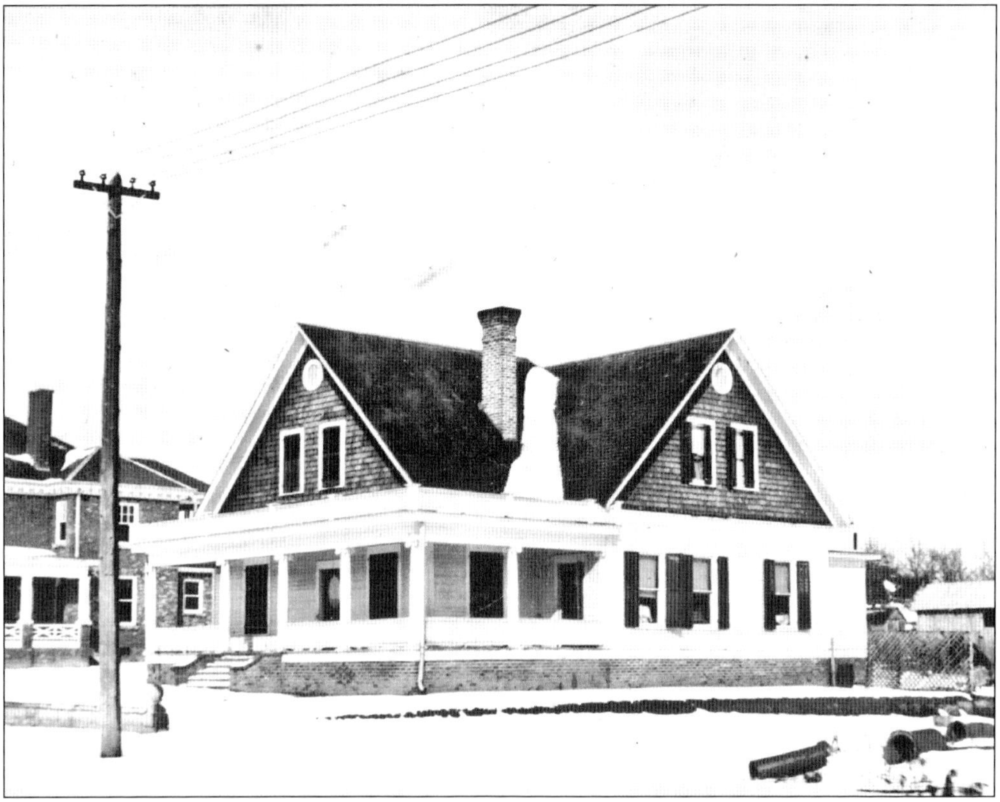

The Skidmore House was located at 129 Montgomery Avenue and North Second Street. (Courtesy of the Stanly County Museum.)

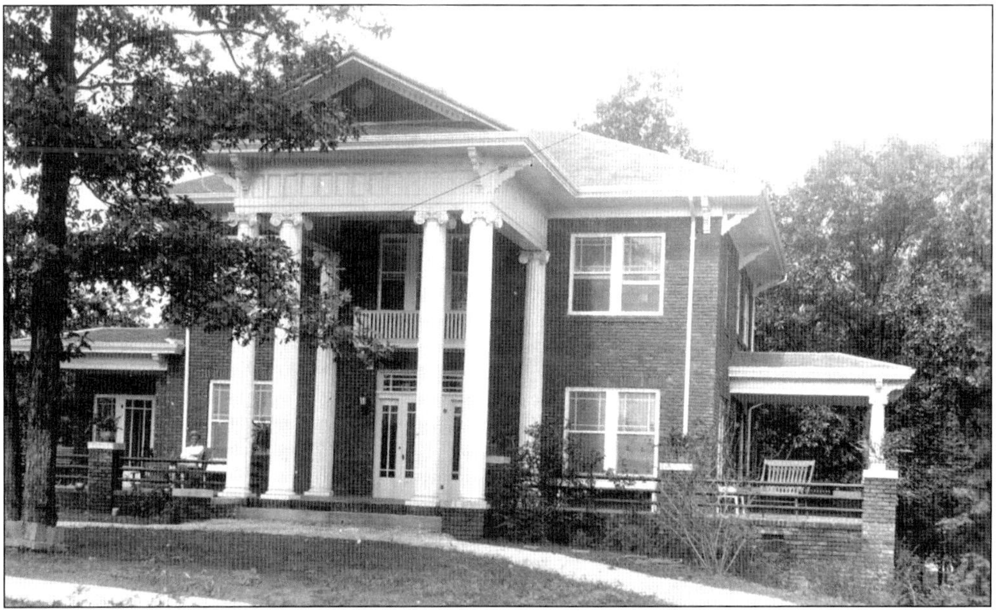

The A.C. Huneycutt house was built in 1923 on 271 North Third Street. (Courtesy of the Stanly County Museum.)

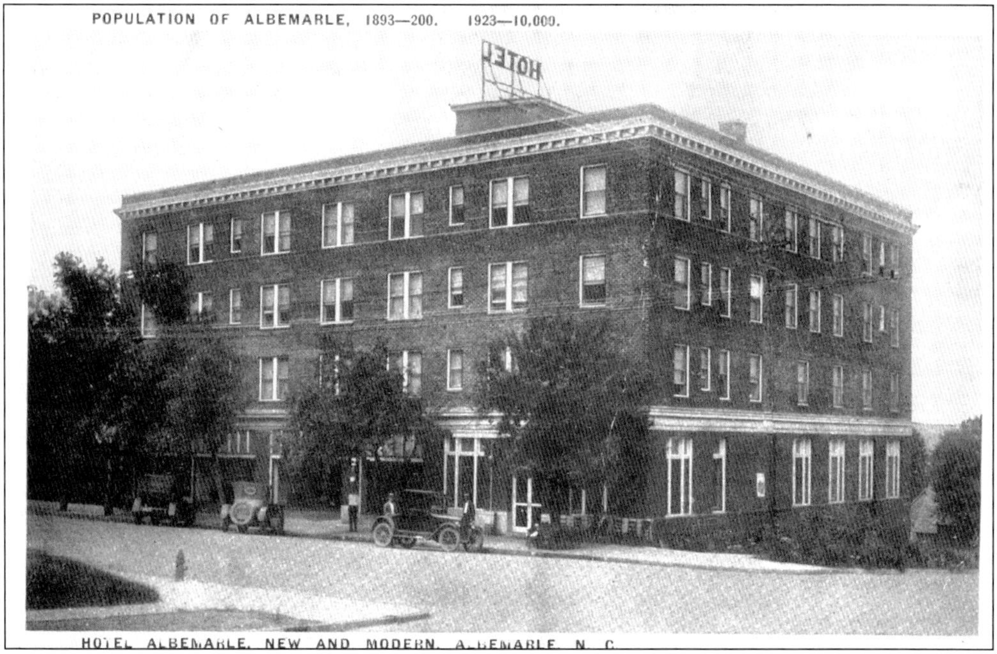

The Hotel Albemarle was built at the southwest corner of North and North Second Street in 1923. (Courtesy of the Stanly County Museum.)

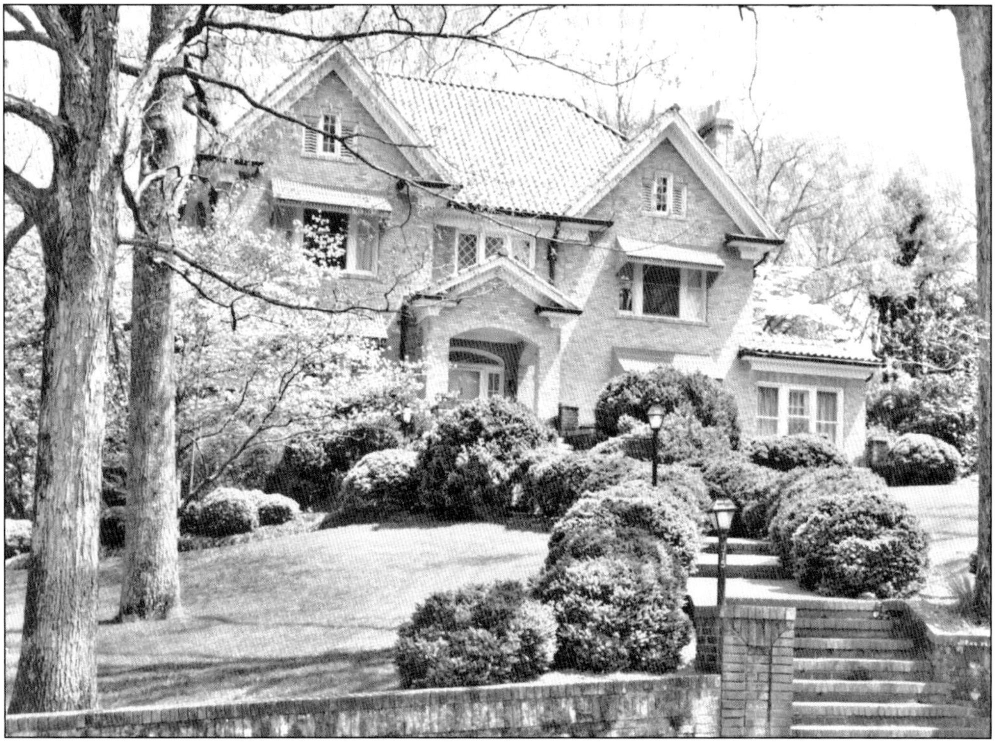

The F.E. Starnes house was located at 315 South Third Street. It was built in 1928 with a female architect, F.L. Bontoey, and contractor J.C. Holbrook. The current occupants are the family of Pat Starnes Bramlett and Chris Bramlett. (Courtesy of Gene Starnes.)